THE END OF JOURNALISM

THE END OF JOURNALISM

News in the Twenty-First Century

Edited by Alec Charles and Gavin Stewart

PETER LANG

Oxford • Bern • Berlin • Bruxelles • Frankfurt am Main • New York • Wien

Bibliographic information published by Die Deutsche Nationalbibliothek.
Die Deutsche Nationalbibliothek lists this publication in the Deutsche National-
bibliografie; detailed bibliographic data is available on the Internet at
http://dnb.d-nb.de.

Library of Congress Cataloging-in-Publication Data

The end of journalism : news in the twenty-first century / Alec Charles
and Gavin Stewart (eds).
    p. cm.
Includes bibliographical references and index.
ISBN 978-3-0343-0261-6 (alk. paper)
1. Journalism--History--21st century. 2. Journalism--Technological
innovations. 3. Online journalism. 4. Digital media. 5. Citizen
journalism. I. Charles, Alec. II. Stewart, Gavin, 1962-
PN4815.2.E53 2011
070.9'051--dc22

                        2011014280

ISSN 1662-7784
ISBN 978-3-0343-0261-6

© Peter Lang AG, International Academic Publishers, Bern 2011
Hochfeldstrasse 32, CH-3012 Bern, Switzerland
info@peterlang.com, www.peterlang.com, www.peterlang.net

Printed in Germany

Contents

vi

Acknowledgments

The editors would like to express their sincerest thanks to their students and colleagues at the University of Bedfordshire who have supported this project, as well as to all of the contributors not only to this collection but also to the 2008 conference at the University of Bedfordshire on which this collection is based, to our friends in the Political Studies Association's Media and Politics Group, and to our colleagues at Peter Lang. Special thanks are due to Professor Les Ebdon, Professor James Crabbe, Professor Mary Malcolm, Professor Garry Whannel, Professor Ivor Gaber, Professor Jon Silverman, Professor Luke Hockley, Professor David Barrett, Professor Mick Temple, Dr Carlota Larrea, Dr Michael Higgins, Dr Dominic Wring, Dr Malcolm Keech, Dr Steve Conway, Dr Heather Savigny, Deena Ingham and Peter Dean, for their encouragement and support, and in particular to Professor Alexis Weedon, Director of the Research Institute for Media, Art & Design at the University of Bedfordshire.

ALEC CHARLES

Introduction: Resistance is Useless

This collection came about as the result of a conference – also called *The End of Journalism* – which we staged at the University of Bedfordshire on 17–18 October 2008. When first we mooted the notion of this project, we found ourselves engaged in hours of pedantic but illuminating debate over its name. We knew that the title would contain the words 'end' and 'journalism' – we were, however, crucially uncertain as to the appropriate articles, prepositions and punctuation. Was it 'an end to journalism?' – or even 'the end for journalism!'? We soon recognized that our stress on the significance of the phrasing originated in a real desire to emphasize the ambiguity of the theme. Do new technologies, new users and new professional practices spell the *end* (the death) of journalism-as-we-know-it? Or do the efforts of bloggers and citizen journalists herald the democratization of journalism – the *end* (the goal) of its defining liberal principles? This may or may not be the end of journalism (either teleologically or eschatologically), but we appear to be witnessing a paradigm shift in the ways in which the world sees the function, nature, status and practice of journalism – and in which journalism sees itself.

This book is not about the death of the newspaper. There are other – many other – studies of that subject. Nor in fact is it about the demise of journalism *per se*. It is about the ways in which journalism is coming to terms with, and learning to take advantage of, new technologies and environments – and how these new conditions may at the same time threaten to undermine or to reimagine the defining traditions and ideals of journalism as profession, industry and political and cultural force.

Power to the people

Andrew Calcutt and Philip Hammond suggest in their chapter of this collection that journalism need not refute that quest for objectivity in which it has traditionally sought to find its authority, while at the same time recognizing that objectivity, while a valid ideal, might not be considered an attainable absolute. As Ivor Gaber and I suggest in our later chapters, journalism might benefit from a sense of its own subjectivity; indeed it can in fact be at its most interesting in its more ambiguous, ironic, symbolic and self-consciously subjective manifestations. From Jonathan Swift and Charles Dickens through Hunter Thompson and Helen Fielding to John Pilger and Robert Fisk, the journalists whose impact we recall very often eschew the standard or stereotypical values of their profession. We might therefore suppose that the trade's dilettantes and arrivistes (from Salam Pax and Matt Drudge to Gavin Stewart's news-gathering Wikipedians, Roy Krøvel's Zapatista activists and Yoani Sánchez, the Cuban blogger described in Clive McGoun's contribution to this book) could be seen as continuing an admirable tradition of individualism and anti-authoritarianism which has underpinned journalism for at least three hundred years. Indeed, as Richard Junger proposes, many of the ostensibly innovatory practices which new media technologies have introduced into journalistic practice have a rich and lengthy heritage. It is, however, sometimes unclear (as Jon Silverman and Marcus Leaning suggest) whether journalism and its news-consuming public are yet ready to benefit from the work of the citizen journalist, the blogger or David Cameron's mobile journalist – and indeed whether that work is as useful, or even as radically unmediated by authority, as it might at first appear or claim to be.

In his exceptional study of *Online Journalism* Jim Hall (2001) proposed – citing cases in the former Yugoslavia, and anticipating those since seen in Iraq – that the weblog might offer a significant alternative source of information and reportage to traditional news outlets. Yet Rupert Murdoch's purchase of the *myspace* blogging platform in 2006 appears to demonstrate that the entrenched institutions of the media are increasingly willing to do their best to assimilate these forms of unauthorized expression. Indeed when one sees Salam Pax, the Baghdad Blogger, filing a series of reports from Iraq for BBC television's *Newsnight* (as he did, for example, in 2006), one is forced to wonder how 'alternative' and unmediated the blog now is. Doesn't such success defeat the weblog's end, by thrusting it into the heart of the mainstream?

In an interview conducted for the purposes of this chapter (1 May 2010) the well-known British political blogger Iain Dale suggested that the political weblog has promoted levels of political engagement among younger voters in the UK: 'I think blogs have engaged people who might otherwise not have become involved in the political process, especially among the 18–25 age group. I know this from dozens of emails I receive from young people, who may be turned off engagement with political parties, but want to involve themselves in the democratic process. They see blogs as a medium for doing this.' Although Dale does not see the blog replacing or even seriously rivalling traditional news services, he acknowledges the weblog's increasing role in setting the news agenda: 'I don't believe that blogs will replace old media, but there's no doubt that new media has had a major impact on the old media. They have provided the old media with new voices to report and engage with and use as independent pundits and commentators.' Dale also recognizes that the weblog phenomenon does not necessarily represent an alternative media form which promises the democratic redistribution of political influence away from the established voices: 'In some ways mainstream journalists have already colonized the blogosphere – so blogs have, to an extent, already become institutionalized. This is inevitable and is neither a good nor a bad thing. It's just a fact.' Modes of resistance to institutionalized power themselves become institutionalized and entrenched: indeed, Dale himself is now something of a recognized figure of the establishment.

The writing has for some time been on the wall for the truly independent news-related blog. For the most part, we have not performed a massive shift in our choice of sources of news. The Internet has provided a different medium through which to access these sources, yet we continue to return to the usual authorities with their same-old stories: *The Guardian*, *The Times*, *The New York Times*, *The Sun*, Reuters, the BBC, CNN. This may not merely be out of an innate conservatism or inertia (or epistemological or ethical distrust of the Internet's less authoritative portals – such as the *Drudge Report* – which, for example, in February 2008 gave wide publicity to the then embargoed news of Harry Wales's sojourn in Afghanistan): it may be because we understand that 'news' is not merely what has happened in the world today, but what has been deemed to be significant, or newsworthy by forms of recognized authority, and thereby becomes part of a shared, global, gate-kept experience.

As the Web's more authoritative news sites increasingly steer clear of steering us towards (by offering us links to) external and 'unofficial' sites – a move the *BBC News* site partially adopted as part of its 2010 relaunch (when it moved those links from a handy sidebar to the bottom of the page) – so they have begun to offer their own informal news(b)logs – such as BBC Political Editor Nick Robinson's on the *BBC News* website. In a newslog entry on political bloggers' vilification of the UK's then Deputy Prime Minister John Prescott, Robinson (2006) argued that 'this is another example of some blogs trying to make the political weather.' Robinson also cited the uses of weblogs by the Conservative Iain Dale, and by *Swift Boat Veterans for Truth*, to tarnish the reputations of Cherie Blair and John Kerry respectively. Robinson distinguished between the professional conduct of journalists and the unregulated activities of bloggers, and proposed that the decision to report unsubstantiated allegations is not a mark of good journalism but of political bias. More recently, Ivor Gaber (Political Studies Association Annual Conference, Edinburgh, 31 March 2010) – in reference to the use of social networking technologies in the campaign against *Daily Mail* journalist Jan Moir's homophobic attack upon the late Stephen Gately (covered by *The Guardian* on 16 October 2009 as 'Twitter and Facebook outrage over Jan Moir's Stephen Gately article') – has spoken in similar terms of the emergence of a demagogic 'Twitter mob rule [...] a Twitter dictatorship'.

In August 2006 Iain Dale publicly defended the rights to 'freedom of speech' of his fellow right-wing blogger Inigo Wilson (Roberts 2006) when the latter was suspended from his job as a result of a poorly written, ill-informed and racially offensive diatribe he posted on the right-wing website ConservativeHome.com. In such a context one might appreciate Nick Robinson's attempt to champion a more formal mode of political writing which eschews blatant prejudice and polemic: yet underlying his argument is the assumption that professional journalism can somehow attain the impossible position of ideological neutrality – and that it thus alone has the right to conjure political storms.

Authoritative yet informal newslogs such as Nick Robinson's provide their readerships with the reassurance of journalistic and institutional authority, while at the same time posing as somehow less mediated or premeditated – less artificial – than straight news. In a way, this activity is no more than a development of the self-conscious subjectivity of American New Journalism, or the extreme (and surely transparent?) editorializing of the likes of Fox's Bill O'Reilly: bringing to electronic mass-media news the openly personal or political modality of the press commentator, columnist or leader-writer. As such, it might be seen to fulfil John Fiske's desire 'to demystify news's discursive strategies and to discredit its ideology of objectivity and the truth' (Fiske 1987: 308). But is this not also a mode of discourse by which the public professional journalist can assume a greater measure of overt subjectivity without surrendering an ounce of authority?

In her weblog of 18 August 2006, the BBC's Head of Newsgathering Fran Unsworth defended the Corporation from allegations posted on 'some blogs' that their journalists in the Israeli-Hezbollah conflict were failing to refer to the fact that they were 'operating under reporting restrictions.' Unsworth argued that the correspondents did not mention the restrictions because the Israelis never actually censored a BBC report – failing to see that the very fact of those restrictions may have resulted in an unconscious or advertent self-censorship (a phenomenon which defamation lawyers refer to as a 'chilling effect'). It might seem odd that the blog – a form once heralded as a viable alternative to moneyed, institutional or state-sanctioned mass-media authority – should be used by such an authority to defend its decision to gloss over the traces of another authoritarianism: but it is a fact of history that potential for subversion tends itself to be subverted.

On 6 May 2010, the day of a general election in the UK, the front page headline of *The Independent* newspaper hailed that event as 'the people's election'. It argued that through the country's first ever series of televized debates between the leaders of the main political parties, and as a result of online activities by individual bloggers and posters which challenged and subverted the propaganda of the established parties, influence over the political agenda had shifted into the hands of the British people. The results of that election, however, did not demonstrate any significant shift in public opinion away from the two largest political parties; the smaller parties and independent candidates did not make the expected electoral breakthroughs which might have diminished the Labour and Conservative stranglehold over the British political system that had endured for the best part of a century. Independent bloggers remain, of course, for the most part unread (how could they all be read?), while the World Wide Web continues to spew forth such democratic delights as the Labour Party YouTube channel (launched by Tony Blair in April 2007), a YouTube version of Prime Minister's Questions (launched by Gordon Brown in May 2008), and, perhaps most disturbing of all, the video weblog launched by Conservative Party Leader (and future Prime Minister) David Cameron in September 2006, Webcameron. In short, new media forms continue, as ever – and as James Morrison and Sonya Yan Song suggest – to be appropriated as tools for the reactionary reinforcement of entrenched power. More worrying for some, however, are the ways in which the journalism itself appears increasingly subservient to that power. This relationship often appears at its most inappropriate when, as has become increasingly common, the Fourth Estate becomes embedded, both ideologically and physically, with the military.

The Dogs of War

The news media no longer seem merely in the background but in the vanguard of the political-military-industrial process, a situation anticipated in the middle of the twentieth century by, for example, Lord Beaverbrook's ministerial portfolio in Churchill's wartime government and mirrored more recently in media tycoon Silvio Berlusconi's Italian premiership. The overlap between the news media and political and military power appears increasingly overt. Reports that the Pentagon liaised with CNN on the timing of the American attack upon Mogadishu – at the start of Operation Restore Hope in 1992 – so as to maximize viewing figures for the live coverage of the beach landings would have seemed absurd just a decade earlier; yet today this situation seems increasingly natural.

In an essay on the coverage of the Falklands/Malvinas conflict, Raymond Williams (1989: 40) wrote of the 'antiseptic presentation of the images of war' – of the media's emotional distancing of that conflict. Williams compares the cold flashes of televized missile hits to the graphics of a computer game – anticipating that mass of footage from the Gulf, first in 1991 and then a dozen years later, of clinical, laser-precision bombings, marvels of postmodern technology, magnificent pyrotechnics, bereft of any sense of human tragedy: footage shot from bombers' perspectives (both physically and morally), provided by the United States military, and disseminated often unquestioningly by the world's media – a stance epitomized, for example, by an *ABC News* report of 9 October 2001 which, in a single headline, celebrated the divine and cinematic glory of the missile technology deployed during the invasion of Afghanistan: 'Guided by the Stars.'

News organizations' involvement with the military represents a consolidation of vested economic and ideological interests. Critical distance has been replaced by a virtual symbiosis. Today's media have moved well beyond, say, the influential appeasement doctrines of *The Times* newspaper in the 1930s; the jingoistic and war-mongering stances of much of the British and American the tabloid press (and, in the United States, of certain TV news networks, most notably the flag-waving Fox – an organization which boasts much-publicized connections with the Bush family) recall Orson Welles's immortal exhortation to a journalist in *Citizen Kane* (1941) – paraphrasing what has been (possibly apocryphally) reported as a line from the real-life newspaper tycoon William Randolph Hearst in 1897: 'You provide the prose-poems. I'll provide the war.' (Or, in Hearst's version: 'You furnish the pictures, and I'll furnish the war.') This is not quite the situation suggested by the James Bond film, *Tomorrow Never Dies* (1997), in which Jonathan Pryce's media mogul attempts to start a war between Britain and China in order to boost newspaper sales and penetrate new satellite broadcasting markets; and yet we are growing ever more acclimatized to that absurdity.

In times of war both journalists and politicians enjoy unprecedented levels of influence, and, as this agglomeration of power dissolves the critical distinctions between the legislators and their gatekeepers, it is perhaps inevitable that some within the news media might be keen to maintain this situation. In extreme cases, this may result in an enthusiasm for, or even an uncritical complicity in, the conduct of military activities. A relatively recent conflict which witnessed the ambiguation of the journalistic role in a number of ways (including the appearance of local bloggers as early citizen journalists) was the war in Kosovo.

The Western involvement in the former Yugoslavia had been directly prompted by the news media, not least by the BBC, whose reports of atrocities in the region had been instrumental in shifting public and political attitudes. It is perhaps therefore unsurprising that the BBC (which famously took a much more critical stance on the Iraq War, a stance shared by few other major Anglophone broadcast news organizations) should in some way act as an apologist for this conflict. On 14 May 1999, for example, when NATO planes mistakenly bombed a convoy of civilian refugees in the Kosovan village of Korisa, an error which (according to the *BBC News* website) resulted in 'up to 100' civilian deaths, the BBC television news reports were somewhat muted in their criticism of the Western alliance. The BBC's reporter on the scene, Jacky Rowland, did her best to play up the positive contribution the West might make to the region: 'As I was driving into Kosovo today, it really recalled scenes from Bosnia, and if you think about how much money the international community has spent rebuilding Bosnia, I think we're going to be looking at similar figures.' The BBC diplomatic correspondent Bridget Kendall went further in her attempts to put a positive spin on events, referring to 'the funeral of just one of many young Serb soldiers killed in this war. Terrible for his family but for NATO a sign its air campaign is working and President Milosevic and his military machine may have been substantially weakened.' Both journalists cast doubt on the veracity of statements emanating from what they appeared to view as the Serbian state propaganda machine, but also appeared to view NATO as a source of independent and authentic information: 'NATO says it's carrying out an investigation into what Serb officials are describing as the worst mistake of the air campaign' – 'the smoke and burning tractors [...] seem to tell their own story, but NATO has still not confirmed its planes were responsible.' Most extraordinary, however, were the apparent obfuscations performed by the BBC's defence correspondent, Mark Laity, who, during the same evening news bulletin, announced:

> No official word, but my understanding is they're having a real problem sorting this out. There has been so many attacks in this area because it's a real hotspot of Yugoslav army and police activity – that there are – it's quite difficult to break it down. Now, my understanding is that there were attacks in the Korica area, but it may well not have been cluster bombs as the Serbs have claimed – so, if there has been a tragedy – it may well not have been cluster bombs, but that is still not confirmed. And the problem is – is that this is one of the intense areas of activity where the battle is really being fought. There's a motorized brigade in that area, a paramilitary gland, a gang, the Black Hand Gang, and also special police units who are trying to create a security zone in that area, and so that's why there's been so many attacks and to distinguish between them is proving quite difficult for NATO.

Despite the footage of the civilian corpses already screened, Laity continued to cast doubt upon whether 'there has been a tragedy'. His perspective seemed indistinguishable from NATO's own; he referred to NATO not as the instigator of a wartime atrocity but (as his BBC colleagues had) as the investigator of this atrocity. In an extraordinary parapraxis, he attempts to cast the blame upon 'a paramilitary gland, a gang, the Black Hand Gang.' It is unclear whether Laity was here referring to the Black Hand (the organization behind Archduke Franz Ferdinand's assassination in 1914) or indeed to *The Black Hand Gang*, a British slapstick comedy of 1930 – a kind of pre-war *Home Alone* – starring Wee Georgie Wood. Mark Laity left the BBC shortly after he delivered this report to take up a position as deputy spokesperson and special adviser to the Secretary General of NATO. The journalist transforms into, in Laity's words, *a paramilitary gland* – an organ of the military authorities.

In an article written for *NATO Review* in 2002, Laity suggested that 'media policy [...] has underpinned NATO's conflict-resolution work in the former Yugoslav Republic of Macedonia.' Laity's point is one to which Paul Reynolds (2006) returns, in his description of the Pentagon's 'media war' – echoing Donald Rumsfeld's announcement (on 17 February 2006) that newsrooms had become crucial battlefields in the War on Terror. As Tumber and Webster (2006: 173) argue the media have become essential to the conduct and success of contemporary warfare.

A classic instance of (and metaphor for) the role of the news media at the forefront of military conflict was the case of the BBC's World Affairs Editor John Simpson's self-proclaimed liberation of Kabul in November 2001. According to *BBC News Interactive* (18 November 2001) Simpson 'said he is "very, very, very embarrassed" after his widely-reported remarks that he liberated Kabul.' The growing public perception – and acceptance – of the complicit relationship between the media apparatus and the military machine appears epitomized by this absurd and infamous example. Yet Simpson has been notable for his refusal to get into bed with the military. As he told *The Guardian* on 15 March 2010, he would not wish to be so morally embedded: 'I don't want to spend my whole time with people to whom I owe my safety, my protection, my food, my transport, and then be expected to be completely honest about them.'

In an online report of 30 November 2004, David Loyn, another BBC correspondent, one embedded at the time with the Black Watch in Iraq, wrote of the British soldiers with whom he was travelling: 'few have more than a fleeting glimpse of the countryside they are living in [...] it is hard to gain any more than a superficial impression of what [Iraqi] people really think.' One wonders whether the partial – or blinkered – perspective Loyn diagnoses is shared by those who see exactly what the soldiers see: the embedded journalists themselves. If the BBC's journalists are now embedded with the military of only one side in any conflict, might that not lead to the very bias – the *one-sidedness* – which the Corporation is pledged to avoid? Are these reporters so profoundly integrated within their military surroundings that they come to assume a double authority: that of the journalist and that of the soldier – the defender not only of the truth but of our very way of life? The costume, the company and the celebrated courage of the embedded journalist add an extra legitimacy (and militarism) to her/his reportage; just as that reportage itself legitimizes its subject.

In his discussion of television news John Fiske usefully refers to a phenomenon which Roland Barthes (1973) termed 'exnomination'. Fiske (1987: 290) writes:

> The impersonal objectivity of this discourse 'guarantees' its truth: it is an example of the ideological practice that Barthes calls 'exnomination' [...]. Exnomination is the evacuation of a concept from the linguistic system with its structure of differences

and alternatives. That which is exnominated appears to have no alternative and is thus granted the status of the natural, the universal, or that-which-cannot-be-challenged.

In the processes of embedded journalism, the soldiers become so intimately associated with the reporter that they assume her/his status as objective, universal and uncontroversial. They, the subjects of the speech, are confused with the speaking subject: these ostensible objects adopt the same sympathetic subjectivity through which the audience identifies with the journalist her/himself. The viewer sees not only through the eyes of the journalist – through the purportedly natural and transparent lens of news reportage – but also, by way of this secondary level of identification, from the perspective of the military personnel themselves. We, the viewers, are in their boots. This dissolution of the distinction and distance between reporter and reported results in a situation in which the armed forces become the very (exnominated) subjects of the news discourse; the enemy are therefore, by extension, consigned to the status of objects, those who have been nominated as different, as otherly. The polarizing opposition between 'us' and 'them' thus comes to dominate the discourse once again.

On 13 January 2010 the then Armed Forces Minister Bill Rammell spoke of the 'sincere mutual trust and respect [...] born of sharing hardship' which develops between embedded journalists and their military hosts; but it might be asked whether such a relationship is necessarily compatible with the principles of critical detachment expected of journalism as the gatekeeper of democracy. As Tumber and Webster (2006: 20) point out, most of the reportage provided by embedded journalists during the early stages of the Iraq War was thus 'largely supportive of the units they were with (and by extension the overall military enterprise).' Fiametta Rocco (2000: 50) has written of a version of the 'Stockholm syndrome' that can arise between a reporter and her subject: 'the psychological condition that describes the mutual dependence between kidnapper and victim [...] the closer the cooperation between journalist and subject, the greater the danger.' The practice of embedded journalism is fraught with a potential for partiality which is prompted not only by the unconscious psychological identifications which may develop between reporter and subject, but also by the regulations upon the freedom of expression which the process openly dictates.

Throughout their coverage of the Iraq War and its aftermath, embedded journalists have referred on camera to the reporting restrictions under which (for *reasons of military security*) they have been obliged to work: although one notes that British correspondents tend to seem more frequently alert to the need to inform their audiences of this censorship than American reporters do. Yet one must not forget in this context that the reporting restrictions enacted by ostensibly repressive regimes for reasons of political censorship are *also* (as journalists have liked to remind us when reporting from the 'regimes' of Slobodan Milosevic and Saddam Hussein) invariably justified by interests of *national security*.

On 13 November 2004, Kevin Sites, a cameraman for NBC television, embedded with the 3rd Battalion, 1st Regiment, of the US Marine Corps, videotaped the shooting by a marine of a wounded and unarmed Iraqi man in a mosque in Fallujah. Although the airing of this tape might present an argument in favour of embedded journalism (the argument that no other form of reporting could have garnered this kind of material), it may be observed that NBC chose to black out the actual moment of the shooting for reasons of public taste – just four days after sixty-six American television stations affiliated to ABC had chosen not to screen Steven Spielberg's World War II film *Saving Private Ryan* for similar reasons: on the grounds that it would be unpatriotic to broadcast a film which showed the horrors of war during a time of conflict. NBC also concealed the identity of the marine who committed the atrocity, reportedly under orders from the Pentagon. These simultaneous processes of censorship and self-censorship reflect the double bind of embedded journalism: the restrictions upon reportage which are imposed both by external power and by emotional proximity.

David Segal, the director of the Center for Research on Military Organization at the University of Maryland, has pointed out the fact that, adding religious insult to mortal injury, the marines involved in this incident had not removed their boots before entering the mosque – and that, while this fact had inflamed Al Jazeera, nobody in the US media had noticed it. Segal argued that 'this is a war where cultural knowledge may be more important than the number of bullets that you have' (CNN, 28 December 2004). The significance of Segal's observation is that the American media saw the incident from precisely the perspective of the military personnel. Like David Loyn's soldiers, they had no sense of the Iraqi perspective.

This is war-reporting in the style of *Black Hawk Down* (2001), Ridley Scott's celluloid dramatization of American military operations in Somalia. While one might forgive the partiality of Scott's blockbuster (which is seen entirely from the perspective of America's armed forces), one's ethical expectations of news journalism may differ somewhat from (or may once have differed from) those one has of a Hollywood action film. Slavoj Žižek (2008: 85) has written of the urgent obligation upon contemporary journalism 'to change [its] subjective position so that telling the factual truth will not involve the lie of the subjective position of enunciation' – but the possibility of such a perspectival shift here seems remote.

A week after NBC broadcast Sites's footage, *Time* magazine published embedded journalist Michael Ware's account of the United States offensive on Fallujah. This article was hailed by the right-wing media (and, in particular, by Fox News's Bill O'Reilly) as a vindication of the American forces' conduct during the attack. Ware (2004) wrote:

> At every stop in its advance, the Wolf Pack [...] found countless bombs, plus doors booby trapped and walls set with explosives. The enemy tactic accounted for the soldiers' unforgiving approach to entering buildings, traversing streets and tackling even lone snipers: if it looks suspicious or shoots at you, blow it up with a grenade, a cannon or the main gun of a tank.

Ware's justification of American military conduct is underpinned by his presentation of their enemy as *the* enemy: no longer just 'them', but now in fact 'it' – an utterly dehumanized object. Insofar as the journalist's survival is dependent upon the conduct (indeed, the self-serving indiscriminate ruthlessness) of the military unit with whom s/he is embedded, this degree of empathy with the military perspective is perhaps inevitable. One recalls in this context Tumber and Webster's suggestion (2006: 55–6) that in the reporting of the early stages of the Iraq War 'U.S. reporters, especially the embeds, depicted little of Iraqi suffering [...]. American journalists were victims of U.S. military and government perception management, particularly due to the constraints that were placed on the embeds. [...]. Mental embedding appeared to accompany physical embedding with the U.S. forces.'

Yet, even considering this, Ware's literary style seems extraordinarily propagandistic, sometimes quite melodramatically so. His reportage is emotive, even at times incongruously romantic: 'Streams of red tracers scorched into the building as a soft golden sun emblazoned a graying sky.' His similarly idealized description of the heroic Staff Sergeant David Bellavia is straight out of a Hollywood screenplay:

> Inside they find Bellavia alive and on the hunt. Upstairs he scans the bedrooms. An insurgent jumps out of the cupboard. Bellavia falls down and fires, spraying the man with bullets. At some point another insurgent drops out of the ceiling. Yet another runs to a window and makes for the garden. Bellavia hits him in the legs and lower back as he flees. When it's over four insurgents are dead; another has escaped badly wounded. To Bellavia, [the platoon's other staff sergeant] Fitts says, 'That's a good job, dude. You're a better man than me.'

One can imagine Clint Eastwood or Arnold Schwarzenegger in the Hollywood adaptation – though they might not have shot a fleeing man in the back. But, of course, this was not a man as such, but an insurgent. The second edition of the *Oxford English Dictionary* defines an *insurgent* as 'a rebel who is not recognized as a belligerent.' This curious term, which has lately gained unprecedented currency – as the Western media have adopted the vocabulary of the US military – appears to be the virtual equivalent, both semantically and ideologically, of that phrase immortalized in Afghanistan and thereafter in Guantanamo Bay: the (unlawful) *enemy combatant* – the fighter who lacks a soldier's, or (for that matter) a prisoner-of-war's, moral status and legal rights. There is nothing new in journalism's apparently unconscious adoption of politically prevalent discourse: such terms as *terrorists, tyrants, regimes* and *military machines* continue to bias journalistic narratives – as they do the opinions and accounts of the blogosphere. As Fredric Jameson (1991: 322) suggests: 'even if Big Brother is not everywhere watching you, Language is: media [...] language that seeks tirelessly to classify and categorize, to transform the individual into the labelled group.' This is the newspeak of news-speak: a politicized media language in which we are all now inscribed.

Sisyphus

How then can we hope to escape this ideological bind? Can the possibilities of a newly self-conscious subjectivity or of a subliminally symbolic discourse help us? Might the possibilities opened up by new media technologies allow the development of forms of expression which transcend the limitations of entrenched institutions and authorities? In some cases – as, later on in this collection, Clive McGoun, James Morrison and Sonya Yan Song suggest – the new media revolution may offer precisely such possibilities – whether in response to the conservatism of China's political structures and media establishment, or, for that matter, as a reaction to the commercial, institutional and professional constraints imposed upon local newspapers in the UK by a combination of national legislation and governmental practices. Yet, although the pragmatic adoption of these technologies may advance solutions to some of the practical problems of society, politics and the journalistic industry itself, can we really hope to witness a revolutionary shift in the nature of journalism, in its relationship with society and in its role as gatekeeper and watchdog – a shift which might offer a remediation of the relationship (and thereby a new covenant) between people and power, a revitalization of the structures and processes of democracy through the regeneration of the openness, accessibility, accountability and transparency of journalistic and therefore political narratives?

Probably not. For every Yoani Sánchez and Bagdad Blogger there are a score of embedded reporters; for every Dale and Drudge a host of entrenched political and journalistic hacks; for every campaigning Wikipedian a Webcameron or a Qianlong; for all the laity a Laity. And yet ....

Haven't we been here before? In truth: have we ever left? At the heart of things are not these debates ones which have been raging for decades, for centuries, and do they not in the end come down to the irreconcilability of truth and power? Reporters and philosophers and artists and poets have been wrestling with this dichotomy since the beginning of recorded history – and, indeed, some might suggest that this struggle is what recorded history is. If that is the case, then, rather than attempting to escape from these ties which bind us inexorably to the processes of history, it might be more useful and interesting to come to terms with, to explore and even to exploit the inevitability of this condition. To accept that the dichotomy of truth and power is a historical prerequisite of the human condition might allow us to come to a greater understanding of, and thereby an enhancement of, our own humanity.

As Albert Camus (1975: 111) suggested in *The Myth of Sisyphus*, the joyful willingness to embrace the impossibility and the futility our condition might be seen as the existential essence of humanity: 'The struggle itself towards the heights is enough to fill a man's heart.' As one hopes that the readers of this collection will appreciate, life isn't about finding all the answers; it is about the nobility of the effort, it is about all of the useful and interesting and wonderful and eye-opening things one discovers on the way. If this is the best that human endeavour and enquiry can hope to achieve, then it is also the end (the goal) and the endlessness of journalism – and, for that matter, the end, the endlessness and the beginning of *The End of Journalism*.

References

Barthes, R. (1973). *Mythologies* (trans. Lavers, A.). London: Paladin.
Camus, A. (1975). *The Myth of Sisyphus* (trans. O'Brien, J.). Harmondsworth: Penguin.
Fiske, J. (1987). *Television Culture*. London: Routledge.
Hall, J. (2001). *Online Journalism*. London: Pluto Press.
Jameson, F. (1991). *Postmodernism, or, The Cultural Logic of Late Capitalism*. London: Verso.
Laity, M. (2002). 'Battling the media' in *NATO Review*. Belgium: NATO Public Diplomacy Division.
Loyn, D. (2004). 'Cold reality of the Black Watch' in *BBC News Interactive*, 30 November 2004.
Reynolds, P. (2006). 'Pentagon gears up for new media war' in *BBC News Interactive*, 31 October 2006.

Roberts, G. (2006). 'Orange suspends blogger over his "Lefty Lexicon"' in *The Independent*, 18 August 2006.

Robinson, N. (2006). 'Prescott for dummies' in *BBC News Interactive*, 5 July 2006.

Rocco, F. (2000). 'Stockholm Syndrome: Journalists Taken Hostage' in *The Penguin Book of Journalism* (ed. Glover, S.). London: Penguin Books, 48–59.

Unsworth, F. (2006). 'Middle East restrictions?' in *BBC News Interactive*, 18 August 2006.

Ware, M. (2004). 'Into the hot zone' in *Time*, 22 November 2004. New York: Time/Warner. 30–6.

Williams, R. (1989). *What I Came to Say*, London: Hutchinson Radius.

Žižek, S. (2008). *Violence*. London: Profile Books.

ANDREW CALCUTT AND PHILIP HAMMOND

Objectivity and the End of Journalism

Traditionally a core tenet of journalistic professionalism, the idea of objectivity has become the target of unremitting attack by academic critics of news and journalism. Today, however, such critics are behind the times. The critique has become the orthodoxy: not only is there a consensus against objectivity among scholars of journalism studies, but journalists themselves have internalized the critique of objectivity. The Society of Professional Journalists, for example, dropped the term 'objectivity' from its code of ethics in 1996, at the same time changing 'seeking the truth' to simply 'seeking truth' (Cunningham 2003: 26). Whatever merits it may have had in the past, the critique of objectivity has become, at best, redundant.

This chapter argues for a new understanding of objectivity – as the corollary of human subjectivity, not its opponent. Subjectivity is not reducible to personal opinion. It is, properly, the consciousness of human subjects acting with other subjects in making the world our object. We subjects first make the world our object; then we make it again, this time as the object of our subjectivity. Objectivity arises from the collective application of subjectivity in the contentious process of producing mental objects – knowledge – designed to capture that material object – the external world – which we subjects have previously made. Objectivity is the condition of those mental objects which are the further objectification of the objective world – the world made into their object by human subjects.

In that journalism is a form of knowledge, it is a particular mental object produced by a specific, designated subject: the journalist. As reporters, journalists apply their subjectivity to that which has already been produced by human subjects. The reporter's job is to identify the primary object resulting from the actions of human subjects – the event – and make it into a secondary object – the story. By a process of mental production, materialized as words, sound, pictures and the arrangement (design) of these elements, journalists transform an object produced by some subjects (actors whose actions have resulted in an event) into another object for the cognition of other subjects (readers, listeners, viewers and users). Although journalism composed of secondary objects – stories – results from a process of transformation, to qualify as journalism it must also reproduce the essential character of original objects – events. Journalism will not pass muster unless it is true to the object (event) that is transformed in the telling of it, and unless the telling of it transforms the object (event) to which the story is also true. Neither a false impression nor a verbatim transcript will suffice as 'journalism'.

Thus the role of journalists is to make mental objects out of events by the application of their subjectivity. The task of these subjects is to objectify. Their objectification process has an objective: to produce a new object which is external to all three sets of subjects (actors in events, journalists acting on events to make them into stories, and readers who may act on knowledge of events as contained in the stories presented to them by journalists). Furthermore, objectivity is the condition of this mental object which journalists strive for on its behalf, i.e. their aim and claim are that their story, produced in the application of their subjectivity, has captured the essential character of the original object (event) from which it is derived. Objectivity is typically the end of journalism, where 'end' is taken to mean 'aim' or 'objective'.

When humanity has seen itself as the subject of history, it has also seen the world of its own making as an object of study: hence objectivity. Conversely, the recent rejection of objectivity is the correlate of the 'end of history', or, the suspension of the idea of humanity as its subject. These are the social origins of objectivity and its discontents. The prospect of the end or demise of journalism is a measure of subjectivity's dislocation from objectivity. In this context, much media content is derivative of journalism but hardly qualifies as journalism. Equally, many of those whose professional lives continually tend towards objective journalism have become less confident about what it is they are doing and what they must do to pursue it. Our contention is that the pursuit of journalism requires the reconfiguration of objectivity; furthermore, that journalism academics should support journalists in the aspiration to provide that quality of new information which complements humanity's capacity to objectify the world, i.e. objectivity. Conversely, if journalists do not succeed in establishing objectivity as their defining aspiration, the work they do may cease to be defined as journalism. Without the core principle of capturing occurrences as they really were, what really is there separating journalism from other kinds of story-telling, or from other modes of self-presentation in social media? Unless objectivity is reconfigured as their essential ambition, journalists may find that they are non-essential to the production of non-journalism on a variety of media platforms. Similarly, if in today's circumstances journalism academics fail to support the call for objectivity, they too are culpable for putting journalism in jeopardy.

The Rise of Objectivity

Historically, journalism's ability to fulfil its democratic role has been constrained by the divisions and tensions of class society; specifically, by the elite's need to marginalize radical opinion and to manage mass public opinion. Historical accounts of the concept of journalistic objectivity (for example, Allan 1997) tend to identify three key moments: the emergence of the bourgeois public sphere in the eighteenth century; the development of the mass-circulation press as a business in the late nineteenth century; and the institutionalization of professional norms of objectivity and impartiality in newspaper and radio journalism in the early twentieth century.

According to Habermas's (1989) account, the identification of the interests of the rising bourgeoisie with the general 'public interest' in the eighteenth century was, though partial (restricted to wealthy white men), also justifiable, to the extent that challenging the *ancien régime* really was in the general interest of society. Once in power, however, the capitalist class became less of a friend to liberty. As described by James Curran and Jean Seaton (2003), in the nineteenth century the commercially oriented, advertising-funded mass circulation press drove out radical newspapers and drastically narrowed the range of what was included in the 'marketplace of ideas'.

The establishment of objectivity as a core professional ethic of journalism after the First World War went hand-in-hand with a concerted and conscious effort to 'manage' a volatile and dangerous public opinion. Stuart Allan (1997: 308) suggests that 'popular disillusionment not only with state propaganda campaigns, but also with the recent advent of press agents and "publicity experts", had helped to create a general wariness of "official" channels of information.' He is no doubt correct, but the underlying issue was not so much popular scepticism toward official channels of information as militant working-class demands for social change. This was, after all, the era of the Bolshevik revolution, the moment when communist parties were being established across the Western world. The explicit promotion of journalistic objectivity was an attempt to cope with this situation by finding ways to retain credibility with the mass audience. It was also a tool for managing public opinion: the rise of Public Relations in the interwar period indicated the elite's pressing concern with handling a new and unpredictable mass public by 'engineering' or 'manufacturing' consent as Edward Bernays (1947) and Walter Lippmann (1997) put it.

In Britain, the birth of broadcasting in this period gave rise to the analogous concept of 'impartiality', which served similar ends. Having been established as a commercial organization (the British Broadcasting *Company*) in 1922, with its potential as a news provider severely restricted on the grounds that it would undermine the press, the BBC's first foray into journalism was during the peculiar circumstances of the 1926 General Strike. The BBC's future direction as a public corporation licensed by Royal Charter had already been decided upon by Parliament earlier that year, but the strike threw all that into doubt. John Reith, the BBC's then managing director, realized that, with newspapers affected by the strike, this was an opportunity to show that 'impartial' broadcasting could be a more credible source of news than the government's propaganda sheet, *The British Gazette*. His implausible formula for BBC 'impartiality' was that 'since the BBC was a national institution and since the Government in this crisis was acting for the people [...] the BBC was for the Government in the crisis too' (quoted in Curran and Seaton 2003: 118). Publicly, the BBC was supposedly above the bitter class divisions of the era, serving 'the people' as a whole. Yet while he fought to prevent the government commandeering the organization, Reith wrote in his diary that 'they know they can trust us not to be really impartial' (quoted in Lewis and Pearlman 1986: 69).

Journalistic objectivity has always had a double-edged character: in part about a genuine extension of public knowledge and informing public debate; but also partly about the narrowing of debate within acceptable parameters. Even as it has called a national public into being, it has also served the interests of the elite. It would be absurd simply to celebrate 'objective journalism' uncritically. Yet it would surely be equally foolish to write off journalism's potential for sustaining the public sphere and informing democratic decision-making.

The Critique of Objectivity

The academic critique of journalistic objectivity has demonstrated how it constrains debate within a 'consensual framework' (Hall et al. 1978) or a 'sphere of legitimate controversy' (Hallin 1986). It has shown how 'objective journalism is a political perspective [...] a perspective most closely associated with political centrism' (Pedelty 1995: 171) and how objectivity became reduced to a 'strategic ritual', a set of routines and a reliance on official sources, rather than a search for truth (Tuchman 1972). Just as the concept of journalistic objectivity has a history, however, so too does the critique of objectivity. Rather than a set of timeless truths, the critique of objectivity needs to be seen in context: indeed, it is our contention that in today's circumstances it no longer makes sense to continue making it.

The critique of journalistic objectivity developed in the 1970s and 1980s was always implicitly undercut by the fact that it did not defend the concept of objectivity as such. As Judith Lichtenberg (1991) observes, it is logically inconsistent to criticize journalism for failing to be objective while also arguing that objectivity is impossible. Yet that has been the thrust of most of the critiques of journalistic objectivity which have come out of Sociology and Media and Cultural Studies. In the past, the implied relativism of the critique was contained or masked by the fact of active political engagement and contestation. News could be criticized for systematically favouring some perspectives and excluding or marginalizing others – trades union or left-Labour views in the Glasgow Media Group's classic (1995) studies, for example. The question of what would constitute an 'objective' account tended to be avoided in favour of amassing evidence of the ways that the 'neutral, unbiased, impartial and balanced' ethos of broadcast news disguised its ideological character (Glasgow Media Group 1995: 367). Radical critics such as those at the Glasgow Media Group made it clear that they were not 'neutral' any more than the news was, but did not clarify the issue of objectivity.

In the absence of the clear Left/Right ideological contest of yester-year, however, that critique becomes much more difficult to sustain. What are the 'alternative' or oppositional viewpoints now being marginalized? Mainstream political debate is narrower than ever, but it is difficult to see this as simply the result of progressive and radical perspectives being marginalized or left out. If anything, today it is those who think of themselves as progressives and radicals who are often the keenest to narrow the sphere of 'legitimate controversy', seeking to delineate the bounds of acceptable debate around issues such as global warming, racism or 'Islamophobia'. Perhaps even more importantly, the majority of people in Western societies are not really engaged or interested in the public sphere.

Habermas's view – that journalism was no longer able to play the role for which it had seemed destined in the Age of Enlightenment, and that the contemporary commercial media had instead given rise to a 're-feudalization of the public sphere' – has usually been seen as overly pessimistic. Today, however, the public sphere does indeed appear to have been 're-feudalized', in the sense that we are more or less passive spectators to a kind of court politics. Yet where Habermas attributed the problem to the media, it seems clear that the real problem is the hollowing-out of political life itself: for this reason, his argument is actually more pertinent to the period after its publication in English in 1989 than it was when it first appeared in German in the early 1960s. After the end of Left and Right, the political class has become increasingly isolated and disconnected from the *demos* it is supposed to represent. Established institutions and sources of authority, from parliament to the press, are called into question, not from a critical political point of view, but simply as an expression of popular cynicism and disengagement. In these circumstances, to go on recycling the critique of objectivity is not simply to miss the point: worse, it is likely to reinforce cynical attitudes toward the media and public life.

The Fall of Objectivity

Stuart Allan suggested more than a decade ago that 'the end of "objectivity" and "impartiality" as the guiding principles of an ethic of public service may soon be in sight' (1997: 319). Even then, there was already plenty of evidence that he was right. In the 1990s, a number of prominent foreign correspondents repudiated the idea of objectivity. The BBC's Martin Bell rejected the 'dispassionate practices of the past' and maintained that he was 'no longer sure what "objective" means'. Objectivity, he suggested, meant having to 'stand neutrally between good and evil, right and wrong, the victim and the oppressor' (Bell 1998: 16–18). Similarly, in the US, CNN's star reporter Christiane Amanpour argued that 'in certain situations, the classic definition of objectivity can mean neutrality, and neutrality can mean you are an accomplice to all sorts of evil' (quoted in Ricchiardi 1996). Being objective, it seemed, meant complicity with evil. Instead, reporters claimed to be listening to their own consciences, which apparently told them to take sides in the wars they covered (particularly Bosnia – the example pointed to by both Bell and Amanpour).

They also sought to make it plain to viewers and readers that they were taking this new approach by couching their reports in personal, often highly emotive terms. Again war reporting threw up some clear examples of this: Fergal Keane's use of a BBC current affairs programme to read out a letter to his newborn son in which he reflected on his experiences covering Rwanda is perhaps the most famous instance of the phenomenon (Keane 1996). The same trend was also visible in other areas of reporting, as objectivity was superseded by the requirements of what Mick Hume (1998) calls 'emotional correctness'. Journalists who did not toe the emotionally correct line risked opprobrium for appearing heartless – as, for example, Kate Adie found in 1996 when her report of the fatal shootings at a school in Dunblane, Scotland, was publicly criticized by a BBC executive as 'forensic'. It seemed that her tone was too cold and factual, failing to hit the right emotional notes (Mayes 2000).

It is notable that the emotional, 'attached' style of reporting that developed in the 1990s did not attract the sort of critique directed at objectivity in the past. Instead, critics sometimes welcomed it as a positive development. John Eldridge et al. (1997: 118–20), for example, after heavily criticizing the 'promotion of the just-war concept' in coverage of the 1991 Gulf War, had nothing but praise for those who ditched the traditional journalistic commitment to objectivity and sought, through their reporting, to influence 'international policy and action' in favour of 'just' war in the Balkans and elsewhere. Reporters who proselytised for international military intervention in the 1990s often saw themselves as critics of Western governments which seemed reluctant to act. Yet in the longer term it became obvious that their moralistic style of journalism coincided with the perspective of powerful states that, by the end of the decade, were justifying NATO's 1999 Kosovo campaign in similar 'ethical' terms (Hammond 2002).

Like political leaders going to war because – as British prime minister Tony Blair said of the 2003 invasion of Iraq – their conscience tells them they must 'do the right thing' (Blair 2003), reporters have attempted to influence policy on the same grounds. The public is often ill-served by such journalism, but this problem is different from the traditional issue of ideological bias. Rather, journalists confront a similar difficulty to that faced by politicians: how to make sense of events when the old framework of political meaning has collapsed. Their response has often been narcissistic, placing their emotional selves at the centre of the story, because the goal has been to resolve this problem of meaning for themselves rather than to inform public debate. The traditional professional routines of journalism were more than mere 'rituals': practices such as fact-checking, or seeking out both sides of a story, offered ways to overcome the limitations of one's own subjective impressions and get at the truth. Today, there is little sense of a necessity to transcend the personal and impressionistic.

The routinism, the reliance on official sources, and the narrowness of debate which critics have associated with the past practice of 'objective journalism' are hardly to be celebrated. And yet, in questioning or abandoning a commitment to objectivity, more recent forms of journalism do not offer an improvement on the past. If objectivity is tied to that active process of rational and critical engagement with public affairs which Habermas locates in the eighteenth century, then objectivity does have a future to the extent that we again come confidently to see ourselves as seekers after truth, able to act on and transform the world.

The Future of Objectivity

We propose that journalism itself can play a significant role in the reconstruction of objectivity. Not in the naïve pretence that reporting is 'real', which would in any case be cynical; but in the recognition of reporting as the deliberate reconstruction of events (necessarily an abstraction from them), which is then the object of scrutiny and deliberation on the part of readers and writers who can now respond to each other in new ways supported by new media technologies. Thus objectivity is reinstated as a social process, and this reinstatement may also contribute to the restatement of humanity as the subject of social reality.

The critique of objectivity was really a critique of objectivity in its alienated form. In the alienated form of objectivity 'hack' journalists were estranged from themselves as subjects producing an object – the story of what happened. Meanwhile readers immobilized by the weight of objects known as facts were equally alienated from themselves as autonomous subjects. Under the terms of alienated objectivity, as writers and readers our own subjectivity became foreign to us. By contrast, today's Western culture is characterized by the restless, weightless movement of subjectivity, in which self-presentation by subjects becomes a continuous process that has no object except the process itself. Not only are we living on thin air (Leadbeater 1999), we are forever blowing bubbles. Moreover, in our bubble made of thin air, as we are estranged from the production of objects by human subjects, so we have replaced alienated objectivity with alienated subjectivity – subjectivity estranged from human subjects producing the world of objects. While this is most readily recognisable in the Western financial economy and its dislocation from production in the East, it is also true of social media and the wilfully inconclusive news process where popular participation has higher status than nailing the story. Hailed as the future of journalism, replacing production with self-perpetuating process – subjectivity without object – is more likely to be the demise of it.

Journalism stands or falls in the attempt to produce a definitive account of events almost as soon as they occur – in other words, journalists applying their subjectivity in the further objectification of the world produced by human subjects. If the world is the object of human subjects, then objectivity is inherent in knowledge which objectifies the actions of human subjects on the world. Thus the tendency towards objectivity occurs spontaneously in the construction of our world for a second time, this time as an object of study. For journalism and also for other forms of knowledge production, the point is to draw out this objective tendency by the further realization of human subjectivity.

Whereas alienated objectivity rested on the denial of human subjectivity, non-alienated objectivity depends on the extension of it. Non-alienated objectivity entails reflexive reporters interacting with a wider range of sources, before and after initial publication, in a concerted, contested attempt to objectify the actions of human subjects. This is objectivity produced collectively by self-conscious subjects – not the pretence that knowledge is a ready-made object which lies on the ground waiting to be picked up and packaged. Non-alienated objectivity is now facilitated by digital technology and the subjective interactions which it enables. It is predicated on human subjects producing the world and it anticipates the possibility of us producing a different one. Posed in these terms, objectivity is not only the end of journalism (its objective); it may also end the prospect of the end (the demise) of journalism.

Furthermore, non-alienated objectivity holds out the possibility of a new relationship between journalism and the academy. In the current context journalists often come close to and sometimes arrive at objectivity in the course of their daily work, yet they are loathe to admit this, or even to volunteer it as their ambition. The critique of objectivity, in which all objectivity was erroneously identified with its alienated form, has helped to put journalism on the defensive. For this the academy is largely to blame – the same academy that previously promoted the alienated objectivity which it subsequently came to reject. Thus journalism has been ill-served by the academy, not once but twice. No wonder there is a vexed relationship between journalism and journalism studies.

But now the further process of objectification by which journalism itself becomes an object of study, can serve both its own interests and those of journalism by reposing objectivity; by recapturing the capacity of human subjects to capture in thought the essence of what they have wrought in practice. Apart from its bracing effect on journalism studies, this approach would also serve journalists by offering them an ambitious but realistic ideal – a guiding principle for their own professional lives, and a weapon to be deployed in the constant skirmishes of office politics. In all these various aspects, the future of journalism lies in objectivity; just as the future of objectivity is partly to be found in journalism.

References

Allan, S. (1997). 'News and the Public Sphere: Towards a History of Objectivity and Impartiality' in Bromley, M., and O'Malley, T. (eds), *A Journalism Reader*. London: Routledge.

Bell, M. (1998). 'The Journalism of Attachment' in Kieran, M. (ed.), *Media Ethics*. London: Routledge.

Bernays, E.L. (1947). 'The Engineering of Consent', *The Annals of the American Academy of Political and Social Science* 250, 113–20.

Blair, T. (2003). Statement Opening Iraq Debate in Parliament, 18 March 2003. Available at www.number-10.gov.uk/output/Page3294

Cunningham, B. (2003). 'Re-thinking Objectivity' in *Columbia Journalism Review, July–August 2003, 24–32.*

Curran, J., and Seaton, J. (2003). *Power Without Responsibility: The Press, Broadcasting and New Media in Britain* (6th edn). London: Routledge.

Eldridge, J., Kitzinger, J., and Williams, K. (1997). *The Mass Media and Power in Modern Britain*. Oxford: Oxford University Press.

Glasgow Media Group (1995). 'Ritual tasks' in Eldridge, J. (ed.), *The Glasgow Media Group Reader Vol. 1*. London: Routledge.

Habermas, J. (1989). *The Structural Transformation of the Public Sphere*. Cambridge: Polity.

Hall, S., Crichter, C., Jefferson, T., Clarke, J., and Roberts, B. (1978). *Policing the Crisis*. London: Macmillan.

Hallin, D. (1986). *The 'Uncensored War': The Media and Vietnam*. Oxford: Oxford University Press.

Hammond, P. (2002). 'Moral Combat: Advocacy Journalists and the New Humanitarianism' in Chandler, D. (ed.), *Rethinking Human Rights*. Basingstoke: Palgrave.

Hume, M. (1998). *Televictims*. London: Informinc.

Keane, F. (1996). 'Letter to Daniel' in *From Our Own Correspondent*, BBC Radio 4, 15 February 1996.

Leadbeater, C. (1999). *Living On Thin Air: The New Economy*. London: Viking.

Lewis, P., and Pearlman, C. (1986). *Media and Power*. London: Camden Press.

Lichtenberg, J. (1991). 'In Defense of Objectivity' in Curran, J., and Gurevitch, M. (eds), *Mass Media and Society*. London: Arnold.

Lippmann, W. (1997). *Public Opinion*. New York: Free Press.

Mayes, T. (2000). 'Submerging in "therapy news"' in *British Journalism Review* 11:4, 30–6.

Pedelty, M. (1995). *War Stories: The Culture of Foreign Correspondents*. London: Routledge.

Ricchiardi, S. (1996) 'Over the Line?' in *American Journalism Review*, September 1996.

Tuchman, G. (1972). 'Objectivity as Strategic Ritual: An Examination of Newsmen's Notions of Objectivity' in *American Journal of Sociology* 77:4, 660–79.

IVOR GABER

Three Cheers for Subjectivity: Or the Crumbling of the Seven Pillars of Traditional Journalistic Wisdom

It is a truism to state that new technology has changed journalism profoundly. But many traditional journalists maintain that despite all the
technological developments – and in particular the rise of the blogosphere
– the practice of journalism remains essentially unchanged. Perhaps more
importantly they argue that there is a fundamental ethical divide between
'journalists' and 'bloggers'. This paper challenges this view and argues,
using the UK's political blogosphere as an example, that the line between
bloggers, blogging journalists, campaigning journalists, commentators and
'journalists' (pure and simple) has become ever more blurred. And this
blurring does not just relate to the expression of opinion and the transmission of rumour and gossip, but also reaches into the dissemination of
news – indeed in some cases bloggers now do news better than journalists.
This blurring also throws into doubt traditional journalistic conventions
of objectivity, truth etc., and, the author suggests, requires the creation of
a new ethical creed to guide journalists and bloggers alike.

One of the fundamental underpinnings of the Anglo-American model
of journalism is the notion of 'objectivity' – described by Michael Schudson (2003: 82) as 'a kind of industrial discipline' for journalists. But it is
the argument of this article that 'objectivity' is based on one of the great
myths of journalism – the 'inverted pyramid' which can be found at the
core of much journalism teaching. This is the notion that a news story must
be structured with the most important aspects of the story coming first –
classically the 'Who, What, How, Where When and Why' followed by the
next most important, with the least important at the bottom – awaiting
the sub-editors ready knife (see Niblock 1996: 14 for a typical example). A
classic example of this format might be: 'Lady Godiva (who) rode (what)

naked (how) through the streets of Coventry (where) yesterday (when) in a bid to cut taxes (why)'. This format superseded the idea that journalists told their 'stories' in more conventional narrative chronologies, and its origins lay either in the US or Britain, depending on which media historian's interpretation is preferred.

In the US it coincided with the growth of the telegraph as means of transmitting news which, because of its expense, required reporters to compress their dispatches into the fewest number of words and, for fear of transmission failures, they sought to get the gist of the story across first so that if the line went down the newspaper would at least have something to print (see Friend and Singer 2007: 6). The British version of the 'inverted pyramid' traces its origins back to the days when sub-editors and printers worked with back-to-front metal type. By this means the letters come out the right way round once printed, but it also meant that they were back-to-front at the pre-printing stage. Thus, when late cuts had to be made the 'stone sub' could make them from the bottom up, safe in the knowledge that the story had been written with the most important elements first.

But the problem with the inverted pyramid is that it conceals the fact that for many news stories, deciding the gist – and hence what should come first – involves essentially subjective judgments. Thus 'Who, What, How, Where, When and Why', far from being simple observable facts, become hugely problematic. Who is the most important character in the narrative? What (and according to whom) happened? How did it happen (it depends on whom you ask)? Where is the most important location for the events described? When was the significant moment and ... why, oh why, oh why? Furthermore, the argument about the relevance, or otherwise, of the inverted pyramid and the traditional notion of objectivity which it underpins are compounded by equally passionate contemporary discussion as to 'what is journalism?' and 'who is a journalist?'

In the pre-digital era these issues were less troublesome – if somebody was paid to write, broadcast or photograph, and they had access to a mass audience via print, radio or television, then they were a journalist and what they did was journalism. But the dramatic changes wrought in the media ecology by the digital revolution have challenged these assumptions.

Traditional Journalism and New Technology

This new ecology of journalism is characterized by four principal developments.

- First, that the traditional media is converging so that a great deal of text (online) is produced by the broadcasters and much audio and video material is to be found on the websites of national and local papers.

- Second, that most (if not all) the traditional media have had to embrace the notion of audience 'interactivity'. This supersedes the notion that journalists 'discover' the news, which they then disseminate. Today journalists receive as much as they give – whether in the form of email responses to stories, participation in blogs, message boards, social networking sites or citizen journalism. The material is coming in all directions, the audience is no longer 'them' and journalists are no longer 'us'.

- Third, that today the audience is no longer dependent on journalists working for the traditional mass media to tell them what is happening. News, unfiltered by journalists is found all over the place and not just on news websites – on sports, entertainment and other sites, on message boards, chat rooms, social networking sites and so on.

- Fourth, and perhaps most significantly, there is the growth of the blogosphere. According to Technocrati, an Internet tracking agency, there is one new blog being created somewhere in the world every 1.4 seconds of every hour of every day – at a recent count, there were up to 200 million active blogs on the Internet.

The Rise of the Political Blogosphere: A Case Study

The election of Barack Obama indicated the power of the Internet as a means of communication, fundraising, mobilization and so on. In the UK the key online activity – in terms of politics – is the political blogosphere. To indicate its size one can note that *Total Politics* magazine publishes an annual list of the 'top' 1,500 political blogs in the UK. These include the 'Top 100 Right of Centre Blogs' the 'Top 100 Left of Centre Blogs', the 'Top 50 LibDem Blogs', the 'Top 20 MP Blogs', the 'Top 40 Welsh Blogs', the 'Top 40 Scottish Blogs', the 'Top 10 Northern Irish Blogs', the 'Top 20 Non-Aligned Blogs', the 'Top 20 Libertarian Blogs', the 'Top 20 Green Blogs' and the 'Top 30 Media Blogs'.

So much for quantity, what about quality? The question thus arises as to what extent the blogs are 'journalism' and these bloggers 'journalists'. Clearly they are part of what Hobsbawm and Lloyd (2008) dubbed the *Commentariat* (albeit, some would argue, the 'rough end'). But they are also breaking news as well. The 2008 British cabinet reshuffle, for example, could be followed on the right-wing *Iain Dale's Diary* blogspot as follows:

Cabinet Reshuffle Open Thread

10.00	Mandelson replaces Hutton at Business, Enterprise & Regulatory Reform – an eye catching, not to say astonishing move. Has there ever been a politician who has come back to the Cabinet after two resignations?
10.05	Jon Cruddas tipped to replace Caroline Flint at Housing – the job he turned down last year.
10.09	Ben Brogan reports that Damian McBride will leave his job as Brown's spokesman. Is he copping it for the Ruth Kelly debacle?
10.15	Geoff Hoon to Transport. Doubt whether he will be very pleased by that.
10.16	Boulton speculating that Margaret Beckett will replace Mandelson as Britain's European Commissioner. This would mean a by election.
10.17	Looks like my friend Mr McNulty is going to miss out.
10.19	Des Browne to leave government of his own volition.
10.21	Oops, forgot to say Nick Brown is tipped to be the new Chief Whip.
10.27	Caroline Flint may go to the Cabinet Office.

10.57	How on earth is Gordon Brown conducting a reshuffle, when he is live on Sky News with the dreadful Michael Winner in Luton?!
11.07	The Labour spin on this reshuffle is that the Tories will be 'nervous' about this reshuffle and will be terrified by Mandelson. You've got to laugh, haven't you? Draper was on Sky earlier saying that this spelled the end of the Tory Party and is a masterstroke by the PM. I wonder if the electorate will be as welcoming.
11.18	A correspondent suggests that it might be Lord Mandelson of Notting Hill!
11.22	Ed Miliband to head up a new department of Energy & Climate Change. Benn to remain at Defra.
11.32	Jeff Rooker (DEFRA Minister in the Lords) is to leave the government.
11.41	John McDonell on Sky saying 'I'm not into criticising personalities, but Mandelson's a ****' or words to that effect.
11.49	Margaret Beckett to the Cabinet Office (so someone says in the comments!)
13.02	David Yelland to be new Director of Communications! Justin Forsyth (who, he) to replace Damian McBride.
13.06	Baroness Cathy Ashton (currently Leader of the Lords) tipped to replace Mandelson in Brussels.
13.24	Adam Boulton withdraws David Yelland story.

This extract highlights some key characteristics of political bloggers. First, during the reshuffle – when the story was moving with great speed – this blog was one of the places in the media where up-to-the-minute reporting of the re-shuffle could be found – even though not all the reports turned out to be accurate. Second, it contained material openly pulled in from other sources – mainstream media, other bloggers and posters (people responding to blogs) – and these are all freely acknowledged. Third, there is the ready admission not only to admit mistakes but to display where text has been corrected (in this case the striking through of the David Yelland story). And finally, there is the injection of comment – some of it useful, some of it gratuitous – mixed in with the reporting. *Iain Dale's Diary* extended this practice further on the night of 4/5 November 2008 as the US presidential election results came through. Dale asked his readers to volunteer to cover a particular TV or Radio channel and then to blog, through the night, both news from the channel and comments on its coverage. This resulted in his website running the most comprehensive live coverage of the results state-by-state as they were being reported by ten UK and US news outlets.

Comparing this mode of coverage to both the mainstream media and perhaps more relevantly to the blogs posted by the mainstream political correspondents, there is a fine line, if any, between what the two groups are doing. One graphic example of this came when there was a minor political splutter in the UK as a junior health minister was forced to apologize for apparently sending emails of a sexual nature to one of his civil servants. Bloggers rushed to suggest that there was more to this than met the eye.

Here are three such examples, all making the same point – two are from right wing bloggers and one from a political correspondent working for the mainstream media. But which is which?

Exhibit A

Ivan Lewis has been a little too outspoken about Gordon's failings, accusing Brown of being out of touch, it was remarkable that he escaped censure at the time. If there is one thing the Brownies excel out, it is malevolence. That the girl isn't quoted means it is not kiss and tell for cash. A few other ministers will be worried that their office darlings could be exposed by vengeful Brownies. This is a warning to other ministers and a score settled.

Exhibit B

A quick thought on Ivan Lewis, the junior Health Minister exposed in the *Mail on Sunday* for 'bombarding a young female aide with suggestive phone messages'. Yes, that's right: the same Ivan Lewis who this summer branded the Prime Minister 'timid' and urged him to show stronger leadership. If the political operation inside No. 10 wasn't so cack-handed these days, I'd suspect that Mr Lewis was the victim of a Downing Street dirty tricks department. Conspiracy theory?

Exhibit C

When I saw the front page headline in today's *Mail on Sunday*, I thought to myself: 'I bet that's Ivan Lewis'. The headline was MINIS-TER: I'M SORRY FOR TEXTS TO GIRL, 24. Now don't get me wrong, I had no prior knowledge of Mr Lewis's text habits, but what I do know is that the junior health minister has angered Number 10 by several off message outbursts about how the government needs to get its act together. Since then, anonymous briefings have suggested he should behave or suffer the consequences. He has just suffered the consequences.

In order, the comments are from blogger Guido Fawke's *Order Order*, *Boulton & Co.* (Sky News) and the third from *Iain Dale's Diary*.

In the United States there have been numerous examples of major political stories being broken by the bloggers and then picked up by the conventional media – these included the start of Bill Clinton's problems with Monica Lewinsky and the revelations that led to the downfall of *CBS News*'s Dan Rather. Recently the 'Draft Sarah Palin for Vice President' blogspot claimed credit (if that's the right word) for securing the nomination of an unknown Alaskan Governor to the Republican Presidential ticket. In the UK the blogs have not, so far, had such high profile stories to boast about (perhaps with the exception of Robert Peston, the BBC's Business Editor's blog) but nonetheless have demonstrated to the mainstream media that they ignore them at their peril.

Political bloggers are often accused of being scurrilous and irresponsible. But what is one to make of the following that appeared on Sky News's Political Blog (13 October 2008) ...?

Osborne: 'Bloody Fool'

UPDATE: A spokesman for Lord Turner has been touch. The head of the FSA insists that our story is 'completely untrue' and 'unhelpful at this time'. Boulton & Co.'s City source stands by what he heard.

Oh dear, it seems the Chairman of the FSA has little time for the Shadow Chancellor. A contact of mine in the city just messaged to say that he witnessed a meeting between Lord Turner and George Osborne this afternoon. I'm told that when the latter was safely out of earshot, Adair Turner muttered 'Bloody Fool' under his breath. Apparently poor George carried on oblivious! But perhaps it's jet lag that's making Lord Turner a little grumpy. He told me he had just got off a plane from Washington when I spoke to him an hour or so ago.

Seven Pillars of Traditional Journalistic Wisdom

Despite this sort of commentary on mainstream media sites, many traditional journalists still seek to distinguish what they do from the bloggers
by asserting that their ethical standards are very different from those of the
blogosphere. Obviously such protestations ignore journalists who blog (as
above) and the fact that many bloggers describe themselves as journalists.
(For example, on the website *Liberal Conspiracy*, ten of the thirty-three
named contributors identify themselves as 'journalists'.)

In the tradition of a Socratic dialogue here is an articulation of 'seven
pillars of journalistic wisdom' that traditional journalists might use to
clarify the difference between themselves and bloggers:

> Journalists seek to be objective, bloggers don't.
> Journalists are interested in 'the truth', for bloggers this is negotiable.
> Journalists are impartial, bloggers are not.
> Journalists seek balance, bloggers don't.
> Journalists are unbiased, bloggers are proudly biased.
> Journalists are independent, bloggers are not.
> Journalists strive to get it right, bloggers don't.

All of these are today, and probably always have been, misconceived.

Objectivity

Objectivity, whether realized or aspired to, is a seductive concept; but like
much that it is seductive it flatters to deceive. (For an interesting discussion about the nature of objectivity in journalism, from a constructionist
perspective, see Poerksen 2008.) It must surely be self evident that objectivity is, and has always been, a meaningless concept. That is because all
journalists – subject to official confirmation – are human beings. That
means they have a gender, an ethnicity, a family, a social background, a
personal history, a set of prejudices etc. etc. that afflict their 'way of seeing'
(cf. Berger 1977). They also have an ingrained sense of 'professional' values

and expectations which colour the way they go about their work. Herman and Chomsky (1994: xii) summarize the pressures thus: 'Most biased choices in the media arise from the preselection of right-thinking people, internalized preconceptions and the adaptation of personnel to the constraints of ownership, organization, market, and political power.' Every attempt by journalists to argue that they are able to put aside their own beliefs and feelings and become, or aspire to become, genuinely 'objective' strengthens a dangerous canard. For it is when journalists believe they have, attained Olympian objectivity that they are in greatest danger of failing to see how their own conscious and unconscious motivations are affecting what and how they report.

Take a simple example of a reporter covering a political gathering. To begin with he or she will probably be part of team, and hence might well be assigned to cover a particular debate, fringe meeting or whatever. So at the very outset the ability to decide what is the most important event at the conference, and to report what he or she regards as the most important event/s of the day, is severely limited. Second, there is the editorial line of the paper (and in the case of the broadcaster, the necessity of attracting and holding an audience) that has to be taken into account in deciding what stories are going to be of interest. Third, there is the prevailing mood of 'today's story' – *Labour in disarray* or whatever – that colours news judgements. And all this before we get to considering how the journalist reports a debate, or meeting, that might have taken place over two hours, involved twenty participants, speaking the equivalent of 10,000 words into 250 crisp and accurate words.

Of course, the way s/he does it, is by making brutal selections of what quotes to use, and by summarizing the broad thrust of the debate in a couple of dozen words. And how is this selection made? 'News judgement' is the usual response. But what is 'news judgement' if it is not a mix of providing the newspaper or broadcaster with what is expected, based on past performance, professional rituals, prevailing moods and a soupçon of personal viewpoint. It is not wrong, there is probably no other way to do it, but 'objective' it is not. To all of which bloggers might respond that since they make no pretence of 'objectivity' none of these difficulties apply to them.

Truth

The notion of the 'truth' is highly problematic – in most situations, there are many truths not one. Deliberate falsity is rare but arguments as to what are the most important elements of a particular event are not. To return to the example of the political gathering – the journalist reporting the fringe meeting at which nineteen speakers said that Labour should stick with Gordon Brown as leader and one that said he should go, would see the 'truth' of the meeting being an overwhelming show of support for Brown. But if the one speaker against was a former cabinet minister, then undoubtedly that would lead the reporter's story. Whose 'truth', then, is right? Bloggers represent the 'truth' by simply reporting everything they hear and then correcting items when they discover them to be untrue.

Impartiality

Impartiality is equally problematic, even if the UK's broadcasting legislation, which requires broadcasters to be impartial in matters of public controversy, implies that it is not. The BBC's *Editorial Guidelines*, for example, state that 'impartiality lies at the heart of the BBC's commitment to its audiences.' Should a journalist be 'impartial' between the racist and the non-racist, the climate scientist and the climate-change sceptic, the eminent historian and the holocaust denier? If the answer is no – as it surely must be – how does the journalist decide which stories require impartiality and which do not? Clearly political stories ought to demonstrate impartiality, but what happens when the journalist works for a newspaper with a political line that requires not just reportage but 'informed comment' as well. And what of the category of 'campaigning journalist' – a badge that many now wear with pride? Is the journalist campaigning against pollution from a local factory required to be impartial in the controversy? And what happens if his or her newspaper, or TV station, decides that it is going to formally back the campaign? Whither impartiality then? The blogger doesn't seek to be impartial and so has no agonising to do.

Balance

The problem with balance is that it implies that all stories have two, more or less valid, sides. As the discussion about impartiality suggests, giving equality of treatment to two sides in a number of areas can be highly problematic. But there is another issue. Many, if not most, controversies that catch the attention of the media have more than two sides to them – situations, once investigated in depth, are generally more nuanced than they might first appear and hence do not lend themselves to simple 'on the one hand, on the other hand' treatments.

Bias

For all the reasons outlined in the discussion about objectivity, journalists are rarely genuinely unbiased. Perhaps in reporting a football match between two teams about which the reporter has no strong feelings, a journalist might begin with an unbiased approach. But during the ninety minutes biases can, and do, develop – this team is playing unfairly, that team is showing more determination, the referee is biased and so on. All (or most) journalists start determined to be unbiased but by the time it has come to start putting the story together, unseen and unheard bias will have reared its ugly head. Online, on the other hand, the biases scream out to be seen and heard.

Independence

Are journalists independent, whilst bloggers are not? Independence implies writing or broadcasting without let or hindrance. But journalists need to reach audiences in order to be journalists. If the TV channel won't commission the programme, the programme does not exist (unless it is streamed on the Internet – as millions of video bloggers are now doing on sites such as YouTube). The columnist might demand that not a word of his or her copy is altered, but if what the writer is writing ceases to please the editor or proprietor, then he or she will lose their column – a thought that is undoubtedly in the back of the minds (if not further forward) of every working columnist. As for the mere mortal hacks labouring away in the foothills of the news, they too have editors and owners and thus no real independence. Conversely, it can be argued that the blogger, with no concerns about being sacked, is far more independent than the journalist. He or she is freer to pursue stories or to vent spleen – freer to write whatever catches their fancy – than their more traditional journalistic cousins.

Accuracy

Finally, do journalists strive for accuracy whilst bloggers don't? On this charge one might argue that both journalists and bloggers try to get it right all the time, even if they also try to put their own spin on the events and select the facts that suit their own particular purposes. The earlier example of the reporter at a political gathering covering a two-hour fringe meeting in 250 words is one example – his or her report might have accurately reported the words he or she chose to select but for anyone who attended the meeting they would, in all probability find that the newspaper report of the meeting bore little relationship to the meeting as they had experienced.

So having destroyed existing journalistic ethics, and even suggested that in the ethics stakes bloggers can claim to be 'ethical' by their own lights, where do we go from here?

Seven Pillars of New Journalistic Wisdom

This author would here like to offer his own pillars of wisdom – applicable to journalists and bloggers alike:

> Thou shalt recognize one's own subjectivity.
> Thou shalt strive to be fair.
> Thou shalt strive to be accurate.
> Thou shalt strive to be thorough.

Thou shalt seek verification.
Thou shalt strive to be transparent.
Thou shalt be accountable.

Subjectivity

Given the previous arguments about the dangers of objectivity, it seems incumbent on journalists and bloggers to recognize 'where they are coming from'. This does not mean writing or broadcasting from a particular perspective *per se*, but it does imply recognizing that, consciously or otherwise, they do have a perspective. In so doing both the journalist and blogger are so much better equipped to counteract it within their own work and ensure that the audience is made aware of the partiality of the journalist or publication. The failure to recognize this can be problematic for journalists and bloggers alike.

Some years ago this author, whilst working for the BBC at Westminster, would observe how some journalists, despite working in a political arena, would declare that they had 'no politics'. Putting aside the issue that everyone in a democratic society has a responsibility to have a view about politics, these journalists were potentially dangerous. They failed to recognize their own prejudices and were thus ill-equipped to monitor their own output to ensure its fairness. Conversely, colleagues who openly declared their own personal politics were better able to monitor themselves to help ensure that their output was less affected (and their colleagues were well-placed to call 'foul' if they thought their prejudices were showing).

Fairness

This brings us to what seems the single most important of the pillars – 'fairness' and its close relationship to subjectivity. For fairness, unlike impartiality, neutrality and so on, is not something that can be established or experienced objectively. By its very nature it is felt. For a broadcast journalist, even working under extreme time pressure, there is always a sense of ultimately how 'fair' or otherwise one is being. Sometimes that awareness only comes to the fore as one watches or listens to the programme on transmission. The overwhelming majority of journalists, one might argue, do set out to be fair; but in the rough and tumble of a news story subjective judgements come to be made about 'good guys' and 'bad guys'. Being aware of such judgements is the key to transcending them. This is done by seeking to attain fairness in the editing which sometimes is achieved and sometimes is not – but the important thing is to be aware when it is not.

Investigative journalism can complicate matters. Most investigations begin with the journalist having some notion of who the 'guilty' man, woman or organization is. The journalist then seeks to uncover the evidence that will sustain that charge. If, in the course of the investigation, he or she finds material that suggests that the original assumption about guilt was mistaken then, as a critical part of the precept of fairness, he or she either ceases the investigation, or produces a story vindicating the subject. If, on the other hand, the journalist does find sufficient evidence of 'guilt' (sufficient to satisfy him or her plus the editors and lawyers) then the story can proceed. Whilst it is important that the subject is provided with some space to state his or her defence, that does not mean equal time and prominence. Of course, should the journalist make the wrong call, then the consequences have to be faced.

Accuracy

The next two precepts – injunctions to be accurate and thorough – are at the heart of ethical journalism and should require little elucidation. Nonetheless, they can conceal as much as they reveal. Accuracy is often assumed to be simply a matter of ensuring that the 'facts' are correct – names, numbers and so on. However, it is worth noting that of complaints to the UK Press Complaints Commission in 2007, 'accuracy' was far and away the largest category, comprising 75 per cent of complaints (in second place, with only 9 per cent of complaints, was privacy). A cursory glance at some of the complaints about accuracy shows that they involved issues such as whether the complainant had said the words attributed to them, or of the complainant denying having given permission for certain information to be used. Thus the term 'accuracy' can conceal as much as it reveals.

However, a simple guideline should be that when reporting matters of fact journalists should take every reasonable care to ensure the accuracy of the information they are reporting – and if in doubt the source of the information should be identified. In an age when much of the information that journalists are using has been obtained online, both checking the information and revealing the sources of information to the audience are significantly easier.

Thoroughness

Thoroughness is more problematic. At what point should the journalist draw the line? This author, on leaving full-time journalism for academia, was asked what the difference was between journalistic and academic research. He answered by saying that it is unlikely that an academic researcher, on ending a conversation with a source who suggested another potential interviewee, would respond, as might a journalist, with: 'No thanks, I've got enough for the piece.' In a journalistic context absolute thoroughness can never be achieved – time and space limitations are always an issue. But a proximity to absolute thoroughness is necessary if the journalist is running an investigation in which allegations of wrong-doing are involved; not only is it editorially necessary but without it, there is little legal cover. (See Welsh et al. 2007: 275–9 for an exposition of the significance of the 'Reynolds Defence' which has made investigative journalism less likely to fall foul of the UK's stringent libel laws.)

Verification

Verification is, in part, another aspect of thoroughness, but it is also an injunction to journalists to only use material from sources they regard as 'reliable', although this raises important issues about the use to be made of material obtained from the Internet – Wikipedia extracts representing only the most obvious example of the problems of verification and provenance online.

Establishing the ideological provenance of, for example, the case study used here – British political blogs – usually appears straightforward. For instance, *Iain Dale's Diary* defines itself as 'Daily political commentary of the Conservative Party activist Iain Dale' whilst Guido Fawkes describes his blogspot as 'Discussion on parliamentary plots, rumours and conspiracy' which, whilst it might not fully indicate his blog's libertarian bent, does at least suggest that it is a long way from 'Here is the News'. On the other hand the world's most popular political blogspot the right-wing *Drudge Report* gives absolutely no indication of its political stance, neither does its opposite number on the blogging left *The Huffington Post*.

But if the blogs are dangerous territory for journalists in pursuit of 'verification' maybe 'old-fashioned' websites represent a safer terrain? It seems not: for there has always been an issue of provenance online. For example, the UK website *Spiked Online* describes itself as standing for 'liberty, enlightenment, experimentation and excellence.' What it fails to explain is that the website grew out of the collapse of the magazine *Living Marxism*, which itself had developed out of a small Trotskyist sect – the Revolutionary Communist Party. But if this sounds like a leftist conspiracy, then think again. *Spiked*'s agenda includes an opposition to environmental-ism, multiculturalism, the European Union and all things it would describe as 'politically correct'. None of this is revealed on its website: indeed, one has to turn to campaigners such as George Monbiot (2003), writing in *The Guardian*, to find this out. So verification is important for both the journalist and his or her audiences, particularly online.

Transparency

From 'verification' to 'transparency' is not a great distance. Transparency has two meanings. One relates to the previous discussion about provenance, the other to the journalist's working methods. It seems important and rela-tively easy (particularly online) to maintain a position of revelation – not so much in terms of content but in terms of method. This involves enabling the audience to make judgments about how information was obtained and where more can be found. Journalists thinking about their working methods need only have one simple criterion in mind when deciding if a particular course of action would be 'ethical' – and that is, 'Would I be comfortable if my working methods were made public, could I justify them in terms of the "public interest"?'

Accountability

Linked to transparency, accountability can be problematic. To what extent is the journalist – offline or online – 'accountable' and to whom? Certainly he or she is accountable to whoever is paying him or her to be a journalist. But there is also, arguably, the more important issue of accountability to the audience. This can be complex. Journalists working for publicly funded or subsidized media – the BBC, for example – have a direct line of accountability to their communities. This is an accountability to the public as their paymasters, in terms of the extent to which their work enhances or detracts from the public sphere.

But do journalists, working outside the public media, have an accountability to society at large? This author would argue that in a pluralist liberal democracy, probably not. Certainly they are accountable to the courts for libel, breaches of privacy and so on, but it is difficult to sustain the argument that they are any more accountable to the public than, say, accountants, solicitors or doctors are. Certainly all such groups are accountable to their 'clients' (not something that directly impacts on journalists as such) and also to the regulators and professional associations that police their professions. In this sense an argument can be made that there is an accountability, once removed. But most journalists – online or offline – would probably see their accountability being simply one of maintaining their audience, both in terms of numbers and of trust. According to Monck (2008: 4), however, even the issue of trust is an outdated concern: 'For me transparency and information supersede our need for trust.'

Conclusion

The debate about trust underpins this whole discussion around the ethics of traditional and new journalism. We are in a time when journalism is undergoing more changes – both in terms of formats and content – than at any time in the past. Of course, change has been a constant factor throughout the history of the media. However, the changes we are now witnessing – and this paper has only focussed on those affecting the reporting of politics – are having a profound impact on our entire understanding of journalism. Is it meaningful, any more, to try to distinguish a particular set of dissemination categories and describe them – and the people who author them – as journalists? And if not then is there any point in trying to establish what is, and what is not, ethical? Beckett (2008: 4, 167) for one argues that this new journalism – what he describes as 'networked journalism' – in fact offers the opportunity of enabling traditional journalism to enhance its own social role by being the spur to creating new ethical standards for all.

That some bloggers, citizen journalists or social networkers do not acknowledge or follow ethical precepts does not invalidate the notion that they should exist. For whilst traditional journalists' own codes of conduct were more often honoured in the breach than in the observance, they did, at least, provide a template for what was to be regarded as acceptable behaviour. Bloggers, and other online contributors, can at times appear to be following an ultra-libertarian philosophy of 'publish and be damned' which creates the real danger of an anarchic tsunami of information which leads the audience, actually or metaphorically, to simply switch off. Surely a far better banner, for bloggers and journalists alike, to be fighting under would be: 'Let's have some ethical standards, for if we don't have any, how do we know when we are breaking them?'

References

Beckett, C. (2008). *SuperMedia*. Oxford: Blackwell.

Berger, J. (1977). *Ways of Seeing*. Harmondsworth: Penguin.

Franklin, B, (2005). *Key Concepts in Journalism Studies*. London, Sage.

Friend, C., and Singer, J. (2007). *Online Journalism Ethics*. New York: M.E. Sharpe.

Herman, E., and Chomsky, N. (1994). *Manufacturing Consent: The Political Economy of the Mass Media*. London: Vintage.

Hobsbawm, J., and Lloyd, J. (2008). *The Power of the Commentariat*. London: O'Mara Associates.

Monbiot, G. (2003). 'Invasion of the Entryists' in *The Guardian*, 9 December 2003.

Monck, A., with Hanley, M. (2008). *Can You Trust the Media?* Cambridge: Icon Books.

Niblock, S. (1996). *Inside Journalism*. London: Blueprint.

Poerksen, B. (2008). 'The Ideal and the Myth of Objectivity' in *Journalism Studies* 9:2, 296–304.

Schudson, M. (2003). *The Sociology of News*. New York: W.W. Norton & Co.

Welsh, T., et al. (2007). *McNae's Essential Law for Journalists: 19th Edition*. Oxford: Oxford University Press.

JON SILVERMAN

Youtube If You Want To: New Media, Investigative Tele-Journalism and Social Control

If one of the principal aims of investigative journalism is to 'speak truth to power' television's voice has become muffled in recent years. In a multi-channel environment with an ever more relentless focus on audience share, the mainstream broadcast media has grasped at techniques, such as secret filming, to deliver its messages. The ubiquity of 3G phones and the global impact of the Internet should subject the 'official account' to more rigorous scrutiny than ever before. The field of crime and policing is especially ripe for a citizens-led attack. But in the UK, the gauntlet has barely been picked up. Can the mobile phone be a more effective weapon against the forces of social control?

In 2007, the mayor of New York, Michael Bloomberg, urged citizens to use their mobile phones to record crimes in progress and send the images directly to the police. In July 2009, the National Association for the Advancement of Colored People launched an online reporting system which enables users to upload cell phone images of alleged police abuse. In December 2009, police in San Jose, California, began wearing miniature ear-mounted cameras to record every face-to-face contact they have with the public. This was a direct response to a rising number of complaints of police brutality, supported by mobile phone footage. In the US, many of the most egregious examples of police free-handedness with batons, Tasers, even guns find their way onto the TV bulletins, both local and national. In one notorious case, the transmission of a fatal shooting by a transit authority officer of an unarmed man in Oakland, California, this led to turbulent protests and a murder charge against the officer.

That situation represents a snapshot of the topsy-turvy picture from the United States where, in 2008, CBS became the first of the traditional

Big Three TV networks to announce the launch of its own dedicated website – Cbseyemobile.com – on which the public could upload video and
still images of 'newsworthy' events from their mobile phones. (CBS was
quite slow off the mark in this regard, having been beaten to the punch
by eighteen months by CNN.)

In the field of crime and policing, Year Zero for the empowerment of
the 'citizen journalist' (or 'witness contributor', as Britain's National Union
of Journalists understandably prefers it) was 1992. And the place was California. In that year, the brutal beating of a black suspect, Rodney King,
by a group of largely white LAPD officers – caught on a home camcorder
and replayed endlessly on the networks – demonstrated that a police force
buttressed and burnished by an expensive press operation and hitherto
defended to the hilt by the mayor could be exposed by a sequence of hazy
live images shot purely by chance. It was a seminal moment.

The distance between the media worlds of 2010 and 1992 is as great
as the possibilities of travel before and after the Wright Brothers' first
flight. But the debate around what Herman and Chomsky famously termed
manufacturing consent (Herman & Chomsky 1992) – i.e. the ways in which
public opinion is manipulated in order to maintain the dominance of the
elite or 'specialized class' – remains as lively as ever. The object of this paper
is to take one aspect of social tension, around policing, as a kind of litmus
test to see how the explosion of new media is playing a part in devolving
and democratizing news gathering, as an element of what has been called
monitory democracy (Keane 2009). And to ask why, at least in the UK, the
process has been slower to emerge than might have been expected.

User-Generated Content: New Wine in an Old Bottle?

In 1992, while working as the BBC home affairs correspondent, a radio
story came my way which demonstrated how the broadcast on national
radio of a clandestinely recorded encounter between police officers and a

suspect could shred Scotland Yard's PR-varnished anti-racism policy in a manner which a reporter's second-hand account could not match. A man of Pakistani origin appeared at Snaresbrook Crown Court, charged with assaulting his wife. It was a routine 'domestic' case. What lifted it out of the ordinary was a cassette recording played to the court in which the two arresting officers could be heard racially abusing the suspect as they transported him in their car to the police station. The judge was so disturbed by what he heard that he ordered a transcript sent without delay to the Director of Public Prosecutions.

Disappointed that the story had got little or no publicity (the adverse effect on court reporting caused by the decline in the number of local newspaper reporters was a matter of concern even twenty years ago), an anti-racism campaigning organization, the Newham Monitoring Group, offered me the recording which I included in a report for the BBC Radio 4 *Today* programme. The story also ran on BBC television news and was picked up by other parts of the national media. The uncomfortable publicity forced the then Scotland Yard Commissioner, Sir Peter Imbert, into his first public admission about the case and led to a disciplinary inquiry.

The time-lag between my becoming aware of the cassette recording and the fully realized story airing on national radio was a fortnight. There were technical issues to surmount. It was a cheap cassette player and the recording quality poor. There was considerable background noise from the car engine. The racial abuse was clear enough but, when the 'victim' shouted several times 'stop beating me' and 'why are you beating me?', was there any evidence to corroborate a physical attack by the officers or was he playing to the gallery? Indeed, why had he hidden the machine in the first place? Was it some kind of reverse sting to entrap the police? All of these considerations needed to be thoroughly checked. The BBC lawyers were closely involved.

Fast forward to 2010 and it is highly likely that the arrested man would have used his 3G phone to record the confrontation in the police car and that the story would break on the Internet, possibly posted on YouTube. With no verification process from nervous lawyers and broadcasting executives, it would certainly see the light of day without a fortnight's delay. On the other hand, it would join the myriad other items of social/political curiosity swirling around cyberspace so its significance might take several days, even a fortnight, to emerge. Perhaps a celebrity Tweeter with an interest in police issues might bring it to wider attention. But, apart from material shot during the G20 protests in London in 2009 (above all, the death of Ian Tomlinson), there is precious little evidence of so-called User-Generated Content (UGC) having the kind of national impact which is going to re-write the rules of engagement between police and society in the UK. Given the ubiquity of the camera phone and the thousands of daily inter-actions between users and the police, this is perhaps surprising.

A search of the YouTube site for the words 'police brutality caught on camera – 2009' (for the purposes of this chapter) produced thirty-four results. The first was from Teheran; one was from a climate camp protest in the UK; all of the rest came from the United States. Even allowing for the fact that, in the main, British police officers do not have the same reputation for violence as some of their American counterparts, and that there is more US-generated material on YouTube, this imbalance is disproportionate.

Added Value – But How Much?

On British television, coverage of a number of high profile stories since 2004 has been enhanced by 3G phone footage – the South-East Asian tsunami, the Buncefield oil depot fire, the UK storms of January 2007, shots taken inside a Ryanair jet which lost pressure and plummeted 30,000 feet. But one story, above all, had a profound impact on the thinking of those who run television and led TV executives to predict that camera phone footage would be increasingly used by all news organizations. It was the 7/7 terrorist bombings in London in July 2005.

Helen Boaden, director of BBC News, said that 'people were sending us images within minutes of the first problems on the tube, before we even knew there was a bomb' (*Independent on Sunday*, 10 July 2005; cited in Allan 2006: 147–8). In all, the BBC received more than 1,000 images from the public, including about twenty videos, as well as an avalanche of

20,000 emails and 4,000 text messages. Referring to the power of some of the digital images captured on mobile phones, Sky News executive editor John Ryley has said: 'It's a real example of how news has changed as technology has changed' (*Independent on Sunday*, 10 July 2005; cited in Allan 2006: 152).

Moreover, it was not just the illustrative effect of these images recorded by ordinary members of the public but the fact that they added to the understanding of the event. For example, most people will recall, without prompting, the picture of the London bus with its roof sheared off. That was not merely a memorable shot (so much so that it was the main picture on the front page of the *BBC News* website for most of 7 July) but, being available so quickly after the first reports were arriving in newsrooms, established that the early explanation that a power surge was to blame was not correct and that the true cause was a bombing. Equally graphic footage from inside some of the tube train carriages helped pinpoint the exact time of the explosions – as well as conveying the atmosphere on the underground.

For the media professionals, there was much to reflect on post-7/7. As early as the following day, Simon Bucks, Sky News associate editor, suggested that the material sent in by the public represented 'a democratisation of news coverage' (*Agence France Presse*, 8 July 2005; cited in Allan 2006: 154). Six months later, at a BBC seminar held at Television Centre in January 2006 to take stock of the new broadcast landscape, one editor said that, before 7/7, he and his colleagues would never have believed that such immediate coverage of a major event was possible. Another editor (cited by Torin Douglas in a piece for the *BBC News* website's *NewsWatch*, 25 January 2006) has said: 'we're not gatekeepers any more, controlling the flow of information. We should use the new technology to engage better with our audience. They can help improve the quality of our journalism.'

It is the concept of democratization and that phrase, 'the quality of our journalism' that this paper will address in order to suggest that, in the five years since the 7/7 bombings, while UGC has certainly made a difference to mainstream broadcasting output in terms of the range of material which gets on air, it has fallen short in providing depth, understanding and empowerment, and that this remains a great unexploited opportunity.

There is no doubt that broadcasters recognize that devices as portable and ubiquitous as a camera phone or the latest generation of camcorders, are potentially useful tools in capturing events, particularly the unexpected ones, which a television camera crew (invariably these days, just one person) could not hope to cover – the more so because the technical quality of the camera phone image has improved significantly in recent years. This is reflected in the sheer number of on-air outlets which, at any one time, have showcased such material. To name just a few, the BBC News Channel has had a weekend segment of thirty minutes, airing first on a Saturday, and repeated twice on Sunday, called *Your News*. Channel 4 ran a programme called *Homemade*, which was billed as YouTube for TV. You can also upload your own videos onto the Sky News website.

All of this is impressively interactive and fulfils the hope of the BBC executive, quoted above, that the broadcasters should exploit the new technology to 'engage better with our audience.' But does it come anywhere close to his other wish – 'to improve the quality of our journalism'? Only if 'quality' is defined in a narrow sense and excludes a collaborative pushing back of investigative boundaries. *Your News* on the BBC News Channel trumpeted the fact that the story ideas came from the public and that each programme was anchored from locations which do not normally feature in BBC News and Current affairs output. But one suspects that this was more to do with the BBC's commitment to move a larger proportion of its programming away from London and the South-East than with providing a platform for 'citizen journalism'. In any case, can it be defined as such when both the presentation and production were still very much in the hands of BBC professionals (as is the case with the Radio 4 equivalent *iPM*)?

The Dark Side of the Mobile

According to the Home Office, network subscriptions for mobile phones in the UK increased from 17 million in 1999 to 72 million in 2007 (Home Office press notice, 109/2007). The mobile is undoubtedly one of the most important cultural artefacts of our time, an indispensable social link and a vital business device. And in Iran in 2009, it became a means, in conjunction with the Internet, by which grassroots activists undermined the hegemonic control of the state, and its compliant media, and kept the world informed of the violence which flowed from a disputed election. It would be hard to imagine a more flexible device than the mobile, as it has transmuted from the unwieldy brick of the 1980s to the slim all-singing/dancing iPhone of today. According to the biennial Oxford Internet Survey (conducted by the Oxford Internet Institute), 51 per cent of those surveyed in 2009 sent photos by mobile phone. In numbers, this amounts (using figures from the Mobile Data Association's UK Mobile Trends Report 2009) to the sending of over 600 million MMS (video and picture messages) in 2009. So why has the camera phone not made a greater contribution to 'citizen journalism' in the UK?

One way of answering that is to consider the various ways in which mobile phones feature in the media. The vast majority are negative. In the early years of the twenty-first century, the context was as likely to be crime as anything else. Briefings at Scotland Yard regularly emphasized the high proportion of street crime and mugging which centred on the theft of a mobile. The Lord Chief Justice issued sentencing guidance prescribing minimum prison terms for such an offence (29 January 2002). Significant sums were spent on researching ways of blocking stolen handsets and the UK mobile phone industry introduced a Crime Reduction Charter (27 July 2006).

Then came the ugly phenomenon known as 'happy slapping' in which people were gratuitously attacked, often by teenagers, and the assault captured on a camera phone and posted on the Internet. Who knows, perhaps it influenced the two young brothers who tortured two children at Edlington in South Yorkshire in 2009, recording the crime on their mobile. Even on 7/7 there were those in the mainstream media who were concerned about the ethics of camera phone footage taken by members of the public – see John Naughton, writing in *The Observer* (17 July 2005), who complained of the 'ghoulish voyeurism' enabled by modern communication technology (cited in Allan 2006: 155–6).

The dangers of using a mobile while driving have featured regularly in government information campaigns. Following a 2008 court case in which a man was convicted of plotting a murder from his prison cell via a mobile phone, the smuggling of mobiles into prison is now considered more newsworthy than the infiltration of drugs. Paradoxically, while drug dealers and paedophiles have used untraceable handsets to disguise their activities, it is a staple of television drama for detectives to be depicted pinpointing the location of the criminal by his mobile phone signal.

The explosion in social networking would not have happened without SMS texting and, for many parents of teenage and pre-pubertal children, the mobile, which is, on the one hand, a reassuring means of keeping tabs on their offspring, has also become a focus of anxiety. In 2009, research published by the charity, Beatbullying, found that 38 per cent of under-eighteen-year-olds had 'received an offensive or distressing sexual image via text or email.' This phenomenon has become known as 'sexting'. In 2008 an inquest in Ohio was told that a teenager hanged herself after a nude photo of her that she had 'sexted' to her boyfriend was circulated around her high school after they broke up. In a less threatening context, school exams, there has been a sharp rise in the number of pupils attempting to cheat by smuggling mobiles into the classroom.

But perhaps it is terrorism, the dominant preoccupation of the early twenty-first century, which is chiefly responsible for taking the utilitarian functionality of the mobile from the private to the public sphere, with so many negative consequences. The revelation that the Al-Qaeda bomb which devastated Madrid rail station in 2004 was triggered by a mobile, retrospectively validated the claims made since the 1990s by security and intelligence agencies, such as MI5 and GCHQ, that the mobile could no longer be treated purely as a tool of personal communication. (The terrorists who attempted unsuccessfully to bomb a nightclub in London's Haymarket in June 2007 also intended to use a mobile to trigger the explosion.) Arguments in favour of logging all mobile calls on a giant database gained ground and police forces began to equip themselves with a new generation of data extraction devices to accelerate the downloading of pictures, personal information and numbers from seized mobile phones.

Transmitting Truth to Undermine Power

The myriad examples given above are an attempt to explain why the mobile phone camera has not, so far, fulfilled its potential in the UK as an aid to 'witness contributions'. So, what are those possibilities which remain tantalisingly unexploited? In 2006 camera phone footage of the *Seinfeld* star Michael Richards responding to hecklers during his nightclub performance in Los Angeles with racist abuse was broadcast within hours on the Internet and the firestorm of criticism badly damaged his career. In 2007 cell phone pictures on YouTube showed a young boy being dragged through a Walmart store in the US by his hair after he had enraged his grandmother by his misbehaviour. A police child abuse investigation ensued.

In an episode with more wide-ranging connotations, a mobile phone smuggled into the execution chamber of Saddam Hussein in 2006 recorded grisly and chaotic images of his last moments, which later appeared in news broadcasts around the world. According to Anna Reading (2009; cited in *The Guardian*, 8 January 2010), the footage 'took away the pretence of civility that some tried to place around the act.'

But it is in the context of interactions between the police and public, of which there are many thousands daily, that you would expect to find the most productive use of the camera phone in challenging the official version of events – or confirming it. A case in point was the arrest, in June 2009, of a man in Nottingham city centre by officers who used a Taser to subdue him. Part of the arrest was filmed and footage appeared on YouTube, leading to allegations of police brutality. An investigation was carried out by the Independent Police Complaints Commission which concluded that the use of the Taser had been justified (IPCC press release, 11 February 2010).

The singer and political activist, Billy Bragg, sees the technology as a new tool to be embraced. On 8 January 2010 he told *The Guardian*: 'Thanks in part to the camera phone, we're all reporters now. And that idea is going to have some pretty radical consequences, especially for police officers. Think about it: only an idiot goes to a demonstration without a camera or a camera phone nowadays. At best, it is subversive in the way it's being used.'

Yet arguably this is not subversive enough. The only example this author could find of camera phone pictures embarrassing the police in 2010 was an incident filmed during the January snow in Oxfordshire. A group of officers was reprimanded after one was pictured on YouTube using his riot shield as an improvised sled to careen down a steep hill. At least, in this instance, the officers were relaxed about being filmed. When a passer-by tried to film the arrest of an unemployed man in a London street, he had the pictures deleted from his 3G phone, the reason, according to London magistrate Simon Neave (in a letter to *The Guardian*, 24 February 2009), being 'to stop police being on YouTube'. Mr Neave went on to argue: 'If we are to have a surveillance society, perhaps the watching should be both ways – monitoring officials as well as the public. '

All the technological ingredients are in place for the professional broadcasters to help nurture this transformative leap in cultural behaviour. Allan (2006: 167) argues that 'in the era of instant communication, when mobile telephone handsets are likely to be camera or video capable, the transfer of communicative power from news organization to citizen is being consolidated.' Nevertheless, in a heavily regulated television environment, there may be institutional limitations on the use to which this 'transfer of power' is put.

Conclusion

According to Director of BBC News Helen Boaden (*The Guardian*, 11 July 2005; cited in Allan 2006: 166), 'people are very media-savvy and as they get used to creating pictures and video on their phones in normal life, they increasingly think of sending it to us when major incidents occur. It shows there is a terrific level of trust between the audience and us, creating a more intimate relationship than in the past. It shows a new closeness forming between the BBC and the public.'

For the BBC, relying as it does on a universal licence fee which is becoming increasingly hard to justify in an age of multi-channel choice, the trust and the confidence of its audience represent a vital commodity. This is equally true of the other mainstream broadcasters. So, to hear senior managers talking about the camera phone in terms of forging closer bonds with audiences is understandable. But it is a narrow frame in which to view the possibilities offered by this technology.

Nevertheless, the subversive potential of camera phone footage to challenge official versions of events deserves to be nurtured by the broadcasters, even at a time when compliance with ever more restrictive in-house rules rather than the courage of their convictions seems to be the watchword. Had the camera phone been invented in 1979, is it likely that the killing of the anti-racism campaigner Blair Peach by a member of the Metropolitan Police Special Patrol Group, would not have been captured by at least one of the many thousands of demonstrators present in Southall that day and led to a criminal prosecution of the officer concerned? The fact that this question is being posed more than three decades later surely demonstrates that in the UK, the empowerment of new technology, revelatory though it has been, still has an awful lot more to offer.

References

Allan, S. (2006). *Online News: Journalism and the Internet*. Maidenhead: Open University Press.

Herman, E., and Chomsky, N. (1992), *Manufacturing Consent: The Political Economy of Mass Media*. New York: Vintage.

Keane J. (2009). *The Life and Death of Democracy*. London: Simon & Schuster.

Reading, A. (2009). 'Mobile Witnessing: Ethics and the Camera Phone in the War on Terror' in *Globalisations*, 6:1, 61–76.

DAVID CAMERON

Mobile Journalism: A Snapshot of Current Research and Practice

Descriptions of journalistic practice have long been compartmentalized according to the media forms in which news output is published. Broad distinctions are often made between print and broadcast journalism, or magazine, newspaper, radio, or TV reporters. Recent variants include references to online or Web journalism, or to newer publication forms such as blogging, micro-blogging ('tweeting') and video and audio podcasting. Journalism is also differentiated by the technological means by which it is produced, such as with the solo video journalist ('VJ') equipped with a compact video camera, or the photojournalist now able to publish digital images straight to our screens via the Internet. The past decade has seen the diffusion of terms such as 'backpack journalism' to describe how a solo journalist equipped with a laptop computer, digital camera and satellite uplink can report across a variety of media from almost anywhere in the world.

Another emerging form is that now described as 'mobile journalism' ('MoJo'). The term has been loosely applied to describe a journalistic practice based on reporters equipped with highly portable multimedia newsgathering equipment, including both consumer and professional devices. This chapter examines a specific form of mobile journalism based on the rapid convergence of handheld and wireless computing, digital photography and mobile telephony. Attention is now turning to the newsgathering potential of highly compact – even pocket-sized – digital field reporting kits based upon mobile phones and tablet devices.

Mobile Journalism Practice

The mobile handset has rapidly moved beyond voice telephony or even simple text-based communication into more complex multi-platform delivery systems; some of the latest smartphone models are portable digital media production and data transfer systems with configurations of features such as still and video camera capabilities, media editing software, multimedia file swapping, global positioning satellite receivers, music players, access to radio and television content, email and Web browsers, databases, address books, calendars, clocks, games and many other downloadable and upgradeable software applications (Cameron 2006). The increased availability of wireless connectivity, Web-based software applications and online storage has fuelled a trend from laptop computers towards more compact netbooks, and more recently to touch-screen tablet devices such as Apple's iPad.

One early example of MoJo practice revolved around an experimental toolkit developed by Reuters. The kit was based on a Nokia N95 smartphone, a small tripod, a compact wireless keyboard, a solar battery charger and an external microphone. In late 2007, selected Reuters journalists used the kit to provide field reports that were published on a website established specifically for the project, and though no longer active it is often cited in descriptions of nascent mainstream mobile newsgathering. Reuters journalists used the MoJo kits as part of their coverage of the Beijing Olympics, though plans to issue MoJo kits to delegates at the 2008 US Democratic and Republican conventions were hampered by a lack of 3G and wireless services in the convention venues (Oliver 2008). *Washington Post* reporter Ed O'Keefe used his mobile phone at the Democratic convention in 2008 to capture footage of Hilary Clinton's endorsement of Barack Obama – this was later edited with TV broadcast footage to form an online news package.

Video is one of the key mobile phone features driving current MoJo practice. The emergence of commercial services and applications such as Kyte's mobile producer application for iPhone or Symbian 60 devices has facilitated reporting from the field, and delivery of that content across multiple platforms such as broadcast, online and mobile. An example is Fox News's use of Kyte to cover the aftermath of the 2010 Haitian earthquake (Hall 2010). In another example of current practice, the Voice of Africa mobile journalism project operating since 2007 describes its reporters as 'camjos' (camera journalists) although they are equipped with mobile devices as an alternative to expensive computers and cameras (Nyirubugara 2008). Stephen Quinn (2008) has outlined other moves towards mobile journalism, all of which centre on video-recording as a key element. These include experiments at Norway's national broadcaster NRK, where various departments considered MoJo content for mainstream platforms like television, while reporters at the online site of the *Philippine Daily Inquirer* in Manila have filed multimedia stories remotely using Blackberry smart-phones (Quinn 2009).

There are also examples of highly productive MoJos working outside of mainstream media, such as Dutch producer Ruud Elmendorp who operates out of Kenya with a website offering more than 180 video news reports from twenty-two countries in Africa. A number of Elmendorp's stories cover the use and diffusion of mobile technology across that continent. In another example cited by Quinn (2008), Californian technology blogger Robert Scoble has been broadcasting live video from his phone since 2007 using the Qik mobile video streaming service. Scoble's work is possibly the inspiration for experiments with mobile journalism by BBC technology reporters (Waters 2008). Other independent MoJos are working more directly with mainstream media organizations. One example was the Berlin Project in 2009, produced by a small collective of multimedia journalists known as Not On The Wires. The team used mobile devices to provide coverage of the twentieth anniversary of the fall of the Berlin Wall, largely in the form of field reporting through images, video, social media updates and audio. Not On The Wires partnered with news wire service Reuters, which used the content to enhance its own coverage of the event.

Increased use of mobile technology by reporters has also started to raise questions about how best to incorporate this form of newsgathering into existing publication activities. To date, much of the professional practice of MoJo appears to have originated within print-based newsrooms that are experimenting with adding multimedia elements to their Web-based publications. Mobile journalists are generally seen as being able to respond quickly to breaking news events, often operating away from the newsroom environment for extended periods of time. For example, a model of the self-sufficient reporter responding to grassroots issues and working with the local community was explored at *The News-Press*, a daily broadsheet newspaper located in Fort Myers, Florida. Although the *News-Press* MoJos did not rely solely on mobile phone technology they believed that untethering reporters from the newsroom could increase their ability to work more closely with the communities in which they operated.

The Pew Research Center's Project for Excellence in Journalism found a growing acceptance of MoJo's among US newspaper editors, despite some dismissing the practice as a fad. Again, the flexibility and speed of the mobile journalist was seen as a key factor to their acceptance in the newsgathering process.

MoJo research

There is still little research literature on mobile journalism. What there is tends to focus upon examinations of so-called citizen journalism or participatory reporting, reflecting recognition of the power of mobile phones as a potential newsgathering device with wide diffusion through the populace. There is an emphasis on the ubiquity of camera-enabled phones, and their impact on the future of newsgathering. In less than a decade, the ability to take still photos and/or video footage with a mobile phone has contributed to the 'radical personalisation of news-gathering' (Goggin 2006: 147).

The combination of wireless communication and compact digital cameras is most apparent in the coverage of crisis situations, or rapidly changing news environments (Pavlik 2003). This is not limited to the use of these devices by journalists and other media professionals to report from the field, as placing mobile communication technology equipped with still and video cameras in the hands of the public has given rise to a new level of eyewitness audio/visual coverage of newsworthy events. Recent examples of the impact of mobile media as news-recording devices include the 2004 South-East Asian tsunami, the 2005 London transport bombings, the aftermath of Hurricane Katrina in 2005, the execution of Saddam Hussein in late 2006, the Virginia Tech shootings in April 2007, and the death of Neda Agha-Soltan during the 2009 Iranian post-election protests. In all these cases professional news coverage initially drew heavily on the resources gathered via mobile phone by eyewitnesses to those events, and in some cases these still and moving images have become iconic representations of those news stories. Commercial services such as Scoopt emerged to act as intermediaries between the mobile-equipped public and news organizations, collecting a percentage of the royalty sales in return. Scoopt was subsequently bought by Getty Images in 2007, and closed down as a separate venture in 2009.

Norwegian newspaper *VG* has developed software called the VG News Portal specifically aimed at helping publications provide the means for mobile-equipped reporters and citizens to submit content to an online publication – again with an emphasis on handling images and video content. An iPhone application called 2200 Tips VG is also available through the Norwegian iTunes store to facilitate the uploading of images, video and text to the *VG* site. Other news organizations have also realized the potential value of tapping into mobile-equipped citizens as eyewitness 'reporters', with iPhone applications released for example by CNN, CBS and the *Straits Times* to encourage and assist people to feed content to those newsrooms.

In the wake of Hurricane Katrina, citizens of New Orleans began using online sites such as Flickr and Blogger to publish their stories, photos and footage of the conditions being experienced in the city as victims waited for assistance. In response some mainstream websites such as CNN.com created their own special Hurricane Katrina citizen journalism sites to tap into this grassroots coverage of the event. Similarly, the bomb attacks on London's transport system in 2005 were seen as a watershed moment in participatory journalism. In addition to the eyewitness mobile phone camera footage and voice reports 'filed' by victims and witnesses to mainstream news organizations, vast amounts of text, images, video and audio

were self-published in the aftermath of the blasts. In particular 'moblogging'
– the combination of mobile media and self-published 'blogs' – proved a
popular and fast way for these accounts and supporting commentary to be
published. It is claimed that the first pictures of the bombings appeared
on a moblog site, and that 3,000 mobloggers contributed content to one
UK moblog site alone (Quinn & Quinn-Allan 2006: 63). Mainstream
media outlets such as the BBC, *The Guardian* and Sky News also attracted
and made use of eyewitness or public-supplied media material, much of it
captured and supplied via mobile media.

A different form of blogging/moblogging is now seen in microblog-
ging applications such as Twitter, which allow users to contribute short text
updates which can include links to other media such as websites, audio,
images and video clips. Although not restricted to mobile devices, a range
of software applications have been developed to facilitate the use of phones,
portable computers and tablet devices to provide content for these information streams. Some device and telecommunication companies market
products specifically on the basis of their support for social media sites such
as Facebook and Twitter. Media organizations are taking greater notice of
these applications as both sources of and outlets for news content.

More broadly the development of social media and content sharing
sites – particularly for video and still images – has provided a significant
publishing outlet for mobile content. YouTube for example allows for simple
and free sharing of video content, including items that could be considered newsworthy, and has introduced tools to facilitate easier uploading
of mobile phone content.

Another emerging research area considers the adoption of mobile
phones as newsgathering and dissemination devices in developing nations.
Across the globe a range of factors such as the prevailing political, economic and social conditions, and the technological infrastructure available
influence the adoption of new technology. Wireless technologies, represented most pervasively by the mobile telephone, are therefore diffusing
at different rates around the world. However, the speed of mobile phone
adoption has outstripped that of other forms of communication technology so far, so that within the past decade 'mobile telephony has moved
from being the technology for a privileged few, to essentially a mainstream
technology' (Castells et al. 2004: 5).

Wireless telephony is increasingly being seen as a means of bridging the 'digital divide' in developing nations by skipping a stage in the development of the telecommunications infrastructure. Rather than spending money on underlying wired systems, which tends to favour major cities or population centres, the GDP available for telecommunications can be spent on developing wireless technology in rural or remote regions. It is possible that the mobile phone will become a grassroots media production and dissemination device in developing nations.

MoJo and the Journalism Curriculum

Consideration of the potential uses of mobile media remains at an early stage among journalism educators. There is increasing awareness of the significance of mobile phones as part of young people's media biographies (Stald 2008), and the potential to co-opt them as learning devices generally (Prensky 2005) and for journalism training in particular. A notable mobile journalism experiment that seeks to address this trend is based at Rhodes University in South Africa. This Knight Foundation funded project will see experiments in citizen-generated content and mobile delivery of news, as well as exploring mobile reporting methods. The project is titled Iindaba Ziyafika, which is normally translated from the Xhosa language as 'the news is coming'. Another experiment based in South Africa was the University of the Witwatersrand's 'Mojozone' campus-based news service, which used Nokia MoJo kits. At the time of the trial, course creator Indra de Lanerolle believed it was important to engage students with the mobile media forms that are transforming journalism: 'The challenges they are grappling with are the same ones that media organisations in print, television and online are also grappling with – how best to deliver content to phones. It's like being around at the very beginning of television – no one knows the answers yet and these students have as good a chance as anyone of finding some of those answers.'

Some of the issues to be considered will be the training of students to understand the technical and practical parameters of producing content for mobile delivery, the nature of mobile media audiences, and the development of cross-platform content. Nguyen (2006) suggests that journalism education would benefit from embracing the theory and practice of participatory journalism, a form that increasingly includes the use of mobile phones. Future journalists will need to act as 'listener, discusser and forum leader/mediator in an intimate interaction with audiences' (Nguyen 2006: 152).

As a production device and a media form the mobile phone is becoming increasingly interesting to news organizations seeking to make use of both professional and amateur content recorded in the field. Software applications to assist people in sharing content from their mobile phones directly with news organizations, or indirectly through media-sharing and social media sites, are becoming increasingly common and freely available for download. Mobile journalism is also becoming an important area of study, as mobile media continue to extend their reach. The impact of the ubiquitous presence of video and still cameras is of particular interest, fuelled by real world examples of eyewitness reporting based on camera phone technology. As mobile technology continues to be taken up by younger users, ensuring the continued development of the technology as new social uses emerge, it is also an area of particular interest to educators both generally, and particularly in the areas of journalism, media and communications.

References

Castells, M., Fernandez-Ardevol, M., Qiu, J., and Sey, A. (2004). *The Mobile Communication Society*. Los Angeles: Annenberg Research Network on International Communication.
Goggin, G. (2006). *Cell Phone Culture*. London: Routledge.

Hall, G. (2010). 'Fox News Reporters Using Kyte Mobile Producer for iPhone to Cover Tragic Events In Haiti'. Available at www.kyte.com/blog/article/fox_news_ reporters_using_kyte_mobile_producer_for_iphone_to_cover_tragic_ev/.

Nguyen, A. (2006). Journalism in the wake of participatory publishing. *Australian Journalism Review*, 28:1, 143–15.

Nyirubugara, O. (2008). 'About Voices of Africa'. Available at www.africanews.com/ site/page/voices_of_africa.

Oliver, L. (2008). 'Reuters using mobile journalism for US political coverage'. Available at www.journalism.co.uk/2/articles/532258.php.

Pavlik, J. (2003). 'New technology and news flows: journalism and crisis coverage' in Kawamoto, K. (ed.), *Digital Journalism*. Lanham: Rowman & Littlefield.

Prensky, M. (2005). 'What can you learn from a cell phone? Almost anything!' in *Innovate* 1:5.

Quinn, S. (2008). 'Why the media is on the move'. Available at www.smh.com.au/ news/articles/why-the-media-is-on-the-move/2008/07/23/1216492457885. html.

Quinn, S. (2009). *MoJo – Mobile journalism in the Asian region*. Singapore: Konrad-Adenauer-Stiftung.

Quinn, S., and Quinn-Allan, D. (2006). 'User-generated content and the changing news cycle' in *Australian Journalism Review*, 28:1, 57–70.

Stald, G. (2008). 'Mobile identity: Youth, identity, and mobile communication media' in Buckingham, D. (ed.), *Youth, Identity, and Digital Media*. Cambridge, MA: MIT Press, 143–64.

Waters, D. (2008). 'Mobile video at Davos'. Available at www.bbc.co.uk/blogs/technology/2008/01/mobile_video_at_davos.html.

RICHARD JUNGER

An Alternative to 'Fortress Journalism'?
Historical and Legal Precedents for Citizen
Journalism and Crowdsourcing in the United States

Most American presidents have made or been involved in off-the-record or leaked comments. Treasury Secretary Alexander Hamilton angered President George Washington in 1794 for leaking information about secret negotiations with the British government (Woestendiek 2003). *New York Herald* reporter John Nugent was arrested by the US Senate in 1848 for publishing information on a secret treaty with Mexico, leaked by a cabinet member of President James K. Polk's administration (Merry 2009). When Commanding General Nelson Miles intimated that American soldiers had inflicted 'cruelties and barbarities' on Filipinos in 1901, President Theodore Roosevelt made an off-the-record remark that Miles's retirement was under consideration, a position he changed when public opinion showed in favour of Miles (Miller 1992). President Franklin Roosevelt leaked details of the Japanese Rape of Nanking in 1938 to bolster efforts to expand the US Navy (Ritchie 1991). In 1961, President John F. Kennedy told newspaper reporters off-the-record that the US had a demonstrable strategic nuclear superiority over the Soviet Union, so angering Soviet President Nikita Khrushchev that the latter ordered nuclear missiles to Cuba (History News Network 2001). And some Russians believed that a 1984 quip by President Ronald Reagan that 'we begin bombing in five minutes', made to technicians prior to a radio speech, was a legitimate threat (Reagan 2007).

But the publishing of off-the-record presidential comments took on a new dimension in 2006 when mobile phone cameras captured humorous moments of the annual Gridiron Club dinner, an off-the-record event for Washington DC insiders since 1885. Two years later, citizen journalist Mayhill Fowler recorded then presidential candidate Barack Obama's observation that 'bitter' small-town Americans 'cling to guns or religion or antipathy to people who aren't like them' and included the quote in a story in the *Huffington Post* (11 April 2008). She also recorded former President Bill Clinton's off-the-record description of a magazine writer as 'slimy' and 'dishonest' (*Huffington Post*, 2 June 2008). Terry Moran, a reporter for cable television's CNBC, 'tweeted' that President Obama had called a rap musician a 'jackass' in what was supposed to be an off-the-record moment in 2009 (*New York Daily News*, 15 September 2009).

Citizen journalists and their works of citizen journalism (CJ), and their kindred online spirit, crowdsourcing, have received cautious mention in mainstream American journalism textbooks. 'Can blogs be considered journalism?' – Carole Rich (2007) asked in *Writing and Reporting News* even as she admitted that a CJ instigated the downfall of television anchorman Dan Rather in 2005 and 2006. The Missouri Group's *News Reporting and Writing* 2008 edition conceded that CJ 'brings a fresh perspective to the news' even as it diminished the practice with the generalization that 'even if journalists don't accept the changes – and some are resistant – it's happening.' 'Journalism is the collection and distribution of information for which one is paid, a trade, a calling, a profession,' media critic Andrew Keen wrote (Keen 2007). CJ has an Orwellian ring to it according to Keen, with the potential to create CJ Big Brothers with omnipresent mobile phone cameras, laptop computers, and related electronic devices. 'The YouTubification of politics is a threat to civic culture,' Keen asserted in 2007, before images of protests in Burma and Iran were disseminated through the website. 'It infantilizes the political process, silencing public discourse and leaving the future of government up to thirty-second video clips shot by camcorder-wielding amateurs with political agendas.' 'Fortress journalism,' the one directional rather than two-directional flow of information involving news providers and consumers (a term coined by Steven Smith of the *Spokane Spokesman-Review* in 1995), remained the preferred model for most American journalism in the early twenty-first century.

By contrast, CJ, the active participation of the public in collecting, reporting, analyzing, and disseminating news, and crowdsourcing, the outsourcing of documents, surveillance, news tips, or story assignments to volunteer groups, have been elements of American political and social culture much longer than Twitter, YouTube, or mobile phone cameras. In reality, the brother of America's 'first printer' Benjamin Franklin produced CJ not unlike that of the *Huffington Post* a few years after the appearance of the first North American newspaper in 1690. Thomas Paine, Alexander Hamilton, frontier newspaper editors, the US Post Office, and social reformer Jacob Riis produced or enabled CJ and crowdsourcing, as did Justice Louis Brandeis, *Village Voice*, underground newspapers, and political activist Daniel Ellsberg. Even though the number of CJ projects declined in the immediate wake of the 2009 recession, the concept remained alive in dozens of online and print incarnations in the United States.

Colonial CJ

Most Europeans recognize the United States' first international celebrity, Benjamin Franklin, but his older brother James is less known. The first issue of James' *New England Courant* appeared in Boston on 7 August 1721. Instead of obeying the religious authorities who ruled the colony with the British government, the elder Franklin allied himself with a group of secular businessmen and published his newspaper without official approval. He invited his business friends to write anonymous letters that he published verbatim. In his first issue, an unnamed CJ attacked a controversial public health practice of the day supported by religious leaders, the use of inoculations to provide immunity against small pox, equating the inoculations to 'the practice of the Greek old women.' Written in the first person, the letter noted that the city council had unanimously voted that the practice was 'rash and dubious, being entirely new, not in the least vouched or recommended.' The majority of residents eventually submitted to the vaccinations and the epidemic was stopped, but Franklin had established a precedent in American journalism, the role of CJ. Franklin ran afoul of the city council the following year for criticizing efforts to defend Boston against pirates and was jailed for contempt. His younger brother Benjamin

briefly filled in for him as editor. The sixteen-year-old Franklin wrote fourteen CJ-type letters under the pseudonym of a middle-aged widow named
'Silence Dogood', the first hoax in the American mass news media history.
Confessing his authorship to his brother, Benjamin moved to Philadelphia
and began his own newspaper career there.

Some fifty years later, an Englishman and three Americans again demonstrated the potential of CJ. Thomas Paine was a failed labour agitator
when he was befriended by Benjamin Franklin in London in 1774. With
a letter of recommendation from Franklin, Paine immigrated to Philadelphia and wrote anonymous articles and poetry for *Pennsylvania Magazine*,
one of the few periodicals produced in the colonies. In January 1776, Paine
wrote *Common Sense* under the pseudonym of 'an Englishman,' phrased
in the style of a church sermon but using newspaper syntax and 'common
sense' analysis. In his pamphlet, Paine ridiculed the imperialistic ambitions
of Great Britain, arguing that physical distance made governance by the
island nation nearly impossible in the distant New World. *Common Sense*
sold more than 500,000 copies with Paine giving his profits to the American
Army. Paine also encouraged unrestricted excerpting and republication,
primitive forms of crowdsourcing. Historian Gordon S. Wood called it
'the most incendiary and popular pamphlet of the entire revolutionary
era.' Paine wrote sixteen more articles in support of the American cause
between 1776 and 1783 that came to be called the *Crisis* papers, again earning no income for his efforts because he encouraged unrestricted republication. A similar provision applied to *The Federalist*, a series of eighty-five
essays appearing under the CJ pseudonym of Publis that appeared in several American newspapers in 1787 and 1788. The articles in support of
ratification of the US Constitution were written at such a rapid pace that
opponents were overwhelmed in responding to them. Only in subsequent
years were politicians Alexander Hamilton, James Madison, and John Jay
identified as the authors.

'Grab & Go' CJs

A new breed of CJs began appearing in the United States after the turn of the nineteenth century, known as frontier or pioneer journalists. These men – there were no women – typically had a mechanic's background in typesetting and printing but little formal education or editorial experience. As new settlements developed along the expanding westward frontier, enterprising printers would hurry to each promising new settlement with what supplies and paper they could carry and establish what they envisioned would be the next great American newspaper. One example was John Calhoun, founder of Chicago's first newspaper, the *Chicago Democrat*. Calhoun learned typesetting and printing as a youth in New York State but had little formal schooling. He had operated a newspaper in upstate New York for less than a year when he heard about frontier Chicago from a friend and journeyed there by boat and stage coach, and on foot. In an office above a hardware store he printed the first edition of the *Democrat* on 26 November 1833. The event was of such importance to the early settlement that spectators cheered as they watched Calhoun peel off the first sticky page from his hand-operated press, vying for the 'first' first issue.

Historians have dwelled on the extreme partisanship of the nineteenth-century American press, but true edge-of-the-frontier editors like Calhoun strived for neutrality and impartiality in their journalism at least until a second, competing newspaper appeared and provided a more traditional two-party political landscape. To build and keep circulation, these pioneer editors endeavoured to offend as few readers as possible, printing eloquent arguments (generally written by anonymous CJs) to attract more settlers and investment capital to their communities. 'More than 800 souls – including the half-breeds – may now be found within the limits that a few months since included less than one-tenth of the number,' an early *Chicago Democrat* issue waxed in prose clearly not written by Calhoun. 'Situated as Chicago is at the mouth of a fine river, on the shore of the noble lake into which the river empties itself; in a country possessing a soil of extraordinary fertility, with a climate whose clear and salubrious atmosphere is almost unsurpassed, it is a matter of wonder that it should be so eagerly sought by enterprising emigrants.' It was only when Chicago's second newspaper, the *American*, appeared in 1836 that the *Democrat* became an adherent to its name. By that time, John Calhoun had sold it to another, better-educated editor named John Wentworth, who went on to become a Democratic congressman and mayor.

Frontier editors were able to distribute their newspapers beyond their tiny settlements through the facilities of what one historian called 'the Manhattan project of communication', the US Post Office (Kielbowicz 1989). Begun by Benjamin Franklin in 1775, President James Madison envisioned a democratic republic of independent, egalitarian towns integrated in space and time by good transportation and an efficient postal system by the early nineteenth century. Using waterways, roads, and railroads, all subsidized to some degree by the federal government, uniform postal rates based on weight rather than distance negated physical proximity as a dimension of communication. Even an edge-of-the-frontier editor could circulate his publication to a broader readership through the cheap mails, and the early nineteenth-century American post office delivered more newspapers than individual correspondence. The result was a nation built if not born on information, the world's first, and that free flow of cheaply-delivered information was enabled by CJ and crowdsourcing.

Behind general circulation newspapers, CJs were involved in the production of specialty American papers. The country's labour movement was aided by pro-labour newspapers staffed and produced by CJs including the *Journeyman Mechanic's Advocate*, which was founded in Philadelphia in 1827, and the *Working Man's Advocate*, started by English printer George H. Evans in 1829. Evans did not have the resources to pay writers and was dependent on CJs from within the ranks of working men for his content. Abolitionism, the social and religious movement against African American enslavement, would not have been possible without CJs as well. William Lloyd Garrison, who had been trained as a printer, began *The Liberator* in Baltimore in 1831, equating abolitionism to the war for independence from Great Britain. His was the most professional of the abolitionist press, but he published CJ contributions and inspired a number of CJ counterparts. Using him as a model, escaped enslaved person Frederick Douglass printed his own paper in Rochester, New York, that routinely featured reports from white and black CJs. 'I write you this letter not because I am a letter writer – by no means, sir, as your readers will learn by reading further,' an African American correspondent in Chicago admitted to Douglass in 1853. As well, CJs were critical to newspapers written for the suffragists' movement, utopian and other dissident religious groups, agrarian and populist political movements, and radical political movements such as socialism, communism, and anarchism.

CJs in the Era of the Professional Reporter

Labour specialization, first described by Adam Smith in 1776, began appearing in American editorial offices during the 1840s and 1850s. The often lengthy, effusive, and occasionally self-serving narrative-writing style provided by CJs disappeared from most American newspapers by mid-century, replaced by more efficient inverted pyramid stories prepared by salaried reporters. Initially, editors, the former *primo uomos* of American newspapering, resisted giving bylines to their reporters, never an issue for CJs, but by the 1880s even the most egocentric editor recognized that bylined stories sold more papers. Letters or correspondent reports that previously manifested a two-way form of communication were condensed and edited, often beyond recognition. A few wealthy men were able to continue the CJ tradition through their own financial support. Former newspaper editor Henry George wrote and published *Progress and Poverty* in 1879, an influential book that highlighted the growing disparity between property owners and what he called wage slaves. Henry Demarest Lloyd, a *Chicago Tribune* editorial writer influenced by the British Christian Socialism movement, quit his newspaper job and wrote an exposé of John D. Rockefeller's monopolistic Standard Oil Company in 1894 called *Wealth Against Commonwealth*. However, few Americans had the ability, time, and financial resources for such efforts.

Another example of CJ produced during the era of the professional reporter was Jacob Riis's 1890 *How the Other Half Lives*. Riis was a Danish immigrant who arrived in the United States in 1871 and lived in poorhouses until he found work as a New York City police reporter. While his day job discounted him as a CJ, Riis taught himself photography, including the cutting-edge technology of flash powder, outside of his regular job. He roamed New York's slums during the 1880s taking spectacular flash pictures of the city's underclass that newspapers could not print because they did not have the necessary reproduction technology. Riis displayed his work in magazines and eventually his own book, *How the Other Half Lives*. His photographs of immigrant life in New York convinced Police Commissioner Theodore Roosevelt to close the city's poor houses, influencing a growing social welfare movement in the United States. When Roosevelt became President a decade later, he called Riis 'the best American I ever knew.'

The Decline of Historical CJ and Crowdsourcing

Crowdsourcing remained commonplace in American newspapers until the late nineteenth century. Beginning in colonial times, editors filled their pages with exchanges, articles clipped from other newspapers. Many were republished verbatim, and amusing stories exist of papers catching competitors stealing their news through the planting of made-up stories. In the spirit of crowdsourcing, many exchanges inspired editorial observations and other forms of journalistic groupthink on topics and issues of the day. Cheap newspaper postal rates encouraged the exchanges. However, such open practices came to an end in the United States when the *New York World* printed the entire text of a poem written by Harriet Monroe, a Chicago poet and newspaper literary critic, in 1893. Monroe had started the copyright process for her poem before it appeared in the *World*, and she sued the newspaper for infringement. The US Supreme Court upheld a lower court verdict in her favour for $5,000 in 1896, declaring that the owner of an original written work had exclusive rights to its use even if it was not formally copyrighted. Within a few years, exchanges effectively ceased as newspapers began copyrighting themselves and everything in them.

However, an early twentieth-century US Supreme Court decision made a case for crowdsourcing. During World War I, British and French authorities barred the American-based International News Service (INS) from the use of their telegraph lines to transmit war reports. To compensate, INS writers rewrote Associated Press (AP) reports (the AP was allowed use of the telegraph lines) that were published in New York papers, inserting their stories in western American papers that were printed three times zones later. The AP sued INS for copyright infringement in 1918 and the US Supreme Court ruled in favor of the AP. While the AP could not prevent what the court called the *publici juris* from copying and repeating the 'history of the day,' it could protect its intellectual property from competitors as long as the news was of commercial or 'hot' value. In a dissenting opinion however, one of the Court's most influential justices, Louis Brandeis, argued in favour of what would come to be called crowdsourcing. 'The fact that a product of the mind has cost its producer money and labor, and has a value for which others are willing to pay, is not sufficient to ensure to it this legal attribute of property,' Brandeis wrote. 'The general rule of law is, that the noblest of human productions – knowledge, truths ascertained, conceptions, and ideas – became, after voluntary communication to others, free as the air to common use.' Brandeis's legal argument has taken on significance as the Internet and crowdsourcing have become more prevalent in the twenty-first century. Meanwhile, the *AP v. INS* ruling resurfaced in 2009 in a case involving an Internet news aggregation service which was redistributing AP dispatches.

In 1925 the *Wall Street Journal* epitomized a low point in the history of American CJ in an editorial written as a response to a comment made by President Calvin Coolidge. Speaking to a meeting of editors, Coolidge criticized the American press for what he considered excessive commercialization. 'A newspaper is a private enterprise, owing nothing to the public, which grants it no franchise,' the *Wall Street Journal* editorialized. 'It is emphatically the property of its owner, who is selling a manufactured product at his own risk.' In response, professional reporters (who had found their own influence diminishing in favour of publishers) began to idolize the so-called 'common man', effectively celebrating the CJs that their predecessors had displaced a half-century earlier. 'I believe that the people's will should be obeyed,' William Randolph Hearst wrote several years later. 'The more I read papers, the less I comprehend, the world and all its capers, and how it all will end,' Ira Gershwin penned to his brother George's music in the 1938 song, 'Love is Here to Stay'. 'Freedom of the press', magazinist A.J. Liebling lamented in 1960, 'is guaranteed only to those who own one' (Brendon 1983: 200).

The Underground Press and its Aftermath

CJ survived the Great Depression in such leftist publications as the *Daily Worker*, *Student Review* and *Champion of Youth*, and CJs were encouraged to contribute to edgy 1950s publications like the *Village Voice*, but they resurfaced in greater numbers as part of the underground or counterculture press during the 1960s and 1970s. Appearing in the UK, Canada, Australia, and other English-language countries as well as the US, most underground publications were produced by college newspaper reporters and editors or others with some journalism training. 'The student journalists who write for the campus papers are working for grades, a degree, and perhaps a little pocket money,' underground historian Roger Lewis (1972: 58–9) noted in his *Outlaws of America*. 'The underground staffers are working solely because it pleases them.' Underground papers routinely shared content through alternative press agencies and exchanges as long as the stories were written in opposition to 'the man.' Labour-intensive to produce, some of the underground papers used the new technology of photocopy machines while others took advantage of offset printing, an older technology that became less expensive in the 1950s and 1960s. 'The more one person does, the more s/he is asked to do,' a CJ staff member complained in a Canadian underground publication (Woodsworth 1974: 47–8): 'If one expresses a millimetre of interest in any subject, ten different groups ask for more [...]. Let me label it the volunteerism syndrome.' CJ-staffed underground newspapers disappeared entirely in the 1970s in favour of professionally-staffed 'alternative' papers that paid homage to the ambiance if not the economics of the underground press. The first newspaper usage of the term 'citizen journalist' appeared in the *New York Times* on 8 September 1976, although it did not enter into common usage until the 1990s (Menand 1995).

Simultaneous to the underground press, two mid-twentieth-century American Supreme Court cases helped to redefine CJ. Beginning in the late 1960s, American prosecutors began subpoenaing evidence from reporters related to illegal drug manufacturing, political radicalism, and other criminal activities. Reporter Paul Branzburg toured a clandestine hashish factory for the *Louisville Courier Journal* in 1969 and was ordered to name his anonymous sources by a state court. A fiercely-divided US Supreme Court ruled in 1972 that the First Amendment did not protect Branzburg and other professional reporters from testifying as required of regular citizens in legal proceedings. One of the most controversial aspects of the decision was alluded to by Associate Justice Lewis F. Powell in notes opened to the public thirty-five years later as published in the *New York Times* on 7 October 2007. 'Who are "newsmen" – how to define,' Justice Powell wrote in reference to a controversy that would grow with the increasing recognition of CJ. In theory, any citizen could call himself or herself a journalist and avoid testifying in court, Powell worried. And as media attorney Floyd Abrams (2005) wrote, American jurisprudence is based in the concept of 'every man's evidence', that every person has to testify in court regardless of profession or social status.

A US Department of Defense citizen employee precipitated the most dramatic episode of CJ in the twentieth century. Economist Daniel Ellsberg contributed to a study of the Vietnam War during the late 1960s commissioned by the Defense Department. Convinced that the war could not be won, Ellsberg used the new technology of photocopying to reproduce 7,000 pages of top-secret documents. With the assistance of fellow researcher Anthony Russo, he gave the photocopies to the *New York Times*, and the paper published summaries and verbatim transcriptions from the

documents in June 1971 until the US government obtained an injunction
against it. Although Ellsberg did not write the actual *Times* articles, he was
intimately involved in their preparation. When the *Times* could no longer
print what came to be called the Pentagon Papers, Ellsberg went to five
other newspapers and helped them continue the series. The newspapers
won in the right to published Ellsberg's documents in a historic decision
on 30 June 1971, although the bulk of the Pentagon Papers remains under
lock and key until 2050. In turn, the Pentagon Papers contributed to the
resignation of President Richard Nixon in 1973 (Ellsberg 1972; Ellsberg
2002).

Conclusion

Recent history has seen a renewed interest in CJ. Protests against a World
Trade Organization meeting in Seattle in 1999 inspired the formation of
a new independent media reminiscent of 1960s underground newspapers, and the development of Internet e-mail lists, message boards, chat
rooms, weblogs, and Twitter 'tweets' expanded the movement. The South
Korean *OhmyNews* website debuted in 2000 with the motto 'every citizen
is a reporter'. The ThemeParkInsider.com website was recognized in 2001
for a crowdsourcing project that tracked personal injuries at amusement
parks. Bloggers questioned the authenticity of documents used in a CBS
report on President George W. Bush's Air National Guard service in 2004,
leading to the resignation of anchor Dan Rather. Mobile or 'mo-jo' photographs and videos of the 2004 Indian Ocean tsunami, the 2005 London
bombing, the 2007 Virginia Tech massacre, the 2007 protests in Burma
and the 2009 protests in Iran have become the accepted images of those
events. CJ platforms such as GroundReport, Global Post, and ProPublica
publish the reports of thousands of voluntary contributors using flexible
copyright licenses that embrace the crowdsourcing philosophy.

Meanwhile, legislation introduced in the US Senate in 2007 sought to define a newsperson as anyone who gathers information of potential interest to the public, uses editorial skills to turn that raw material into a distinct work, and distributes that work to an audience. Yet a bill pending in the US House sought to protect only those who were engaged in reporting, editing, and publishing activities 'for dissemination to the public for a substantial portion of the person's livelihood or for substantial financial gain.' Crowdsourcing has been confused in the United States in the wake of the 1998 Copyright Term Extension Act and the companion Digital Millennium Copyright Act which protect works that have passed into the public domain in European and Asian countries, and which legislation critics have called a form of corporate welfare. If, as Richard Gant (2007) maintained, the mantra that *We're All Journalists Now* has become the case, then further historical and legal research on CJ and crowdsourcing is a necessity, not just in the United States but in European, Asian and other nations as well.

References

Abrams, F. (2005). *Speaking Freely: Trials of the First Amendment*. New York: Penguin.

Brendon, P. (1983). *The Life and Death of the Press Barons*. New York: Atheneum.

Ellsberg, D. (1972). *Papers on the War*. New York: Simon & Schuster.

Ellsberg, D. (2002). *Secrets: A Memoir of Vietnam and the Pentagon Papers*. New York: Viking Press.

Gant, R. (2007). *We're All Journalists Now: The Transformation of the Press and Reshaping of the Law in the Internet Age*. New York: Free Press.

History News Network (2001). 'Leaks to the Media ... An Old Story?' Available at www.hnn.us/articles/342.html.

Keen, A. (2007). *The Cult of the Amateur: How Today's Internet is Killing Our Culture*. New York: Doubleday.

Kielbowicz, R. (1989). *News in the Mail: The Press, Post Office, and Public Information, 1700–1860s*. Westport: Greenwood Press.

Lewis, R. (1972). *Outlaws of America: The Underground Press and its Context: Notes on a Cultural Revolution*. Harmondsworth: Penguin.

Menand, L. (1995). 'The Trashing of Professionalism' in *The New York Times*, 5 March 1995.

Merry, R. (2009). *A Country of Vast Designs: James K. Polk, the Mexican War and the Conquest*. New York: Simon & Schuster.

Miller, N. (1992). *Theodore Roosevelt: A Life*. New York: Morrow.

Reagan, R. (2007). *The Reagan Diaries* (ed. Brinkley, D.). New York: HarperCollins.

Rich, C. (2007). *Writing and Reporting News*. Belmont: Thomson Wadsworth.

Ritchie, D. (1991). *Press Gallery: Congress and the Washington Correspondents*. Cambridge, MA: Harvard University Press.

Woestendiek, J. (2003). 'Secret Weapon' in *The Baltimore Sun*, 14 October 2003.

Woodsworth, A. (1974). 'Volunteerism' in *Booklegger Magazine* 1.

MARCUS LEANING

Understanding Blogs: Just Another Media Form?

In recent years weblogs or blogs have attracted a great deal of attention in relation to their perceived ability to radically transform politics and culture. As a topic of academic study blogs are conceived as a form of media that will impact upon all areas of traditional media studies enquiry: blogs will impact upon media audiences, fracturing traditional divisions between media audiences and media producers (Jenkins 2006; Papacharissi 2007); blogs offer a multiplicity of new forms of text for a variety of analytic practices (Herring et al. 2004; Herring et al. 2005; Herring et al. 2007). But it is the impact that blogs may have upon media institutions that arguably has attracted the most analysis. Blogs are understood to have a considerable impact upon the practice of journalism, the 'traditional' media industries and the relationship of these industries to systems of political power and the actors in such systems. Central to this argument is the assertion that blogs are a form of media technology that alters how people engage with mass media. Blogs are understood to be able to 'reposition' the citizen into a new and dynamic relationship with political power (Tremayne 2007). Where in traditional media systems the citizen was broadcast *to*, blogs along with other forms of new media empower the citizen in the face of corporate and governmental media control. As Rettberg (2008: 31) argues:

> Blogs are part of a fundamental shift in how we communicate. Just a few decades ago, our media culture was dominated by a small number of media producers who distributed their publications and broadcasts to large, relatively passive audiences. Today, newspapers and television stations have to adapt to a new reality, where ordinary people create media and share their creations online. We have moved from a culture dominated by mass media, using one-to-many communication, to one where participatory media, using many-to-many communication, is becoming the norm.

Blogs are of course not the first media form credited with potential to radically challenge the status quo. Indeed, it seems almost a 'rite of passage' for any new media form or technology to be considered dangerous, radical or subversive (Carey 1989). Carolyn Marvin's (1990) study of two emergent technologies of the nineteenth century, the telegraph and the electric light, revealed how the technologies were imagined and constructed in a multiplicity of ways. This chapter will argue that we are witnessing a similar process with blogs: they are imagined in a variety of ways and in many instances are imbued with transformative potential. This act of imagination mirrors that which occurred with preceding media forms – blogs are viewed as a media form that will transform life and the social practices that we engage in. One particularly strong assertion is that blogs will impact upon civil society in an overtly positive manner and that they will revitalize political life and assist in the fracturing of existing power systems.

This chapter will sketch the arguments that have been proposed that support this claim and the counter-arguments that challenge it. It is important to note the discursive nature of contemporary networked communications (Mitra 2008). Internet communications, of which blogs are just one part, are a constantly changing and transforming system of social practice. Indeed the technologies that are used to communicate are subject to the continually 'rolling' process of innovation, adoption, adaptation and obsolescence (Dean 2010). Consequently the task of detailing all of the texts that contribute to this debate is beyond the scope of this chapter or indeed any academic publication that is 'fixed' in time and space by print. Therefore, the texts used here have been selected as they represent the dimensions of the debate if not all of the nuances within it.

This chapter is broadly divided into three sections: section one provides a brief history of blogs and an examination of the term 'blog'. Interestingly, while seeming a rather pedestrian activity, examining the history and definition of blogs does reveal a number of contentious issues. Sections two and three explore the different arguments put forward concerning the transformational power of blogs. Section two examines the case for the power of blogs to transform civic life while section three looks at those arguments proposed to counter such claims.

The History and Nature of Blogs

For a phenomenon of such recent historical genesis the history of the blog is surprisingly muddled. In the most pragmatic and prescriptive senses blogs are generally understood as a type of website or page with a specific form of content. This content consists of descriptions of events, links to other pages, graphics, sound files, other forms of multimedia and, most importantly, a commentary upon these items. Blog entries appear in reverse chronological order with the most recent entry appearing at the top. Blogs also commonly (but not always) contain a number of features that serve to distinguish them from other types of web page: blogs permit comments to be left by readers; they often have archives of older postings and content; there are often links to other similar blogs; they permit 'feeds' – the automatic publication of content from other sites and blogs; similarly the content of a blog may be syndicated or sent to other blogs for publication there.

What complicates the history of blogs is that a number of the characteristics of blogs appeared in earlier Internet media forms. One 'ancestor' is the usenet newsgroup *mod.ber* that dates from as early as 1983. In this pre-*http* Internet, newsgroups offered a text-only, many-to-many communication system. For the most part newsgroups were 'moderated' with all posts being under the editorial control of an administrator. In the vast majority of cases newsgroups functioned as discussion fora allowing for debates and argument. This form of communication has been extensively researched and lauded for its ability to facilitate virtual communities (Fernback 1997), preserve existing communities (Jankowski 2002) and enable political debate (Dahlberg 2001a; Dahlberg 2001b; Dahlberg 2001c). *Mod. ber* differed from other newsgroups in that its content consisted not of debate between a number of people but of information and links posted by one individual, Brian F. Redman (the name of the newsgroup refers to 'mod' for moderated and 'ber' for Redman's initials). While not technically a blog (it cannot be claimed to be a blog as it was not part of the web for the simple reason that the web had not then been invented), *mod.ber* did have two of the key characteristics of blogs: it contained links to and commentary on external newsgroup posts, mailing list posts and news stories. In 1992 Tim Berners-Lee, inventor of the key protocols that are used in the world-wide-web (Berners-Lee et al. 1994) started keeping a webpage of new Internet and web-specific developments. This page was the first of innumerable web-based online diaries, regularly updated personal or organizational journals detailing developments in a particular area. Such online journals were usually kept and edited by one person or a small group of individuals. In the late 1990s a number of companies released software specifically designed for the production of blogs. The availability of such tools and the sites to host blogs meant that the technical skill required to produce blogs was reduced considerably. Consequently, the number of people writing blogs increased dramatically.

While regular statistics are produced by organizations such as Technorati.com concerning the number of blogs in existence – the size of the 'blogosphere' – trying to calculate the current total number of blogs is problematic if not impossible for a number of reasons. First, a percentage of blogs consist solely of stories drawn from other sites and collated automatically with no additional comment. The practice of copying, reproducing and repackaging content that occurs on the Internet and is arguably a distinctive feature of contemporary culture (Jenkins 2006) adds to the sheer volume of web pages and content but does not add to the amount of discursive practice occurring. Second, blogs are written in many different languages and there is no central system that registers their establishment. Technorati.com, a website dedicated to such a task has been heavily criticized for missing large sections of the Internet in its counting of blogs, though it remains an authoritative and influential site (de Judicibus 2010). Third, many blogs are started and abandoned after a very short period of time, the existence of such 'orphaned' blogs is un-measurable and undoubtedly inflates number of reported blogs.

Origin of the Term 'Blog'

Most histories and accounts of blogs and blogging (for example, Baker 2008; Blood 2002; Herring et al. 2004; Rettberg 2008; Wortham 2007) indicate that the first use of the term 'weblog' can be attributed to Jorn Barger in his 'Robot Wisdom' website. Barger, an influential blogger in his own right, first used the term on 17 December 1997. The attribution to Barger is widely accepted and appears in many accounts and dictionaries and seems for the most part uncritically used.

However, the attribution to Barger of the term 'weblog' in its current meaning can be questioned. The first description of a specialized application available over the web that meets the contemporary definition of a blog and employed use of the term 'WebLog' was made in an academic conference paper by Raikundalia and Rees entitled 'WebLog: exploiting the Web use interface for document management in electronic meetings'. This paper was delivered on 21 August 1995 (Raikundalia and Rees 1995), though the paper had been advertised in a newsgroup posting on 6 August that year (Rees 2007).

The term was abbreviated by web designer Peter Merholz in a side-bar to his site in April or May 1999 – Merholz claims he cannot remember which month exactly (Merholz 2002; Baker 2008). Merholz split the word into 'we blog', though as Merholz himself acknowledges such word play would not be significant if a blogging tool named Blogger not been released by Pyra Labs in August 1999 and the word spread with the tool's success (Merholz 2002).

The Power of Blogs

In a similar way to how newsgroups and other preceding forms of computer-mediated communication were understood, the potential of blogs to bring about change is an intensely debated area within the academic fields of media studies and journalism. It is possible to discern two broad camps in this debate. One school of thought regards blogs as possessing an enormous transformational potential – blogs are seen to possess certain characteristics and are used in ways that will bring about a transformation, they will restructure journalistic and media practice. A second school of thought challenges this interpretation and argues that blogs must be considered in concert with other forms of media and social practice.

The argument that blogs bring about change in practice invokes a particular version of technological determinism: that a particular type of technology will bring about a form of social action. Technological determinism has proven a strong and persistent strand of thought in understanding the role of media technology within modern Western society even though it seems rarely explicitly stated (Marx and Smith 1996: ix–xv). In terms of how blogs transform media and journalistic practice four key arguments can be identified.

First, blogs are thought to encourage civic participation and involvement. Drawing upon a long tradition of political thought that regards contemporary political culture as deficient and political engagement by citizens as restricted and limited, blogs are regarded as a medium that will help to restore civic culture. Through blogs people can be re-empowered and civic culture revitalized (Blood 2002; Colvile 2008). This argument centres upon the idea that blogs have an inherent democratic aspect to them. Blogs allow for a 'passive' public to engage with, and not just receive, information; blogs are one of the key new social media that are driving a 'shift' in communication practice. Audiences are being transformed; the nature of engagement with media is shifting from a passive mode to an active one (Barlow 2007; Benkler 2006; Blood, 2002; Blood, 2003; Gillmor 2006; Jenkins 2006; Keren 2006; Kline 2005; Rettberg 2008; Hall 2006). Moreover blogs allow people to comment upon and publicly engage in debates taking place in mainstream media. Accordingly blogs are understood to foster debate and an interest in politics that has previously been presented *to* the public by the media – instead blogs allow one an opportunity to engage with key issues and to have one's opinion disseminated. As Blood (2003: 61) contends, blogs have 'given millions of people the equivalent of a printing press on their desks.' This ability to comment is thought to engender a greater sense of participation in the political process and to foster civic engagement reversing the long-noted trend of disengagement from politics. Such a re-engagement will result in a revitalization of civic culture, a keener sense of being linked to decision-making and being part of the political process (Hewitt 2006).

Second, a further elaboration of this position is that blogs will allow for a rejuvenated sense of journalistic practice to emerge (Blood 2003; Gillmor 2006). While Pavlik (2000) argues that new technologies essentially change the relationships between journalists and their publics, blogs challenge the power of mainstream media by offering a means by which individuals are able to engage in journalistic activities external to the large media industry gatekeepers (Singer 2005). Such 'citizen journalists' undermine and highlight the problems of selectivity, partisanship, bias and prejudice in mainstream journalism. Similarly, Wall (2005) contends that blogs will bring about a new form of journalism, one endowed with more relevant, postmodern sensibilities. Indeed, Gillmor (2005: 1) contends that for journalism to prosper or even survive it must engage with the participatory culture:

> It's essential for professional journalists to adapt to what's happening, to use these techniques themselves, of course, but also to become allies of the grass-roots practitioners. Bringing more voices into the conversation is smart from a journalistic point of view. It's also part of a survival strategy. The long-range financial salvation of what some people sneeringly call the MSM, or mainstream media, may depend – at least in part – on a collaboration with what I like to call the 'former audience'.

While the majority of (US) bloggers do not consider themselves journalists (Lenhart and Fox 2006), Rettberg (2008: 86) develops a threefold typology for the nature of the interaction between journalism and bloggers and the way in which blogging can resemble journalism. In the first instance blogging can provide eye witness reporting in a way in which traditional journalism would be hard put to match. Indeed Rettberg notes how many news organizations now make widespread use of such eyewitnesses to supplement their own content, an argument supported by Sambrook (2005) in relation to the BBC. The second iteration of the link between blogging and journalism concerns the manner in which social networks afford bloggers the ability to explore stories ignored by mainstream media channels. Finally Rettberg notes how the differing standards or codes of practice between journalists and bloggers means that in certain instances journalists are challenged by bloggers for the stance adopted on a story. Deuze (2003) notes the distinction between blogs as citizen journalism and other forms of online media, while Bentley et al. (2007) note a further distinction between the edited nature of citizen journalism sites and blogs which typically articulate the views of an individual.

The third argument for the potency of blogs to transform is the ability of blogs to bring in a new level of accountability for politicians (Colvile 2008; Kline 2005). Blogs are thought to extend and rejuvenate the 'watch-dog' aspect of the media. The surveillance and monitoring of politicians and the reporting of their activities and comments through blogs is broadly understood to bring a new level of responsibility to politics. The history of politics and the media indicates that initially politicians encountered problems with broadcast media; however the use of public relations and media management agencies has resulted in the production of more coher-ent and controlled messages (Curran and Seaton 2009). Indeed one of the major criticisms of contemporary political activity is that politicians look too 'slick' and polished (Jones 2000). The emergence of innumerable and interlinked blogs concerned with politics means that the claims of politi-cians can be more fully investigated (Colvile 2008). Furthermore, instances in which politicians err, make 'off-message' pronouncements or make inju-dicious decisions are recorded and soon disseminated (Keren 2006).

Fourth, blogs erode the influence and power of formal groups and existing power structures (Hewitt 2006) and challenge corporate media power (Gilmor 2006; Hall 2006). The potential of blogs to allow for innumerable 'voices from below' means that existing power structures and dominant forms of communication are undermined. As with several other forms of Web 2.0 media systems, blogs constitute a challenge to traditional systems of expert knowledge (Benkler 2006). Andrews (2003: 64) contends that blogs move commentary from 'a centralized, top-down, one-way publication process to a many-hands, perpetual feedback loop of online communications.'

From this broad perspective blogs are understood to present a new and definite challenge to the existing systems of power, politics and existing frameworks of communication and cultural operations. In contrast to this optimistic interpretation of the power of blogs to transform, a number of counter-arguments have been raised. These arguments articulate a less celebratory approach to blogs and continue a more reserved examination of blogs, the Internet and new media in general (Leaning 2009). Indeed many of the arguments that have been raised in opposition to the euphoric accounts of the Internet are also valid when applied to blogs.

Cautionary Accounts

The more cautionary or critical interpretations of blogs and the activity of blogging can be grouped into three key arguments. First, rather than being seen as a new form of social activity blogging should be understood as a continuation of a particular style of writing or journalistic practice. Barlow (2007) argues that blogs do not present a new form of journalism but represent (and restore) a theme of 'citizen journalism' in American political life. Citizen journalism is of course not a new occurrence but draws upon a long tradition in alternative media practice and civic action (Downing 2001). While it important to recognize that the perceived binary divide between mainstream and alternative media is problematic and ideological in nature (Downing 2001), alternative media may be considered self-consciously 'outside' the mainstream. Atkinson (2006: 252) defines alternative media as 'any media that are produced by non commercial sources and attempt to transform existing social roles and routines by critiquing and challenging power structures.' This description strongly echoes the 'pro-blog' rhetoric. In many accounts noted in the previous section blogging is conceptualized as a decidedly alternative form of media engagement. Blogging is presented as a form of resistance media, a form of oppositional or counter-cultural practice. However, this is a position that has been strongly challenged:

Kenix (2009: 815) proposes that rather than being an alternative media form blogs are 'firmly grounded within the ideological mainstream.' A number of authors show how blogs and mainstream media are deeply linked and that blogs draw from mainstream media rather than oppose them or offer an alternative to them (Delwiche 2003; Haas 2005; Reynolds 2005). From these perspectives, blogs are posited within a cultural milieu; they are not a new radical force. This idea that blogs perpetuate a mainstream form of communication and political activity is important as it interprets blogs as being situated within a political framework and not in some way outside of society.

Second, a strong area of criticism of the potential of blogs is the impact of commercial pressures upon them. Wilhelm (2000: 6) identifies numerous problems in the cultural imprint or baggage that comes with new technology and asserts that 'new information and communication technologies, as currently designed and used, pose formidable obstacles to achieving a more just and human social order.' A further criticism is the identification of a number of limitations imposed by commercial interests upon online communication that restrict and challenge open debate. Phenomena such as overt commercial interests stifling free comment (Dahlberg 2005), commercial influence affecting information retrieval (Hargittai 2000; Hargittai 2007), overt regulation of Internet content consumption (Gomez 2004) and monopolistic ownership of media organizations (Bagdikian 2004) all pose challenges to the idea of unfettered communication. Dean (2010: 5) goes further and in his development of a critical theory approach to the study of blogs he situates them deeply within 'communicative capitalism'. Further, issues of access and skills deficits (Selwyn 2004) and power relations within online groups (Dahlberg 2007) also point to the deep influences of cultural and capitalist systems of power in the regulation of blog activity.

The third key critical argument concerns the consideration that blogs constitute an actualized public sphere. A number of authors have theorized blogs within a model of the public sphere (Froomkin 2003; Ó Baoill 2005). Indeed Tremayne (2007: vii) notes the term 'blogosphere' is clearly a derivative of the public sphere. However, for authors such as Keren (2006) celebrating blogs for their potential to rejuvenate the public sphere may be a little premature. This division continues an earlier debate on the possible impact of new media on the public sphere. Here the direct and progressive linkage between the Internet and a resurgent public sphere has been extensively challenged. One of the key problems in considering blogs as comprising an actualized public sphere lies in the fragmentation and partisanship of online communication. Internet audiences and blog audiences in particular are notoriously partisan. Participants in online deliberative environments tend to stick within their community of interest (Hill and Hughes 1998; Wilhelm 1999), 'pockets of interest' (Selnow 1998), 'deliberative enclaves' (Sunstein 2001) or an 'online echo chamber of mass-mediated political views' (Singer 2005: 192). Indeed mutually supporting belief groups may seem to exacerbate differences and lead to extremism (Tateo 2005), a far cry from the development of citizenship and of rational discourse that Habermas identified as the goal of deliberative action. Instead Habermas (2006: 423–4) interprets the communicative systems of the Internet, of which blogs are but one aspect, as dangerously fragmenting of politics and at best as little more than ancillary to mass media in the development of civic discourse:

> the rise of millions of fragmented chat rooms across the world tend instead to lead to the fragmentation of large but politically focused mass audiences into a huge number of isolated issue publics ... the online debates of web users only promote political communication, when news groups crystallize around the focal points of the quality press, for example, national newspapers and political magazines.

If this argument is applied to blogs Habermas's comment is particularly illuminative. It indicates that we should consider blogs not as an alternative to mainstream media forms but as part of a broader media ecology. Blogs should be understood in concert with other forms of media, be they traditional mass media forms or other forms of new media. Furthermore, the potential impact of blogs upon the practice of journalism may be seen to be mitigated by their being considered not as an alternative to traditional journalism but as an aspect of public deliberation that is founded upon 'focal points' initiated by traditional journalistic practice, a point noted by Haas (2005).

Blogs are conceptualized as part of complex media ecology and we may better understand blogs if we refuse to see them as separate or alternative media forms but instead as a component of a mesh of interacting media forms. Indeed, we may find a more useful approach to understanding the interactions of blogs, other media forms and social practices by drawing upon the idea of 'media meshing' (Lerma 2005), a concept developed in advertising to understand the interplay of offline and online media. Media meshing seems to present a viable model with which the power and social impact of blogs may be theorized.

Conclusion

The brief descriptions of the contrasting perspectives on blogs noted here are indicative of a larger and far from homogeneous understanding of how blogs function socially and how they impact upon the social practices of media and journalism. Furthermore, in addition to actually examining the impact of blogs, the debate between the two camps is informed and nuanced by differing political perspectives, philosophies and epistemologies. Bolter argues that academic attempts to explain new media and specific instances of technology such as blogs can be divided into two broad camps: 'formalist' approaches – theories that 'appear to focus on 'internal' or even 'inherent' characteristics of the media – and 'culturalist' approaches – theories that focus on characteristics that are 'external' (Bolter 2002: 77). Indeed, perhaps the best way to understand the current argument is to view it as the latest incarnation of the debate that took place between McLuhan and Williams at the dawn of the new media age in the early 1970s (Lister et al. 2006) – a debate that was never fully resolved. If this is the case then the current debate on blogs is far from concluded and is perhaps unlikely ever to reach a resolution.

References

Andrews, P. (2003). 'Is blogging journalism?' in *Nieman Reports*, Fall.

Atkinson, J. (2006). 'Analyzing resistance narratives at the North American Anarchist Gathering' in *Journal of Communication Inquiry* 30:3, 251–72.

Baker, J. (2008). 'Origins of "Blog" and "Blogger"' in *American Dialect Society Mailing List*, 20 April 2008.

Barlow, A. (2007). *The Rise of the Blogosphere*. Santa Barbara: Praeger.

Bagdikian, B. (2004). *The New Media Monopoly*. Boston: Beacon Press.

Benkler, Y. (2006). *The Wealth of Networks*. New Haven: Yale University Press.

Bentley, C., Hamman, B., Littau, J., Meyer, H., Watson, B., and Welsh, B. (2007). 'Citizen Journalism: A Case Study' in Tremayne, M. (ed.), *Blogging, Citizenship and the Future of Media*. Abingdon: Routledge.

Berners-Lee, T., Cailliau, R., Luotonen, A., Nielson, H., and Secret, A. (1994). 'The World Wide Web' in *Communications of the ACM* 37:8, 76–82.

Blood, R. (2002). *We've Got Blog: How Weblogs Are Changing Our Culture*. New York: Perseus Books.

Blood, R. (2003). 'Weblogs and journalism: do they connect?' in *Nieman Reports*, Fall.

Bolter, D. (2002). 'Formal Analysis and Cultural Critique in Digital Media Theory' in *Convergence* 8:4, 77–88.

Carey, J. (1989). *Communication as Culture: Essays on Media and Society*. New York: Routledge.

Colvile, R. (2008). *Politics, Policy and the Internet*. London: Centre for Policy Studies.

Curran, J., and Seaton, J. (2009). *Power without Responsibility*. Abingdon: Routledge.

Dahlberg, L. (2001a). 'Computer-mediated Communication and the Public Sphere: A Critical Analysis' in *Journal of Computer-Mediated Communication* 7:1.

Dahlberg, L. (2001b). 'Democracy via Cyberspace' in *New Media & Society* 3:2, 157–77.

Dahlberg, L. (2001c). 'The Internet and Democratic Discourse: Exploring the prospects of Online Deliberative Forums extending the Public Sphere' in *Information, Communication & Society* 4:4), 615–33.

Dahlberg, L. (2005). 'The Corporate Colonization of online Attention and the Marginalization of Critical Communication' in *Journal of Communication Inquiry* 29:2, 1–21.

Dahlberg, L. (2007). 'Rethinking the fragmentation of the cyberpublic: from consensus to contestation' in *New Media & Society* 9:5, 827–47.

de Judicibus, D. (2010). 'Technorati: the War of Languages' in *L'Indipendente*.

Dean, J. (2010). *Blog Theory: Feedback and Capture in the Circuits of Drive*. Cambridge: Polity Press.

Delwiche, A. (2003). 'Reconstructing the Agenda in the World of Participatory Media', paper presented at the *Annual Convention of the Association of Internet Researchers*, Toronto, Canada.

Deuze, M. (2003). 'The Web and its journalisms: considering the consequences of different types of news media online' in *New Media and Society* 5:2, 203–30.

Downing, J. (2001). *Radical Media: Rebellious Communication and Social Movements*. London: Sage.

Fernback, J. (1997). 'The Individual within the Collective: Virtual Ideology and the Realization of Collective Principles' in Jones, S. (ed.), *Virtual Culture*. London: Sage.

Froomkin, M. (2003). 'Habermas@Discourse.Net: Toward A Critical Theory Of Cyberspace' in *Harvard Law Review* 16:3, 749–873.

Gillmor, D. (2005). 'Where Citizens and Journalists Intersect' in *Nieman Reports*, Winter.

Gillmor, D. (2006). *We the Media: Grassroots Journalism by the People for the People*. Sebastopol, CA: O'Reilly Media.

Gomez, J. (2004). 'Dumbing Down Democracy: Trends in Internet Regulation, Surveillance and Control in Asia' in *Pacific Journalism Review* 10:2, 130–50.

Habermas, J. (2006). 'Political Communication in Media Society: Does Democracy Still Enjoy an Epistemic Dimension? The Impact of Normative Theory on Empirical Research' in *Communication Theory* 16:4, 411–26.

Haas, T. (2005). 'From "Public Journalism" to the "Public's Journalism"? Rhetoric and reality in the discourse on weblogs' in *Journalism Studies* 6:3, 387–96.

Hall, R. (2006). *The Blog Ahead: How Citizen Generated Media Is Tilting the Communications Balance*. New York: Morgan James.

Hargittai, E. (2000). 'Open Portals or Closed Gates? Channeling Content on the World Wide Web' in *Poetics*, 27:4, 233–54.

Hargittai, E. (2007). 'The Social, Political, Economic, and Cultural Dimensions of Search Engines: An Introduction' in *Journal of Computer-Mediated Communication* 12:3.

Herring, S., Scheidt, L., Bonus, S., and Wright, E. (2004). 'Bridging the Gap: A Genre Analysis of Weblogs' in *Proceedings of the 37th Hawaii International Conference on System Sciences*.

Herring, S., Scheidt, L., Bonus, S., and Wright, E. (2005). 'Weblogs as a Bridging Genre' in *Information, Technology and People* 18:2, 142–71.

Herring, S., Scheidt, L., Kouper, I., and Wright, E. (2007). 'Longitudinal Content Analysis of Blogs: 2003–2004' in Tremayne, M (ed.), *Blogging, Citizenship and the Future of Media*. Abingdon: Routledge.

Hewitt, H. (2006). *Blog: Understanding the Information Reformation That's Changing Your World*. Nashville: Nelson Business.

Hill, K., and Hughes, J. (1998). *Cyberpolitics: Citizen Activism in the Age of the Internet*. Lanham: Rowman and Littlefield.

Jankowski, N. (2002). 'Creating Community with Media: History, Theories and Scientific Investigations' in Lievrouw, L., and Livingstone, S. (eds), *Handbook of New Media: Social Shaping and Consequences of ICTs*. London: Sage.

Jenkins, H. (2006). *Convergence Culture: Where Old and New Media Collide*. New York: New York University Press.

Jones, N, (2000). *Sultans of Spin: Media and the New Labour Government*. London: Gollancz.

Kenix, L. (2009). 'Blogs as Alternative' in *Journal of Computer-Mediated Communication* 14, 790–822.

Keren, M. (2006). *Blogosphere: The New Political Arena*. Lanham: Lexington Books.

Kline, D. (2005). 'Toward a more participatory democracy' in Kline, D., and Burstein, D. (eds), *Blog!: How the Newest Media Revolution Is Changing Politics, Business, and Culture*. New York: CDS.

Leaning, M. (2009). *The Internet, Power and Society: Rethinking the Power of the Internet to Change Lives*. Oxford: Chandos.

Lenhart, A., and Fox, S. (2006). 'Bloggers: A Portrait of the Internet's New Storytellers' in *Pew Internet and American Life Project*.

Lister, M., Kelly, K., Dovey, J., Giddings, S., and Grant, I. (2002). *New Media: A Critical Introduction*. London: Routledge.

Lerma, P. (2005). 'Media Meshing: An Evolution in Media Consumption' in *ClickZ*, 28 June 2005.

Marvin, C. (1990). *When Old Technologies Were New*. Oxford: Oxford University Press.

Marx, L., and Smith, M. (1996). 'Introduction' in Smith, M., and Marx, L. (eds), *Does Technology Drive History? The Dilemma of Technological Determinism*. Cambridge, MA: MIT Press.

Merholz, P. (2002). *Play with Your Words*. Available at peterme.com/archives/00000205.html

Mitra, A. (2008). 'Using Blogs to Create Cybernetic Space: Examples from People of Indian Origin' in *Convergence: The International Journal of Research into New Media Technologies* 14:4, 457–72.

Ó Baoill, A. (2005). 'Weblogs and the Public Sphere' in Gurak, L., Antonijevic, S., Johnson, L., Ratliff, C., and Reyman, J. (eds), *Into the Blogosphere: Rhetoric, Community and the Culture of Weblogs*. Available at blog.lib.umn.edu/blogosphere/weblogs_and_the_public_sphere.html.

Papacharissi, Z. (2007). 'Audiences as Media Producers' in Tremayne, M. (ed.), *Blogging, Citizenship and the Future of Media*. Abingdon: Routledge.

Pavlik, J. (2000). 'The Impact of Technology on Journalism' in *Journalism Studies* 1:2, 229–37.

Raikundalia, G., and Rees, M. (1995). 'WebLog: exploiting the Web use interface for document management in electronic meetings', paper presented at *Queensland Computer Human Interaction Symposium*, Bond University.

Rees, M. (2007). 'A Father of the word Weblog?' Available at mrees.wordpress.com/2007/08/18/a-father-of-the-weblog/.

Rettberg, J. (2008). *Blogging*. Malden: Polity Press.

Reynolds, R. (2005). 'Agenda-setting the Internet: political news blogs and newspaper coverage of the 2004 U.S. democratic presidential candidates', paper presented at the *Annual Convention of the International Communication Association*, New York.

Sambrook, R. (2005). 'Citizen Journalism and the BBC' in *Nieman Reports*, Winter.

Selnow, G. (1998). *Electronic Whistle Stops: The Impact of the Internet on American Politics*. Westport: Praeger.

Selwyn, N. (2004). 'Reconsidering Political and Popular Understandings of the Digital Divide' in *New Media & Society* 6:3, 341–62.

Singer, J. (2005). 'The Political J-Blogger' in *Journalism* 6:2, 173–98.

Sunstein, C. (2001). *Republic.com*. Princeton: Princeton University Press.

Tateo, L. (2005). 'The Italian extreme right on-line network: an exploratory study using an integrated social network analysis and content analysis approach' in *Journal of Computer-Mediated Communication* 10:2.

Tremayne, M. (2007). 'Introduction: Examining the Blog-Media Relationship' in Tremayne, M. (ed.), *Blogging, Citizenship and the Future of Media*. Abingdon: Routledge.

Wall, M. (2005). 'Blogs of War: Weblogs as News' in *Journalism* 6:2, 153–72.

Wilhelm, A. (1999). 'Virtual Sounding Boards: How Deliberative is Online Political Discussion?' in Hague, B., and Loader, B. (eds), *Digital Democracy: Discourse and Decision Making in the Information Age*. London: Routledge.

Wilhelm, A. (2000). *Democracy in the Digital Age*. New York: Routledge.

Wortham, J. (2007). 'After 10 Years of Blogs, the Future's Brighter Than Ever' in *Wired*, 17 December 2007.

CLIVE MCGOUN

From Cuba with Blogs

In January 2007 the website desdeCuba.com was established on a server in Berlin, Germany. It was a development of the work of a small group of writers in Cuba which began with the publication of an online journal called *Consenso* (Consensus) in 2004. That publication aimed to 'enable us to agree, from our differences, about the fundamental questions: what kind of country do we want for ourselves and our children? What do we need to do to achieve it?'

From its beginnings *Consenso* was dedicated to providing a space for the diversity of progressive ideas in Cuba: a space, according to its editor Reinaldo Escobar, which was 'plural, respectful and serious'. *Consenso* continued publishing bi-monthly for two years, but by the end of 2006 it was clear that not only did the name *Consenso* fail to mirror the aspirations of its founders and contributors, but also that the digital tools for publication on the web had evolved. The central publication on desdecuba.com became *Contodos* (Together), emphasizing plurality and solidarity without the necessity of accord, whilst the website itself became a host and gateway to a variety of content including archives of debates, image galleries and blogs. Its purpose also began to be articulated in more overtly political tones: from 'a space for reflection and debate' in 2006 to 'a journal about politics – independent [...] a distinct panorama to that offered by the Cuban government' in 2007 to the more recent 'portal for citizen journalism' in 2008. In this same period the digital tools used expanded, most conspicuously with the inclusion of links to blogs hosted on the site.

The desdecuba.com project then has been designed to provide a publishing platform for Cubans on the island who have been unable to communicate publicly outside and against official media. Whilst the editorial board of *Contodos* includes a (former) journalist, a (former) lecturer in philosophy and a graduate of the University of Havana, it makes no claims to be journalistic or 'of the press'. Instead it has chosen to reconfigure the criteria for involvement with the site from journalists and 'experts' to those who 'live the reality about which they write and live in the epicentre of those problems and situations that are the subject of their debates.'

The Internet and politics

In some respects this choice is unsurprising. Developments in communications technologies have regularly inspired the kinds of aspirations expressed by desdecuba.com towards a more pluralistic media ecology (Castells 2002; Grossman 1995; Hanson 2008). Telegraph and radio technologies have often been hailed as agents of social change, harbingers of enhanced freedoms of expression and communication; the introduction of the Internet into the public domain was very quickly accompanied by some lofty claims as to its democratizing potential, especially where media diversity has been threatened by autocratic governments. As early as 1989 Ronald Reagan proclaimed that 'information is the oxygen of the modern age. It seeps through the walls topped by barbed wire, it wafts across the electrified borders [...]. The Goliath of totalitarianism will be brought down by the David of the microchip' (cited in Kalathil and Boas 2003: 2). Ten years later, on 4 December 1999, George W. Bush, in a presidential campaign debate, asked his audience to 'imagine if the Internet took hold in China. Imagine how freedom would spread.' Expanding to reporters after the debate, he added: 'unleashing the Internet in a country like China is going to be like unleashing freedom's genie out of the bottle.'

In the decade since Bush's cyber-optimism the debate over the democratizing impact of digital media has opened up its own digital divide between those heralding an age of horizontal politics in which citizens' voices disrupt elite media and governance (Bimber 1998; Gillmor 2006; Hall 2006; Hewitt 2006; Reynolds 2007) and those more sceptical as to the birth of a new plural politics (Barney 2001; Davis 1999; Hill and Hughes 1998; Kalathil and Boas 2003; Margolis and Resnick 2000; Sunstein 2007) or even those who dismiss the idea that new media are significantly different in kind to traditional mass media (Hindman 2008).

Recent research into the impact of the Internet on politics has fragmented towards more focused agendas such as: the role of social networking in political motivation (Boyd 2008; Montgomery 2008); the political potential of mobile technology (Castells, Fernandez-Ardevol et al. 2007; Gergen and Katz 2008; Rheingold 2002; Rheingold 2008; Rizzo 2008); and the political uses made of such social technologies as Twitter (Huberman, Romero et al. 2008) or YouTube (Burgess and Green 2009). Research on blogs, blogging and bloggers has similarly fragmented with research on political blogs (Bahnisch 2006; Drezner and Farrell 2008), the relation between blogs and journalism (Lasica and Blood 2002; Rutigliano 2006) and analyses of emerging structural networks engendered by blogs and the meanings and practices these may generate socially and politically (Hodkinson 2002; Rutigliano 2006). Whilst a great deal of this research has focused on the US and the UK, case studies of language-specific blogospheres (Merelo, Orihuela et al. 2004) and international blogging practices are beginning to emerge (Russell and Echchaibi 2009).

This chapter contributes to that literature by examining the oldest, most prolific and most lauded of the blogs hosted by desdecuba.com: *Generación Y*, begun by Yoani Sánchez in April 2007. By placing the rising international visibility of *Generación Y* within the context in which the Internet operates in Cuba, and by exploring the ways in which its writing opens up spaces for the discussion of a Cuban/Citizen identity for the twenty-first century, some tentative suggestions will be offered as to why both *Generación Y* and desdecuba.com can be understood to be impacting on the public sphere in Cuba.

Generación Y

The title of the blog '*Generación Y*' references a generation of Cubans that have names which either begin with, or include, the letter 'Y'. With their Russian overtones, Yamil, Yanisleidi, Dayron, Yunieksi, Yudelkis and Yoani became fashionable names during the 1970s and 1980s when the influence of Soviet politics, culture and trade was at its height. This is a generation in Cuba that has been shaped through adolescence and early adulthood by such influences together with waves of emigration and a period of economic crisis known as the 'Special Period' provoked, in part, by the collapse of Eastern Europe. It is a generation at odds with those, now in their seventies and eighties, who shared the hopes and idealism of the early years of struggle against Batista and the establishment of the Cuban Revolution in 1959 or with those much younger, many of whom, born into the economic crisis after 1990, now dream of a future abroad. The generation invoked by Yoani Sánchez 'came of age' as Cuba, the socialist survivor, struggled to re-define itself in a world increasingly enraptured by globalization. Such struggle also became personal as people coped with the deprivation, frustration and hopelessness brought about by the lack of everyday resources. If the 1990s were a 'defining decade' for Cuba (Hernandez-Reguant 2009) they were so in particular for this generation. Decades, in the sense used here, are rarely chronologically self-contained. Arguably, the 'Special Period' that began in 1991 continues to prevail and 'normality' has yet to be established. Whilst the state continues to subordinate economic policy to the political survival of the government and its socialist project, the social interregnum continues to focus on the intractable problem of 'transition' to more open and plural spaces for civil expression.

With *Contodos*, desdecuba.com created a publication for the discussion of that problem. With *Generación Y* Yoani Sánchez created a blog for its individual expression, its manifestation in the routines and struggles of everyday life. Sánchez herself describes the reason for beginning the blog as highly personal: 'an individual exorcism, a type of therapy that I prescribed to myself early last year [2007]. I arrived at this medicine that would cure a horse after verifying that the Internet was the only opening through which an alternative, critical and inconvenient opinion could jump the fence of censorship in Cuba.' This theory of writing resonates with evidence suggesting that over 50 per cent of bloggers blog as a form of self-therapy (AOL 2005) and that the kinds of cathartic writing once limited to the private diary are now emigrating to the web. In a discussion of blogging as self-therapy, Tan explores the way one such blogger, Jenny, 'turned to blogging as a means of dealing with the tension, frustration and distress of not being able to speak her mind or own a voice' (Tan 2008: 155). Whilst the self-censorship of Jenny is different in kind to the censorship experienced by Sánchez, the underlying motivations are similar; the desire to create a safe place from which to speak freely.

Since the blog appeared in April 2007, Sánchez has published an average of just over two blog posts per week. Many of these are grouped so that two or even three posts appear on one day. Its blogroll has grown steadily to include fourteen blogs and websites authored on the island together with links to fifty sites in the Cuban diaspora indicating a self-ascribed Internet community of interest. The length of the posts on *Generación Y* rarely exceeds two hundred and fifty words and almost all include a photograph taken by the author documenting her daily movement around the city of Havana. In the period examined here (April 2007 to February 2009) no posts contain links to sites external to the host domain desdecuba.com. These characteristics are, in part, dictated by the circumstances in which *Generación Y* is produced. Posts are invariably written and saved to a storage device off-line to be loaded up to the blog on its server in Germany when the limited access to the Internet available to the author allows. Whilst the avowed intent of *Generación Y* is to provide a platform for personal expression, such circumstances influence the kinds of conversations and social ties that Sánchez can form and contribute to in the blogosphere. Yet, in some ways, these circumstances have proved far from a limitation. In October 2007 Reuters reported the presence of *Generación Y* and the emergence of an incipient blogosphere in Cuba. The article, syndicated throughout the world, resulted in numerous emails being sent to Sánchez in support of her efforts and through CubaNet.org, the blog was ensured further exposure in the Cuban diaspora blogosphere (in particular through PayoLibre.com, Directorio.org and CubaEncuentro.com).

In response to this growing interest, *Generación Y* was re-designed in November 2007 using the popular, open-source blog publishing application Wordpress, and readers encouraged to link to it. In the same month posts began to be translated into English (with translations into Italian, German, French, Polish, Lithuanian, Japanese and Portuguese following in 2008). On 10 December 2007, nine months after starting *Generación Y*, Sánchez announced the inclusion of a feature allowing readers to comment on posts to the blog. Various interviews with the author appeared in the mainstream media in December 2007 including one with the *Wall Street Journal* which led to further exposure and debate on the authenticity of *Generación Y* and the political motivations of its author. This debate became particularly vigorous on the forum of the site, *Secretos de Cuba*, where suggestions ranged from Sánchez being a puppet of the government of Cuba allowed to filter news from the island to the notion that she was working for the CIA. Her response, 'Without Pedigree', failed to assuage the unconvinced and the debate has rumbled on in comments from readers on and off the island since.

One effect of this exposure and subsequent online buzz can be measured by the growing number of requests to deliver the blog by its host server, also known as 'hits'. In March 2008 *Generación Y* reported receiving four million such hits. The number of comments left on the blog was startling. From 10 December 2007 to the end of March 2008, Sánchez published forty posts which received 20,882 comments: an average of 522 comments per post. In April 2008 Sánchez won the Ortega y Gasset prize for digital journalism. The award, sponsored by the Spanish newspaper, *El Pais*, praised 'the shrewdness with which the journalist Yoani Sánchez, author of the blog *Generación Y*, has overcome the limitations to freedom of expression in Cuba' and referred to her as a citizen-blogger who has been able to insert herself into the global media-scape (*El Pais*, 5 April 2008). In May 2008 *Time* magazine placed Sánchez thirty-first in their fifth annual list of the world's most influential people stating that 'under the nose of a regime that has never tolerated dissent, Sánchez has practiced what paper-bound journalists in her country cannot: freedom of speech.' Once again it would seem that coverage in the mainstream media had an influence on the number of comments left on *Generación Y*. Between April and September 2008, 186,628 comments were submitted to 81 posts, an average of over 2,000 comments per post. The trend continued into 2009: from September 2008 to February 2009, 214,000 comments were made to 112 posts again averaging over 2,000 comments per post.

Whilst the numbers here may indicate a solid following amongst the readers of *Generación Y*, some caveats are clearly needed. The number of hits cited above is an assertion of popularity gained from a reading of the server log analysis. The number of hits does not necessarily correspond to the total number of unique visitors to the blog nor the number of pages viewed. Also, whilst comments are filtered for spam by the publishing platform, comment numbers do not take into account multiple comments from single commentators. Posts can become the stimulus for a forum-like response where dialogues and debates take place between commentators. Such debates can range some distance from the topic of the original post serving either as personal soapboxes and/or including vitriolic criticisms of other participants. Initially, comments were not moderated due, in part, to the unusual circumstances in which the blog was managed and the obvious difficulty of one person moderating such a significant number of comments. Only at the end of May 2008 did Sánchez announce that future comments would be moderated by a group of volunteers according to guidelines aimed, she maintained, not at censorship, but at creating a common 'netiquette'.

The growing visibility of *Generación Y* tracked through its comments is also paralleled by its popularity as measured by Google, Alexa and Technorati. These services use hyperlink-based algorithms to establish the impact of blogs and domains across the web. In the period examined, Google's PageRank placed *Generación Y* at 6/10, on a footing with popular political blogs in the UK (Guido Fawkes's blog) and the US (Joshua Marshall's Talking Points Memo). Data from Alexa ranked traffic to desdecuba.com (it measures traffic only to principle domains) at a three-month average of 86,899 and the percentage of global Internet users visiting the site at 0.00156 per cent. Again, comparison with the UK and US bloggers above suggests that the domain is particularly well embedded in the blogosphere especially given its short history and the circumstance in which it is managed and authored. Alexa locates the source of the traffic to desdecuba.

com interestingly as 24.6 per cent from the US, 15.7 per cent from Spain, and 8.3 per cent from Cuba. Finally, Technorati, the search engine that indexes over 100 million blogs, ranked *Generación Y* in the top 2,000 blogs (1,463) in September 2008. This compares with a ranking of 4,836 for Guido Fawkes and 542 for Talking Points Memo.

Why have a little over two hundred blog posts amounting to a total of less than 75,000 words garnered such a response from the blogosphere? What is the relationship of that response to Cuban politics on the island? And more specifically, how can *Generación Y* be understood to be contributing, if at all, to a re-shaping of the public sphere in Cuba?

The Media Landscape in Cuba

For almost fifty years Cuba has fed on and been nourished by a polarization. On the one side those who revere the government and the process whereby the Cuban Revolution has struggled, and continues to struggle, to secure the sovereignty and independence of the island against an arrogant neo-colonial overlord. On the other, those who view the Castro dynasty as a bastion of totalitarian dictatorship whose hold on a bankrupt political and economic model is maintained through coercion, control and repression. The terms of the split were established by Fidel Castro himself: 'within the revolution everything; against the revolution nothing' (Castro 1961: 11) and its interpretation has galvanized support and opposition (from 'sacrifice' to 'exile') in equal measure.

Clearly this conventional polarization is simplistic, a caricature of complex political issues and values. Yet it is one that frames understandings and explanations of events on (and off) the island. To take just two examples from an extensive literature: Antoni Kapcia in *Cuba: Land of Dreams*, whilst noting the ambiguity of Castro's words, argues that, in the main, the limits to dissent have been coherently maintained. He considers that periods of debate during the past fifty years have involved competing discourses of development and definitions of what it means to be Cuban (*Cubanía*). On the one hand, there have been dissenting voices embedded in a tradition of externally-oriented discourses that define what it means to be Cuban in terms of exogenous cultural and political models. For the Cuban state such voices themselves become exogenous, external and marginal. On the other hand, there are voices of dissent embedded inside internally oriented discourses that seek a definition of *Cubanía* which is local and sovereign. According to Kapcia (2000: 224), the tensions between these discourses have neither been unhealthy nor unproductive:

> It is important to see the question of 'dissent' as one of 'ins' and 'outs', with periods of isolation and crisis often producing a narrower definition of the 'ins' (resulting in exclusion, and even marginalization and antagonism), but with subsequent periods of 'inclusion' and even rehabilitation.

In her discussion of 'artistic public spheres' in Cuba during the 1990s, Sujatha Fernandez (2007: 12) updates and focuses this theory by exploring the ways in which the Cuban state has co-opted and incorporated critical and oppositional expression in order to re-draw and strengthen its hegemony:

> The Cuban state tolerates counterhegemonic cultural practices such as critical art because they can be reincorporated in official institutions, traditions and discourses in ways that bolster the state's popularity, delineate the boundaries and limits of contestation and promote national unity.

Whilst Fernandez illustrates in great detail the dynamics of an ever-shifting *cultural* citizenship between the 'ins' and the 'outs', her discussion throws into relief the dearth of such dynamics in *political* citizenship. In the words of Cuban art critic Gerardo Mosquera (cited in Navarro 2002), parodying Castro's rhetoric, 'As strong as this [artistic] expression turns out to be, it is a questioning that emerges within socialism and for socialism.'

Whilst critical artistic dissent can co-exist inside the hegemonic project of the Cuban state when that criticism lies within the parameters established by the state, social and political criticism in print outside of those parameters must instead be neutralized. This can be seen in practice with the closure in 1961 of *Lunes de Revolución*, the literary magazine of the newspaper *Revolución*, the fate of *Pensamiento Crítico*, the final edition of which appeared in 1971, and *Cuadernos de Nuestra América*, whose reformist academic editorial group was disbanded by the government in 1996 (Perez 2008: 121). These state-owned publications were considered by their writers and editors to be successfully navigating a difficult line of ideological plurality from within, yet all ultimately suffered from the narrowing of the parameters for inclusion.

There have never been claims in Cuba since 1959 that the press or the media in general could ever be anything but an organ of state ideology. Indeed there is little disagreement between Hugh Thomas's claim in *Cuba or the Pursuit of Freedom* that 'May [1960] saw the end of the free press in Cuba' (Thomas 1998: 1280) and Fidel Castro himself who, in an interview with US photojournalist Lee Lockwood, proclaimed in 1965 that 'an enemy of socialism cannot work in our newspapers – but we don't deny it, and we don't go around proclaiming a hypothetical freedom of the press where it actually doesn't exist' (Lockwood 1990: 114).

Since the nationalization of the Cuban press in 1965, both national and local newspapers have been regulated by the Communist Party of Cuba and content filtered through the Ideological Department of the Central Committee. This ideological imperative is formally represented in Article 5 of the 1976 Cuban constitution which grants to the Communist Party the duty to organize and control all the resources for communication in order that they benefit the state. The Union of Cuban Journalists is the only legal professional organization for journalists in Cuba and the centralization of education for media professionals safeguards the ideological loyalty of its graduates working in the press and television (Nichols and Torres 1998; Ripoll and Ratliff 1987).

Whilst the government maintains a press monopoly there is no specific censorship law prohibiting the activities of independent journalism on the island. Given the monopoly, however, such independence has always been extremely circumscribed and was largely limited, before the advent of the Internet in Cuba, to feeding foreign-based media outlets in the US and Europe such as the US-based CubaNet and Encuentro de la Cultura Cubana in Spain. The dilemma in doing so, however, lay not only in the harassment and persecution from the government that accompanied it, but also with the fact that such publications themselves had ideological bias: a virulent anti-Castroism. The possibility of 'independence' always remained slim against the ideological battleground of *pro* and *contra*. With the creation of the independent news agencies Cuba Press and Havana Press in the mid-1990s as well as the appearance of *De Cuba* and *Vitral*, the first privately owned magazines since 1959, grassroots journalism began its own tentative steps to organize and test the tolerance of the government to criticism. The response, known as the 'Black Spring', resulted in 75 arrests in March 2003. By April of that year 29 journalists began serving prison sentences of between 14 and 27 years for acting as 'mercenaries' at the service of the United States. The charge for which the journalists were found guilty related directly to the Cuban constitution which states that it is against the law to collaborate with foreign media with the intent of destabilizing the country and destroying the socialist state; to provide information directly or indirectly to the US in order to facilitate the objectives of the Helms-Burton Act; or reproduce or distribute material deemed to be subversive propaganda from the US government (Laws 80/88 of the Cuban Constitution).

If the imprisonments represented a crackdown on independent journalism, they were also a symbolic message to critics in general. Navarro (2002: 193) wrote:

> Even when the intellectual's critical role is explicitly recognized in a theoretical way, it is immediately neutralized through diverse restrictions and reservations, and carrying it out in concrete social practice becomes the target of all kinds of political and ethical accusations.

The symbolic response seemed designed to renew and reinforce state authority. If social criticism in the public sphere can be used by the enemies of the Revolution as propaganda to destabilize the country, threatening its sovereignty and autonomy, then such criticism becomes counter-revolutionary and marks a *de facto* collaboration with the enemy. Where national strength is achieved by collective unity, such collaboration can only be destabilizing. Even when, as is often the case, much social criticism in Cuba is an 'open secret', its expression in printed, distributed form and discussion in the public sphere on the island remains rigorously resisted.

In the light of the above, it is not difficult to anticipate the reactions to *Generación Y* by both the Cuban state and those media outlets who had supported independent journalists. However, CubaNet very quickly welcomed Sánchez into its fold and that affiliation doubtlessly contributed to her growing visibility in the Cuban-American blogosphere. Although reported on CubaNet on 27 October 2007, it was the post of 10 September 2007 ('I abstain!') which was highlighted as worthy of the solidarity of the anti-Castro community:

> Neither Yoani nor the other bloggers [in Cuba] are alone. Without them knowing it there are thousands of other Cubans who have said the same as she has alone in front of her computer: abstaining from voting, saying no to a farcical election, looking for freedom, trying to find it.

Equally clear in his characterization, Fidel Castro identified *Generación Y* as 'proof of the confusion and trickery spread by imperialism' and complained that the worst aspect of the blog was not the immediacy with which imperialist mass media was able to spread opinions but the fact that young Cubans could actually think ideas such as those expressed by Sánchez in her blog. He described her as an example of the 'special envoys used to do the work of interference and neo-colonial reporting of the ancient Spanish metropolis that then awards them prizes.'

However, we should be wary of these attempts to position *Generación Y*, in reading Sánchez as a dissident of neo-colonialism or as an independent journalist under the tutelage of the Cuban exile community. She herself claims neither to be a dissident nor a journalist:

> I have denied in numerous interviews that I'm 'in opposition' because I don't have a political programme, political policies nor even a political allegiance [...] I don't belong nor have I ever belonged to a political group. I was never a member of the Young Communist Union. I never tried to be militant in the Communist Party. I was only a 'pionera' because it was obligatory up to the age of 16 [...] I believe that one of the things that characterises postmodernity and the present moment is that the great definitions, right and left, green, red, are outdated.

Sánchez attempts to capture a place outside of the conventional *pro/contra* polarization which for those 'polarised' is deeply disconcerting. She lives in a world of 'postmodernity' of which writers such as Jameson (1991), Giddens

(1991) and Friedman (1994) have observed, the grand narratives of modernity have given way to the personal, reflective and reflexive projects of the self. Social order, in this understanding, is less about collective, ideological scripts and more about the interlinking global and local networks of personal narratives. This view of the self not only conflicts with the polarizations characteristic of the dominant narratives of a Cuba tied into a continued Cold War relationship with the United States, it is also suggestive as to why a communication medium such as a blog might be seen as an appropriate medium for the inscribing of those identity projects. Sánchez did not start her blog in order to discover a postmodern identity: she was inclined to start the blog because of an awareness of living in postmodernity.

The naming of her activities on the blog as 'citizen journalism' follows a similar pattern: 'I didn't know that getting "my own grip on information" was something that had a name: citizen journalism.' She neither contests nor consciously adopts the ascription. Her reaction is similar to other younger generation activists whose activities ('networking', 'flash-mobbing' or 'denial of service attacks') have often been named after the events in which they played a part and which, only subsequently, become ritualized or rule-governed. Being called a citizen journalist seems not to have influenced Sánchez's understanding of what she thought she was doing on *Generación Y*. Once again, her inclination towards using the medium is an illustration of her personal concerns and desires to inscribe her personal narrative. Sánchez did not start the blog in order to practice citizen journalism. It will, however, be interesting to chart the influence that the ascription has in the future. Will she write differently knowing that she is being thought of and read as a citizen journalist?

The Internet in Cuba

Fidel Castro's criticism of *Generación Y* reaches to the core of the specific socio-political context from which the blog has emerged. If Sánchez sees the network society as the connections between personal narratives, the

Cuban government has seen the Revolution as a project unified around a leader, an ideology and the mobilization of mass participation in clearly demarcated social and political groups. The perceived dangers of the Internet to such a project were expressed by Castro as early as 1995: 'They [the United States] speak of 'information highways', new ways that serve to fortify this economic order, which they want to impose on the world, through propaganda and the manipulation of human mentality' (cited in Hoffmann 2004: 205).

At the same time the benefits of an albeit rudimentary connection to the Internet that began in 1992, were becoming evident and Cuba was beginning to ruminate on how to maximize those benefits. In establishing the priorities for the development of information technology on the island during the mid-1990s it was made clear that any economic, political, social and intellectual arguments in favour of the implementation of the Internet should be subservient to the political, ideological and security imperatives that would protect the Cuban Revolution.

The discussions that took place at this time did so against the background of the 'Special Period', a time of extreme economic and social crisis. In 1996 Law-Decree 209 was passed, establishing the structures and regulating the processes for the introduction of the Internet on the island. Access to the Internet would be limited to official institutions and state companies. This policy was legitimized on two fronts. First, the telecommunications infrastructure and the type of connection to the Internet (satellite) were inadequate to support widespread access. Second, the potential of the Internet to contribute to a development programme in a materially impoverished country needed to be channelled to those organizations most able to harness that potential. As Sergio Perez, Director of the state Internet provider Teledatos, told the Communist Party daily newspaper *Granma* in March 2001, 'Cuba is a poor and economically blockaded country that rations its food and has shortages of medicine. How could citizens' access to the Internet not be limited?'

Government policy concerning the development of the Internet was to be no different to the allocation of other scarce resources on the island: central control and rationing. State ministries, universities and government research centres began to be connected to the Internet during the late 1990s. Accreditation for its use was required by Law-Decree 209. Any use that violated 'Cuban society's moral principles or the country's laws' or which might 'jeopardize national security' was outlawed. Civil society organizations can and have applied for Internet access using government authorized Internet Service Providers. However, they are unlikely to have their application approved unless they are seen to support the government's political guidelines for the informatization of Cuban society (Kalathil and Boas 2003: 59). Residential access is extremely rare and limited to those authorized by prioritized government agencies.

Whilst connection to a transnational Internet created a dilemma for the government, the development of domestic local and wide area networks linking institutions and businesses, which had begun in the 1980s, has continued and grown (Hoffmann 2004: 216). This network, also known as the Cuban Internet or CUBANET, is the net that the majority of Cuban users not accredited for the Internet access through public access points. These access points include a small number of cyber-cafés which are mostly restricted to particular organizations and computer rooms that have been gradually integrated into the post office service since 2001. Internet access here is limited to international email and access to CUBANET. It is very slow and carefully monitored through the requirement to register with a name and national ID. Unsurprisingly, clamour for more extensive Internet access has resulted from these initiatives. The post office service is deluged with requests for increased access, discussions in cultural and artistic fora continually call for more inclusive accreditation for Internet use, and although penalties if discovered are high, the development of a black market for Internet access has become more and more sophisticated (Kalathil and Boas 2003: 61). Yet Cuba's policy seems little changed since the mid-1990s when the attitude was to 'accept and incorporate the technologies, but minimize their negative effects through authoritarian socio-political mechanisms of control' (Hoffmann 2004: 207).

The emergence, or rather the limited presence, of the Cuban blogosphere on the island can be more readily understood from this context. Very few blogs are visible in the top-level *.cu* domain and are all contained within the online editions of government press and media channels. There are also issues concerned with identifying blogging in Cuba. Establishing the provenance of a blog in terms of where it is authored is notoriously difficult. Blog publishing platforms such as Blogger and Wordpress make geographic anonymity the rule rather than the exception. Blogs that are home-spun and created on local servers are equally difficult to identify. Enterprising and IT-competent teachers and students at the University of Havana are known to keep blogs and there may be blogs kept (well-hidden) by Internet-savvy users on black market connections as well as proxy blogs fed from Cuba but maintained abroad. Clearly, these factors make it is impossible to know exactly how many blogs are written from the island of Cuba. However, from 2003 examples of blogs kept by Cuban journalists began to appear using third party hosts such as blogia, blogspot, ya.com and Wordpress. Such blogs are directly influenced both by the normative role ascribed to accredited journalists and enshrined in the code of journalistic ethics, as well as by the government's policy at the beginning of the 2000s of increasing Cuba's presence on the Internet. This initiative, which produced a dramatic growth in the number of sites at .cu can be seen as an example of using the Internet to amplify existing communication routines (Bennett 2003: 145). It was designed to improve Cuba's image abroad, attract tourism, and counter propaganda aimed at destabilizing the government.

Civic Engagement/Critical Ethnography

It is against this background that the management of *Generación Y* and desdecuba.com operate. Law-Decree 209 does not permit the hosting of public citizen content on the Cuban top-level domain .cu without government authorization. Because of this the site is hosted on a server in Germany and posts are written to be later uploaded when access to an Internet account can be found. On the majority of occasions such access is to be found in hotel Internet cafés which are both expensive and often reserved for hotel residents. However, if access is achieved, largely unfettered and unmonitored contact with the Internet is possible. The singularity of such an experience was not lost on the initial press reports on *Generación Y* – as Reuters reported in October 2007, 'when 32-year-old Yoani Sánchez wants to update her blog about daily life in Cuba, she dresses like a tourist and strides confidently into a Havana hotel, greeting the staff in German.'

Nor is it lost on Sánchez herself, although her thinking is clearly more deeply embedded in the experience of a tourism industry that has become emblematic of the dual economy where market economics in (convertible) dollar-currency enclaves such as tourism sit parallel to socialist state enterprises in Cuban pesos. The social and political consequences of such a system have been documented by various commentators (Taubman 2002; Venegas 2004). The crisis of legitimation that has gripped the country since the 'Special Period' and that has continued with the erosion of relative social equality into the present is the stuff of everyday experience and conversation in Cuba: the 'open secret' about which it is impossible to talk. Yet, Sánchez, in her blog does so. The insider view renders the invisible visible and exploits the vagueness implicit in blogging; that blog posts should be at one and the same time biographical but also report on the world outside:

He's 28 and works at a hotel pool because his stepfather bought him a job in the tourism industry. His command of English is awful but with the two thousand pesos he paid to the administrator, he didn't have to prove he could speak it. More than half the bottles of rum and coca cola he sells at the snack bar he bought himself at the retail price. His colleagues taught him how to sell his own 'merchandise' first, over that which the State sells to tourists. Thanks to this trick, on every shift he pockets what a neurosurgeon would earn in a month.

His rhythm of spending is tied to his illegal profits, so he tries to comply rather than clash on the plane of 'ideological unconditionality'. He's one of the first to arrive when called to a march or to the May-Day parade. In his wardrobe, for when needed, he has a pullover with the Five Heroes, another with Che's face, and a dark red one that says 'Battle of Ideas'. If his boss tries to catch him diverting resources, he wears one of those shirts and the pressure eases. At his young age, he already understands that it doesn't matter how many times you cross the line of illegality as long as you keep applauding. Some slogans shouted at a political event, or that time he spoke out against a counterrevolutionary group, have helped him keep his lucrative employment. His hands, that today steal, cheat customers, and divert goods from the state, six years ago these same hands signed a constitutional amendment to make the system 'irreversible'. For him, if they let him continue to line his pockets, socialism could well be eternal.

The post is an example of a kind of literary reportage blending observation, experience and anecdote into an evocative narrative. Its power is derived both from the (assumed) credibility of its source together with its succinct summary of a 'case' that illustrates the political logic of a tolerated informal economy that is able to reproduce existing political power: socialism is safe in the hands of this twenty-eight-year-old. Three thousand three hundred and thirty one comments attest to the resonance of such a story amongst readers of *Generación Y*. Many posts echo this approach. Whether a description of a doctor's surgery, commentary on political billboards in the neighbourhood, or the scrutiny of her son's graduation diploma, the writings seek to open a space with a locally embedded voice: a situated voice receptive to local context, person specific yet rarely personal. To return to Sánchez's notion of therapy: the therapy here is in voicing the unvoiced/ unvoiceable as well as in the reciprocity to be found in the thousands of comments the blog receives. The development of voice is key. It is that which, cultivated over time in a blog, enables an identification by a readership; a readership that can respond directly. Another post illustrates the way in which the insider view is given its setting in much the same way that classical ethnographies introduce their readers to the field:

> Habanero Boulevard, on Wednesday night, was the stage for a couple with their son, looking for a little fresh air. It is only nine o'clock, but judging by the atmosphere it seems like three in the morning. The smell of urine from every corner confirms that the drunks have started early and that public bathrooms continue to be an illusion. The abundance of prostitutes causes the mother to hurry through the passage, but the child manages to witness a very direct transaction between a pimp, his 'girlfriend' and a tourist.

Whilst its voice gives the post an authenticity and credibility, its significance lies in it introducing another 'open secret' into the public sphere: in enabling a 'public' collectively to discuss a phenomenon that has been taboo

since the government claimed that the Revolution had eradicated a practice symbolizing the neo-colonial exploitation of Cuba during the 1950s.
Sánchez is not the first to do this. Other writers and artists have explored
these issues before her. She is, however, the first to do so in a blog.

Blogs are essentially textual media in which the use of language plays
a central role. Although Sánchez does use photographs in her posts, her
craft in using a camera is clearly less consciously elaborated than is her use
of language. She tends for the most part to avoid the polarization of 'us'
and 'them', refusing to be placed at either end of the dichotomy whilst at
the same time continually constructing and affirming a sense of *Cubanía*
through the language she uses. Clearly this represents a challenge to the
translator and arguably it is only through the original posts that the more
subtle nuances of this use can be appreciated. A posting in September 2008
illustrates this point. After two hurricanes hit the island in that month,
the mainstream media were anxious to reassure a speedy return to normality. Sánchez was quick to question the reassurance and listed the ways in
which life has been 'abnormal' during the preceding three decades. That
list – including 'los mítines de repudio', 'mis amigos armando una balsa
para echarse al mar' and 'las colas perennes' – is notoriously difficult to
translate because each element is embedded in the consciousness of those
who recognize or identify with *Generación Y*. Each has an emotional as
well as a social history that resonates with multiple individual stories,
personal trauma, and private sadness. Each codes a particular sense of
shared *Cubanía* which has been denied space in the public sphere on the
island where such public invocations as 'Socialismo o Muerte' (Socialism
or Death) have dominated one-dimensional understandings of national
identity. On *Generacion Y* Sánchez affirms a *Cubanía* through her experiences of the past three decades, validating exactly these experiences as ways
of being Cuban on the island. In refusing the exit option (physically or
mentally) and instead giving voice to her *Cubanía* in the public domain
she establishes a form of civic participation in the political processes that
surround her.

El Caso Gorki

Could then the argument be extended to suggest that *Generación Y* is re-shaping the public sphere in Cuba? Is Sánchez contributing to political processes on the island? The belief that the blogosphere in general and individual blogs in particular are influencing political processes often rests on anecdotal evidence built from a number of 'foundational stories'. The Trent Lott case and the questioning of President Bush's National Guard Service, Howard Dean's use of the blogosphere in the 2004 Presidential primaries, legal cases such as that of Cory Maye, and the actions of bloggers in stopping the European sale of arms to Venezuela, are examples of such stories raised retrospectively to foundational level. One episode fuelled by and reported on in *Generación Y* might lay claim to being such a 'foundational story' in the emergence of the influence of blogs on political and legal processes in Cuba.

On 26 August 2008 Sánchez wrote in *Generación Y*: 'They took him because nothing destabilizes the intransigents more than a man in his most free state' – referring to Gorki Águila, a guitarist and singer with the punk-rock band Porno para Ricardo, arrested on 25 August on the charge of 'peligrosidad social pre-delictiva' (pre-delinquent dangerousness), a law introduced to counter anti-government behaviour. Over the next forty-eight hours more than 4,000 comments were left on *Generación Y* in response. Aggregated and syndicated throughout the blogosphere, the following days saw online reports by major media outlets in the United States and Europe. Open letters of support sent by musicians and activists, a 'Free Gorki' blog and a Wikipedia article on Gorki attest to the interest in the case and its increasing international visibility. On Thursday 28 August a protest was held at an open-air concert in Havana. Banners with the name of Gorki were briefly displayed before some protesters were taken away to be detained by the police, and others chronicled the events on the blogosphere through telephone contacts to friends with Internet access. The following day, at the court hearing to decide Gorki's fate, a number of protesters arrived together with the press from various international agencies. The initial charge of pre-delinquent dangerousness was dropped and

Gorki was subsequently fined 600 Cuban pesos (just over 20 US dollars) for 'disturbing the peace'. For the protestors involved, including Sánchez, the outcome was understood as a victory for a very new form of civic engagement on the island. She describes it in a post on 26 September:

> What I do not want to fail to say is that never before, as in these last few days, have I seen international public opinion, the media, and part of Cuban civil society come together and unite. Yesterday we demonstrated that the wall can be pushed if we do it together. We have forced them to retract, to undo the injustice, and this is a very good precedent for us and extremely dangerous for 'them'. The Internet proved that it can act, in the Cuban case, as a virtual environment for joint efforts. I hope that these centimetres we gained by pushing the boundaries will be followed by metres and metres of reclaimed freedoms.

Perhaps this is a foundational story and one that will be cited in future discussions of the emergence of an influential blogosphere in Cuba. Perhaps the Internet's potential to change the practice of politics radically because of its interactive and participative attributes is being realized by bloggers in Cuba. Perhaps it is just wishful thinking on the part of a small group of Internet-savvy individuals. Clearly, it is too early to know.

Conclusion

The limited access to the Internet presently available to Cubans in Cuba greatly constrains its potential for becoming a platform for any expression unsympathetic to the government's political agenda. Until that access changes, the notion that politics and policies may be influenced by it remains remote. During her chronicling of the Gorki case Sánchez reflected on her own role as a writer, journalist, and blogger:

> Looking at those foreign correspondents confirmed that I'm not made of the right stuff to be a journalist. I cannot stay behind the lens without getting involved. This work of entomology that consists of observing and reporting but not intervening, is definitely not for me. Being a blogger allows me to be a part of what's happening and that's why I am stuck with this role.

In maintaining the blog, she is pushing at the edges of definitions of journalism, of citizen journalism and civic participation. She is even pushing at the edges of what a blog actually is for herself and her readers. *Generación Y* has become a platform for a community to exchange ideas, yet due to organizational constraints, her role is more of writing *to* rather than writing *with* that community. The community itself is disproportionately international and despite efforts to distribute the blog postings within Cuba on disk, such limitations no doubt greatly reduce its influence on a local public sphere. Perhaps more important, however, is the visible attempt by *Generación Y* to challenge the dichotomies that have characterized and sustained the media in Cuba over many years. In affirming her 'Third Way' of *Cubanía*, in resolutely choosing voice over exit, in demanding her right to communicate, and doing so in a transnational medium, she may just be creating a space where a plurality of forms of civic engagement can take root.

The public sphere has not changed significantly in Cuba. But perhaps in altering her own relationship to the Cuban public sphere, Yoani Sánchez is suggesting a direction in which it may change in the future.

References

AOL (2005). 'AOL Survey Says: People blog as Therapy'. Available at corp.aol.com/press-releases/2005/09/aol-survey-says-people-blog-therapy.

Bahnisch, M. (2006). 'The Political Uses of Blogs' in Bruns, A., and Jacobs, J. (eds), *The Uses of Blogs*, New York: Peter Lang, 139–49.

Barney, D. (2001). *Prometheus Wired: The Hope for Democracy in the Age of Network Technology*. Chicago: University of Chicago Press.

Bennett, W. (2003). 'Communicating Global Activism' in *Information, Communication & Society* 6:2, 143–68.

Bimber, B. (1998). 'The Internet and political transformation: populism, community, and accelerated pluralism' in *Polity* 31:1, 133–60.

Boyd, D. (2008). 'Can social network sites enable political participation?' Available at rebooting.personaldemocracy.com/node/5493.

Burgess, J., and Green, J. (2009). *YouTube: Online Video and Participatory Culture.* Cambridge: Polity Press.

Castells, M. (2002). *The Internet Galaxy: Reflections on the Internet, Business, and Society: Reflections on the Internet, Business and Society.* Oxford: Oxford University Press.

Castells, M., Fernandez-Ardevol, M., Qui, J., and Sey, A. (2007). *Mobile Communication and Society: A Global Perspective.* Cambridge, MA: MIT Press.

Castro, F. (1961). *Palabras a los intelectuales.* Havana: Ediciones del Consejo Nacional de Cultura.

Davis, R. (1999). *The Web of Politics: The Internet's Impact on the American Political System.* New York: Oxford University Press.

Drezner, D., and Farrell, H. (2008). 'Introduction: Blogs, politics and power: a special issue of Public Choice' in *Public Choice* 134:1–2, 1–13.

Fernandes, S. (2007). *Cuba Represent!: Cuban Arts, State Power, and the Making of New Revolutionary Cultures.* Durham: Duke University Press.

Friedman, J. (1994). *Cultural Identity and Global Process.* London: Sage Publications.

Gergen, K. and Katz, J. (2008). 'Mobile Communication and the Transformation of the Democratic Process', in Katz, J. (ed.), *Handbook of Mobile Communication Studies.* Cambridge, MA: MIT Press, 297–310.

Giddens, A. (1991). *Modernity and Self-Identity: Self and Society in the late Modern Age.* Cambridge: Polity Press.

Gillmor, D. (2006). *We the Media: Grassroots Journalism By the People, For the People.* Cambridge, MA: O'Reilly Media.

Grossman, L. (1995). *The Electronic Republic: Reshaping American Democracy for the Information Age.* New York: Viking.

Hall, S. (2006). *The Blog Ahead: How Citizen Generated Media Is Tilting the Communications Balance.* Garden City, NY: Morgan James Publishing.

Hanson, E. (2008). *The Information Revolution and World Politics.* Plymouth: Rowman & Littlefield Publishers.

Hernandez-Reguant, A. (2009). 'Writing the Special Period: An Introduction' in Hernandez-Reguant, A. (ed.), *Cuba in the Special Period: Culture and Ideology in the 1990s.* Basingstoke: Palgrave Macmillan, 1–18.

Hewitt, H. (2006). *Blog: Understanding the Information Reformation That's Changing Your World.* Nashville: Nelson.

Hill, K. and Hughes, J. (1998). *Cyberpolitics: Citizen Activism in the Age of the Internet.* Lanham: Rowman & Littlefield.

Hindman, M. (2008). *The Myth of Digital Democracy.* Princeton: Princeton University Press.

Hodkinson, P. (2002). 'Subcultural blogging? Online journals and group involve-
    ment among U.K. Goths' in Blood, R. (ed.), *We've Got Blog : How Weblogs Are
    Changing Our Culture*. New York: Perseus Books, 187–97.
Hoffmann, B. (2004). *The Politics of the Internet in Third World Development: Chal-
    lenges in Contrasting Regimes – Case Studies of Costa Rica and Cuba*. London:
    Routledge.
Huberman, B., Romero, D., and Wu, F. (2008). 'Social networks that matter: Twitter
    under the microscope' in *First Monday* 14:1.
Jameson, F. (1991). *Postmodernism, or, the cultural logic of late capitalism*. Durham:
    Duke University Press.
Kalathil, S., and Boas, T. (2003). *Open Networks, Closed Regimes: The Impact of the
    Internet on Authoritarian Rule*. Washington, DC: Brookings Institution.
Kapcia, A. (2000). *Cuba: Island of Dreams*. Oxford: Berg.
Lasica, J., and Blood, R. (2002). 'Blogging as a form of journalism' in Blood, R. (ed.),
    We've Got Blog: How Weblogs Are Changing Our Culture. Cambridge, MA:
    Perseus Books, 163–70.
Lockwood, L. (1990). *Castro's Cuba: Cuba's Fidel*. Boulder: Westview Press.
Margolis, M. and Resnick, D. (2000). *Politics as Usual: The Cyberspace 'Revolution':
    The Cyberspace Revolution*. London: Sage Publications.
Merelo, J., Orihuela, J., Ruiz, V., and Tricas, F. (2004). 'Revisiting the Spanish
    Blogosphere' in Burg, T. (ed.), *Blog Talks 2*. Norderstedt: Books on Demand,
    339–52.
Montgomery, K. (2008) 'Youth and Digital Democracy: Intersections of Practice,
    Policy, and the Marketplace' in Bennett, W. (ed.), Civic Life Online. Cambridge,
    MA: MIT Press, 25–50.
Navarro, D. (2002). 'In Medias Res Publicas: On Intellectuals and Social Criticism
    in the Cuban Public Sphere' in *Boundary* 29:3, 187–203.
Nichols, J., and Torres, A. (1998). 'Cuba' in Noam, E. (ed.), *Telecommunications in
    Latin America*. Oxford: Oxford University Press, 17–35.
Perez, O. (2008). 'The Media in Castro's Cuba: Every Word Counts' in Lugo-Ocando, J.
    (ed.), *The Media in Latin America*. Oxford: Oxford University Press, 116–30.
Reynolds, G. (2007). *An Army of Davids: How Markets and Technology Empower
    Ordinary People to Beat Big Media, Big Government, and Other Goliaths*. Nash-
    ville: Nelson Current.
Rheingold, H. (2002). *Smart Mobs: The Next Social Revolution*. Cambridge, MA:
    Perseus Books.
Rheingold, H. (2008). 'Mobile Media and Political Collective Action', in Katz, J.
    (ed.), *Handbook of Mobile Communication Studies*. Cambridge, MA: MIT Press,
    225–40.

Ripoll, C. and Ratliff, W. (1987). 'The Press in Cuba 1952–1960: Autocratic and Totalitarian Censorship', in Ratcliff, W. (ed.), *The Selling of Fidel Castro: The Media and the Cuban Revolution*. New Brunswick: Transaction Books, 83–108.

Rizzo, S. (2008). 'The Promise of Cell Phones: From People Power to Technological Nanny' in *Convergence* 14:2, 135–43.

Russell, A., and Echchaibi, N., eds (2009). *International Blogging: Identity, Politics and Networked Publics*. New York: Peter Lang.

Rutigliano, L. (2006). 'Emergent Communication Networks as Civic Journalism', in Tremayne, M. (ed.), *Blogging, Citizenship, and the Future of Media*. London: Routledge, 225–38.

Sunstein, C. (2007). *Republic.com 2.0*. Princeton: Princeton University Press.

Tan, L. (2008). 'Psychotherapy 2.0: MySpace blogging as self-therapy' in *American Journal of Psychotherapy* 62:2, 143–63.

Taubman, G. (2002). 'Keeping out the Internet?' in *First Monday* 7:9.

Thomas, H. (1998). *Cuba or the Pursuit of Freedom*. New York: Da Capo Press.

Venegas, C. (2004). 'Will the Internet Spoil Castro's Cuba?' in Jenkins, H., and Thorburn, D. (eds), *Democracy and New Media*. Cambridge, MA: MIT Press, 179–202.

ROY KRØVEL

The War in Chiapas:
The Fall and Rise of Independent Journalism

On 1 January 1994 armed peasants from the Ejercito Zapatista de Liberación Nacional (EZLN) attacked police stations and army bases in the Mexican state of Chiapas. It did not take long before the army had the rebels on the run, and the EZLN retreated into the jungle. The Mexican regime tried to control the information seeping out of the war zone, but soon realized that this was not possible. Information kept coming from the jungle, distributed on the Internet, a technology which had only recently been introduced in Chiapas. Global networks of organizations and activists began organizing activities supporting the EZLN, using news lists and later homepages to mobilize support.

A number of studies have concluded that the Zapatistas' use of the Internet and other new communication technologies broke the authoritarian grip on the media. Indeed, the Zapatistas have been dubbed the world's first post-modern guerrillas (Burbach 1994); other studies have noted how activists have used the Internet to support the Zapatistas (Olesen 2004; Olesen 2005). Such studies have pointed to the fact that news audiences now have many alternatives to traditional journalism, and even the opportunity to communicate directly with the participants in conflicts.

This chapter is informed by interviews conducted with members of five Zapatista communities. The first interviews were conducted a few weeks after the war broke out and have since been followed up through annual rounds of interviews. Interviews have also been conducted with activists in North America, Latin America and Europe.

A Historically Docile Press

The often authoritarian Partido Revolucionario Institucional (PRI) governed Mexico from 1929 until 2000. Mexico experienced many social
and political protests, but the PRI had a firm grip on the media and very
few protests were ever given attention in the media. The regime did not
permit extensive freedom of speech, especially before the Internet came
to Mexico.

Lucio Cabañas was the leader of a movement of peasants and teachers
in Guerrero in the late 1960s and early 1970s. His Partido de los Pobres
(Party of the Poor) kidnapped an influential member of the governing
party, Rubén Figueroa Figueroa, in 1974. The kidnapping provoked a violent and extensive military response, which ended in the death of Cabañas
in December 1974, and the 'disappearance' of several hundred guerrillas
and their supporters. It took almost twenty years before the events were
systematically investigated, and a further nine years before the results of
the investigation were made public. The Party of the Poor in many ways
resembled the EZLN. Both organizations were made up mainly of indigenous peasants living in regions where local landowners ruled as if they
were feudal lords. Both the Party of the Poor and the EZLN demanded
the redistribution of land to the peasants, as well as political reforms. But
there are important differences in the ways the conflicts unfolded.

The conflict between the Mexican army and the Party of the Poor was
reported in relatively few articles in the press. In one of the earliest examples (in *Excelsiór*, 24 August 1972), the guerrillas were simply referred to as
'hooligans' and 'bandits', and the newspaper cited only the Mexican army's
General Hermengildo Cuenca Díaz as its source. General Cuenca Díaz was
also the only source for two articles published by the same newspaper in the
autumn of 1974 on army operations to release the politician held hostage by
the guerrillas. The newspaper *El Heraldo* also reported on the operations
to free Figueroa, reporting the deaths of five 'criminals' in the fighting. *El
Heraldo* also used the term 'bandits' to describe the guerrillas.

The Party of the Poor made several attempts to break the regime's iron grip on the dissemination of information. The organization sent out a communiqué to give its version of the kidnapping and the subsequent events. This communiqué does not seem to have been used by any of the newspapers at the time. It was ten years before the communiqué was published, and then only in scholarly books. The conflict in Guerrero was generally ignored by European and other North American media.

Similar stories have been told of many other revolutionary groups in Mexico during these years (Castellanos and Jiménez Martín del Campo 2007). The Zapatista case is therefore particularly interesting as it has indicated a fundamental change in the relations between social movements, the media and government in Mexico.

The Internet in Chiapas in 1994 and 1995

The war in Chiapas broke out almost exactly twenty years after the events in Guerrero. This time, though, the war did not last long; it took less than two weeks before the parties agreed a ceasefire. This short-lived war proved that many things had changed in Mexico. A number of Non-Governmental Organizations in Chiapas had been connected to the Internet through a project called *La Neta* only months earlier. These organizations could therefore communicate directly and at low cost with partners in Latin America, the US and Europe. EZLN soon learnt to exploit this new mode of communication.

The Mexican authorities tried to apply similar media management tactics to those employed in the conflict with the Party of the Poor. The first press releases from the Ministry of Defence used the term 'criminals' instead of 'guerrillas'. The Ministry claimed that 'foreigners' had 'seduced' certain members of the indigenous population of Chiapas, and that the guerrillas were receiving support from countries 'to the south of Mexico'. These claims were reported in both the Mexican and international media,

and were followed up with the arrests of a few suspicious-looking foreigners. But as the cases of the arrested foreigners were investigated, these
claims proved to be unsubstantiated, and the government's media strategy
received a devastating blow.

While a few newspapers and magazines played an important role in re-
framing the news agenda during the first few days of the conflict, Internet
communications became increasingly significant. The news list Chiapas-L
was started in August 1994 and administered from the national university
of Mexico by Arturo Grunstein. The news list was open for anyone to post
messages on it and had no editor. Chiapas-L distributed news from various sources, including NGOs, international solidarity groups, indigenous
groups, churches and peasant organizations. One large group of postings on
the list comprised eyewitness accounts from activists. A second large group
of postings offered news produced by independent NGOs in Chiapas. A
third group consisted of news clipped and pasted from local, national or
international news media.

The ceasefire held from January 1994 to February 1995. In February
1995 the army went on the offensive to arrest the leaders of the EZLN.
Most Mexican news media avoided publishing information provided by
the EZLN or their supporters during the first few days of the offensive,
but information kept flowing on the Internet, instigating protests both in
Mexico and overseas (Cleaver 1998; Russell 2005).

The journalist Amado Avendaño, for example, held a press conference
in San Cristóbal de las Casas to call for protests against the offensive the
same day as the army was sent into the jungle on the hunt for the guerrillas.
His appeal was distributed un-edited on Chiapas-L. The first mobilizations
for protests therefore began even before the offensive had had much effect
on the rebels. The production of alternative information happened fast
enough to have an effect on the conflict itself. The existence of a global
solidarity network meant that the information quickly found an interested
audience around the world.

Problems Assessing the Quality of Information

The activists used Chiapas-L as a tool to verify news and rumours circulating on the Internet. Wayne Pitt at the University of New Mexico posted a message on Chiapas-L on 11 February 1995 about rumours he had heard from a friend in Mexico. The rumours claimed that local hospitals were filling up with victims of the latest military offensive. Bonnie Schrack answered a few hours later. She pointed to several earlier news items that seemed to overstate the gravity of the situation. Several activists using Chiapas-L were aware of the danger of turning Chiapas-L and the Internet into tools for spreading unsubstantiated rumours. A message on the possible use of biological weapons against the indigenous population led to strong reactions from other users of Chiapas-L. Within a few hours five postings were made criticizing the message for lacking credibility and trustworthy sources. The writer had to issue a statement on Chiapas-L the same day expressing regret for posting unsubstantiated rumours. Harry Cleaver later used a similar case to warn the activists on Chiapas-L of the dangers of spreading false information.

This example illustrates a dilemma for those using the Internet to spread or find information. While it was necessary to produce and disseminate information fast enough to have an effect on what was happening in Chiapas, it was also of great importance that the information was trustworthy. The activists in the solidarity network needed the information to support their protests and campaigns, but they also had to feel confident that they could trust the information. Therefore, they spent much time trying to verify the quality of information received through these alternative channels of information.

Using Chiapas-L proved more effective when trying to gather information to correct or repudiate claims in the mainstream media. The activists had a long and exhaustive exchange in relation to an article in *The Washington Post*; mistakes were pointed out and tactics to dispute claims made by the article were discussed. It became a collective effort, thereby multiplying and clarifying the arguments to be used in the 'counter-attack'.

The network's response to a report issued by Chase Manhattan illustrates how the network could work together as a collective. The report was written by Riordan Roett (Director of Latin American Studies at Johns Hopkins as well as a consultant for Chase Manhattan) four weeks before the offensive against the EZLN. The report seemed to argue for a tougher Mexican policy against the EZLN. The report was first leaked by a small, independent magazine, *Counterpunch*, but received a much bigger audience after being posted on Chiapas-L by Harry Cleaver on 14 February. The Internet proved a useful tool in organizing protests against Chase Manhattan. As the protests grew in strength, Chase Manhattan distanced itself from the implicit recommendations of the report (Associated Press, 13 February 1995).

The first reports on torture were posted on 13 February 1995. The National Commission for Democracy in Mexico issued a series of interviews with suspected supporters of the Zapatistas. They had been arrested at the beginning of the military offensive, but were later released. Several of the suspected members of the EZLN claimed to have been pressured to sign declarations connecting them to the EZLN. Claims of torture reached the mainstream media while the military offensive in Chiapas was still underway. Testimonies of torture and human rights abuses had an important effect on the conflict in Chiapas. They led to protests from human rights organizations which resulted in restraints on army activities.

The Mexican army failed to arrest the leaders of the EZLN. President Ernesto Zedillo finally stopped the offensive, and Mexico's Congress passed a law granting amnesty for those arrested for being members of the EZLN. The conflict was back at square one, but the events had long-lasting effects on the freedom of the press in Mexico. New technology had laid the foundations for global networks which undermined much of the Mexican state's formal and informal control over the production and distribution of information. Slowly, newspapers, radio and television became less inclined simply to parrot official information.

Technology and Optimism

Such internationally famous academics as Manuel Castells and Harry Cleaver became intrigued by the developments in Chiapas. According to Castells (1996), the EZLNs success was founded upon their information strategy. Castells suggested that the production of information had become the most important resource in the 'network society' and predicted that hierarchical and rigid forms of organization in the future would be no match for flexible networks organized around symbols of identity. Castells also felt that a handful of 'prophets', such as the EZLN's military leader Subcomandante Marcos, might act as the protagonists in the construction of new symbols of identity. Harry Cleaver (1998) meanwhile wrote that 'today those networks are providing the nerve system of increasingly global challenges to the dominant economic policies of this period.' According to Cleaver (1998), the Zapatistas had demonstrated how the 'fabric of politics [...] is being rewoven.' This process was now challenging the 'existing political, social and economic order' (Cleaver 1998). These writers tried to show how information technology had stimulated the growth of new global networks able to alter fundamental power relations in society.

Such an understanding of the power of the Internet also has implications for the understanding of journalism and its position in society. Castells describes a situation in which participants themselves can distribute important information directly to their audience without the mediation of journalists. Activists, for instance, can produce and distribute information swiftly and effectively in a way that can have an effect on ongoing events. Who then needs journalists?

The Return of Journalism

During his successful election campaign of 2000, Vicente Fox promised to solve the problem in Chiapas in fifteen minutes. After the elections, President Fox presented a somewhat half-hearted proposal to Congress, based on the results of earlier negotiations between the government and the EZLN to give indigenous peoples collective rights over territories, including natural resources, in line with international conventions that Mexico had already signed. However Mexico's Congress was not willing to give indigenous peoples such far-reaching autonomy. The EZLN therefore decided to send their entire leadership to Mexico City to put pressure on Congress, joining forces with other indigenous organizations to demand better protection for collective rights in Mexico's Constitution. In 2001 the EZLN organized a caravan of buses to transport its leaders and supporters from Chiapas to Mexico City. This became a massive media event as the buses slowly toured from state to state on their way to the capital, with journalists from dozens of countries following the caravan. The caravan was received by some 200,000 people when it finally reached Mexico City. Among these were famous authors, Nobel Prize winners, artists and musicians. However, in spite of the massive media coverage of the Zapatistas and their demands, Mexico's Congress failed to pass a law in line with the original deal between the EZLN and the government. The EZLN refused to accept the resulting compromise, and returned to Chiapas without signing a formal peace agreement.

The activity in the global solidarity network had intensified as the caravan had prepared to set out on its journey to the capital. Italian anarchists from the organization ¡Ya Basta! took responsibility for the security of the caravan. Observers came to join the caravan from a number of countries, including Ireland, Spain, Great Britain, Norway and the United States. Several NGOs sent representatives to travel with the caravan, publishing daily updates online as the caravan advanced towards Mexico City. *La Neta* made sure the caravan was more or less constantly connected to the Internet, so that speeches and announcements could be published almost without delay. In addition, journalists from major national and international news outlets – including *Time, Newsweek, The Times, The Guardian, La Jornada,* CNN and the BBC – followed the caravan from town to town. Such well-known writers as Naomi Klein, José Saramago and Gabriel García Márquez wrote articles discussing the caravan and its potential effects. The Associated Press began one of its items by announcing that 'anti-capitalist rebel Subcomandante Marcos, who wooed the world with his poetic Internet communiqués, is on his way to becoming the most marketable man on the planet' – suggesting that Benetton was even interested in using Marcos in its commercials (Associated Press, 28 February 2001).

Such online news lists as Chiapas-L again played an important role, gathering information from many sources and distributing it to organizations and activists in their networks. However, much less information was produced by activists and organizations in these networks than six years earlier, in spite of the large number of activists travelling with the caravan and observing events at first hand. This may have resulted from the presence of the large number of news outlets also in tow, producing relatively independent and reliable information. Mexican newspapers, radio and television had by this time become more independent and offered information that even the activists in the networks found increasingly useful. Therefore, there was less need for the production of alternative news.

By 2001 mainstream news media had become the primary sources of information distributed through these online activist networks. In 1995 every fourth posting was cut and pasted from mainstream news media; by 2001 the proportion of articles pasted from the mainstream media had increased to 44 per cent of the total number of postings. Furthermore, the activists had gradually turned away from left-leaning media outlets: by 2001 Reuters and the Associated Press had become their most influential sources of news. Reuters and the Associated Press offered the activists access to sources within both the Zapatistas and the Mexican authorities, in addition to foreign governments.

Online networks have not therefore finally come to replace mainstream journalism. Indeed, one of the most important long-term effects of the Internet in Mexico has been to create conditions for the development of a robust mode of independent and critical journalism within the traditional institutions of professional news production.

References

Burbach, R. (1994). 'Roots of postmodern rebellion in Chiapas' in *New Left Review* 205, 113–14.

Castellanos, L., and Jiménez Martín del Campo, A. (2007). *México armado 1943–1981*. Mexico: Ediciones Era.

Castells, M. (1996). *The Rise of the Network Society*. Cambridge, MA: Blackwell Publishers.

Cleaver, H. (1998). 'The Zapatista Effect: The Internet and the Rise of an Alternative Political Fabric' in *Journal of International Affairs* 51, 621–40.

Olesen, T. (2004). 'Globalising the Zapatistas: From Third World Solidarity to Global Solidarity?' in *Third World Quarterly* 25, 255–67.

Olesen, T. (2005). 'Mixing Scales: Neoliberalism and the Transnational Zapatista Solidarity Network' in *Humboldt Journal of Social Relations* 29, 84–126.

Russell, A. (2005). 'Myth and the Zapatista movement: exploring a network identity' in *New Media Society* 7:4, 559–77.

GAVIN STEWART

'I cant belive a war started and Wikipedia sleeps': Making News with an Online Encyclopaedia

If you had been reading the newly created Wikipedia article called '2008 South Ossetia war' at exactly 21:47 UTC on 7 August 2008 you would probably have seen two very short sentences saying that a war had broken out between Georgia and South Ossetia. You might also have seen a short-lived plea, in bold, that read:

> Admins. I am a new User but at the Russian TV right now they show it. Right now a few hours ago Georgia started a War on Ossetia. The western media yet published it, the Russian intensivly publishes and that brings confusion with the sources. Those who now Russian, Osseatian,Georgian, please come in. I cant belive a war started and Wikipedia sleeps. (Wikipedia A)

This somewhat awkward call-to-action is interesting as it defies a number of the norms of an encyclopaedia article. Indeed, the direct address to the administrators of Wikipedia, the call to certain ethnic identities, the use of the first person, the unusual grammar, the non-standard spellings and the lack of any references or information will no doubt do much to confirm many deeply-held prejudices about the overall reliability of the writing in Wikipedia. However, this short-lived paragraph is also significant as it clearly draws attention to the fact that this editor believed that Wikipedia should be 'covering' an on-going war.

The notion that Wikipedia has a role in reporting a major news story is not an original one; in fact, this idea has been expounded by a number of advocates of the online encyclopaedia. For example in his book *The Wikipedia Revolution*, Andrew Lih argued that 'wikipedia wouldn't be as popular today without being timely and cataloguing events as quickly as the news happens' (Lih 2009: 7). Similarly, Sue Gardner, the executive director of the Wikimedia Foundation, is quoted in a Haaretz.com article as saying that Wikipedia was 'just another mainstream news medium' (Liphshiz 2009). Even journalists writing for mainstream media outlets have described the encyclopaedia as a news organization. For example, a Reuters article from 2007 titled 'Wikipedia remains go-to site for online news' reported research by Nielsen/NetRatings that placed Wikipedia as the 'top online news and information destination' (Woodson 2007).

Academic commentators have also made this claim for Wikipedia. In his book *Here Comes Everybody* Clay Shirky argues that it 'has now transcended the traditional functions of an encyclopaedia' (Shirky 2008: 116). Shirky provides the example of the 7/7 bombings in London. He notes that within minutes of the bombs going off a page had been created and it received more than a thousand edits during its first four hours as it responded to the latest news reports. Shirky (2008: 117) concludes that 'what was conceived as an open encyclopaedia in 2001 has become a general-purpose tool for gathering and distributing information quickly.'

This framing of Wikipedia as a 'top' news provider is significant for a number of reasons; first, because it re-opens the issue of the reliability of Wikipedia as a source of information; second, because it adds cultural significance to the overall popularity and search engine ranking of the site; third, because this claim highlights a number of tensions that lie at the heart of the Wikipedia project (which arise out of the policies, guidelines and procedures of the project and their interpretation through the local norms of its editors and wider user base); and, fourth, because it draws attention to the important issues that arise out of framing 'online journalism' as the act of news dissemination. This chapter will explore these issues, using the '2008 South Ossetia war' page as a case study of a large-scale news event reported by Wikipedia.

Wackypedians

It will come as no surprise to many readers to learn that Wikipedia has been subject to a number of trenchant criticisms. The most well-worked criticisms of the project include the claim that it is often inaccurate, that it is written by people who are not experts, that its content is often plagiarized from other sources and that it is subject to acts of vandalism. For those who are interested, the editors of Wikipedia have provided an extensive list of references on their page dedicated to critical analysis of the project (Wikipedia B).

Perhaps the most notorious example of inaccurate information being displayed on Wikipedia is the version of the biography entry for John Seigenthaler edited by Brian Chase, a manager at a small delivery service in Nashville, which falsely alleged that Seigenthaler had been implicated briefly in the Kennedy assassinations (Page 2005). According to an article written by John Seigenthaler in *USA Today* (29 November 2005), this 'character assassination' was up on Wikipedia for 132 days before being corrected. Another widely reported incident raised questions about the reliability of the editors of Wikipedia. A prominent editor, called Essjay, claimed to have a PhD in theology on his user page, but subsequently turned out not to be qualified in this or any other relevant subject (Lih 2009: 194–200). Wikipedia has also had a number of problems with 'premature obituaries'. For example, in January 2009 Wikipedia reported that Senator Edward Kennedy had died (Rajan 2009). Likewise, another premature obit reported that Alexander Chancellor had died on 10 December 2009, which afforded the veteran journalist the opportunity to emulate Mark Twain and write, 'the report of my death is an exaggeration' (Chancellor 2009).

It is not surprising, therefore, that some commentators regard Wikipedia as something of a joke. The blogger Mark Kraft, for example, gave the title 'Wackypedia' to a short post in which he noted that 'following the election of the new Pope Benedict in April, a user substituted the pontiff's photo on the Wikipedia site with that of the emperor from *Star Wars*' (Kraft 2008). Likewise, the editors of Uncyclopedia have developed their wiki-based site as a parody of Wikipedia, with the strapline 'the content-free encyclopedia that anyone can edit'.

Not everyone is laughing, of course. The basic thesis of Andrew Keen's book *The Cult of the Amateur* (2007) is that any engagement with amateur user-generated content is bad. It is particularly bad, he argues, in the public sphere because it replaces the well researched, well-edited pieces written by professional journalists with the work of amateurs. Keen reserved some of his best invective for Wikipedia. In a blog posting in 2006 he argued that:

> The open source encyclopaedia infantilizes knowledge. On Wikipedia, we all become children, playing at being adult, slipping into an Alice in Wonderland version of reality. If you're Alice, it might be fun. But for the grown-ups, it is worse than bad.

It is, however, possible to make too much of some of these headline-grabbing deficiencies. It is not as though traditional media outputs are free of errors. The eminent scientific journal *Nature* conducted a comparison between the scientific information presented by Wikipedia and online material presented by *Britannica* from which it concluded that they had a similar level of accuracy (though these findings were subsequently disputed by *Encyclopædia Britannica* and then defended as being valid by *Nature* in 2006 – see Giles 2005, *Encyclopædia Britannica* 2006 and *Nature* 2006).

It is quite striking, given the widespread criticism noted above, that there are a number of commentators willing to speak up in favour of Wikipedia. Charles Leadbeater, for example, praised Wikipedia for its egalitarian aspirations. Leadbeater quotes founder Jimbo Wales's aim to put 'the knowledge contained in a large encyclopaedia in the hands of everyone on the planet for free' (Leadbeater 2008: 14–15). Leadbeater then developed this point further by praising Wikipedia for already being free to access (Leadbeater 2008: 18), globally available (Leadbeater 2008: 18), popularist (Leadbeater 2008: 16) and non-elitist (Leadbeater 2008: 15) and for creating a positive 'wiki' culture (Leadbeater 2008: 19). Leadbeater (2008: 19) noted that as 'Wikipedia spreads around the world not only does it carry knowledge, it teaches habits of participation, responsibility and sharing.'

Key commentators have also praised the economics of Wikipedia. Writing in the *Wealth of Networks* in 2006 Yochai Benkler (2006: 71) argued that its 'open, peer-produced model proved enormously successful.'

Making a similar point, Leadbeater (2008: 14) drew attention to its amazing expansion, noting that the rate of growth for articles English between 2001 and 2007 was five million percent. Leadbeater (2008: 19) also noted that it has achieved this growth with few staff and little funding. Writing in *Print is Dead*, Jeff Gomez (2008: 83) argued that it was able to expand so rapidly because it harnessed collective intelligence. Leadbeater also praised Wikipedia for its ability to 'heal' itself. He pointed to the attacks made by Robert McHenry, the former editor-in-chief of *Britannica*, on Wikipedia, and the rapid incorporation of his criticism into the text of the updated version of the encyclopaedia (Leadbeater 2008: 17).

Turning to the public sphere, Cass R. Sunstein (2006: 152) noted the importance of the ability of Wikipedia to 'elicit widely dispersed information.' Sunstein (2006: 219) sees this as being important because it aids the development of effective deliberation in which 'people can obtain immediate access to information held by all or at least most, and in which each person can instantly add to that knowledge.' Furthermore, Sunstein has seen this wiki-enabled deliberation between differing perspectives as being important for the effectiveness of contemporary democracy as it serves as a corrective to problems of 'information cocoons' and 'echo chambers' that limit the effectiveness of the political blogosphere (Sunstein 2006: 191).

Sunstein presents a positive notion of the deliberations of the editors. However, in practice this can be highly variable from page to page. The talk pages of the '2008 South Ossetia war' article demonstrate how difficult it is to create the necessary dialogue around a conflict. There are inspiring passages in which there are genuine attempts at deliberation. However, some of the interchanges are like listening to a graduate student argument: there are impressive presentations of information in the form of links and Wikipedia guidelines (with an amazing attention to detail) but there are also obvious irresolvable assumptions of position. For example, in one of a multitude of arguments about the name of this article, one editor ends their contribution with a contentious statement, noting: 'After all of the conflict is restricted to South Ossetia, which is not part of Georgia' (Wikipedia C). Predictably, given the subject of this article, the next editor replies: 'You're totally wrong: South Ossetia is a part of Georgia' (Wikipedia C). Furthermore, there are also asides, endless claims of bias and propaganda, rhetorical flourishes and barbed put-downs. For example, a short interchange about the claim that 90 per cent of Ossetians carry Russian passports ends with the suggestion that: 'I strongly urge you to take a math class. Cheers!' (Wikipedia D).

Wonderpedians

Given the well-publicized criticisms noted above, one of the most striking things about Wikipedia is how popular it has become in the last five years. Statistics from Alexa have suggested that approximately 9 per cent of all global Internet users visited Wikipedia in 2008. Indeed, Wikipedia has become so pervasive that on occasions it has become a victim of its own success. For example, whilst covering the death of Michael Jackson, Tech Reporter Declan McCullagh observed that there were times during that day when Wikipedia 'appeared to be temporarily overloaded' (McCullagh 2009).

It is further testament to the rising importance of the site that a number of countries have taken notice of Wikipedia. The site claims that it has been blocked at various times by the People's Republic of China, Iran, Tunisia, Uzbekistan and Syria (Wikipedia E). Moreover, the Wikiscanner project (2007), created by graduate student Virgil Griffith, provided a fascinating insight into how government agencies, corporations and politicians regularly altered material on Wikipedia.

This author's own interest in Wikipedia arose out of research project that undertaken in 2007/8 which developed a critical view of the corporate use of community media (Stewart 2008). This research involved the culture of Search Engine Optimization (SEO). Reports of these practices (including one article on a blog called 'What To Do When Your Company Wikipedia Page Goes Bad' – Bowman 2007) suggested that the encyclopaedia had become a focus of attention for practitioners seeking to edit its contents solely to improve the rankings returned by search engines for their own sites. Methods recommended by these SEO practitioners include identifying and then deleting links to the competing Wikipedia page from other parts of Wikipedia and posting competing links in fora and blog comments linking to the Wikipedia site (see Blue Hat SEO 2008; Rafiq 2008). These competitive practices are not entirely surprising, for, as Wikipedia notes on its page dedicated to the subject, 'the growth of Wikipedia has been fuelled by its dominant position in Google search results; about 50% of search engine traffic to Wikipedia comes from Google' (Wikipedia F).

The dominance of Wikipedia in Google's rankings can be seen clearly in the results provided by RankPulse. This service tracks one thousand key search terms and reports on the site allocated the top spot at any particular time. On 21 July 2010, this site reported that Wikipedia occupied the first slot for 229 out of its 1,000 keywords. To give an idea of the nature of this achievement, Google returned Wikipedia as the first site for the search term 'America'. This made it the number one site out of a total of 574,000,000 sites listed by the search engine for this term.

The strategic importance of an online encyclopaedia to a search engine is also not lost on Google. Google created an online knowledge-sharing project called Knol. More recently, they have also acknowledged (tacitly) the value of Wikipedia to their enterprise by making a $2 million donation to the Wikimedia Foundation (Parr 2010).

It is not entirely surprising, therefore, that Wikipedia is having an impact on the wider public sphere. Reporters at the *New York Times* claim that they were able to manipulate news coverage of the kidnapping of their reporter David Rohde in Afghanistan by repeatedly removing reports of the incident from Wikipedia (Perez-Pena 2009). There are also some reports of the encyclopaedia being used in US intelligence documents (Aftergood 2007). Likewise, Wikipedia is being used as a source for journalists working for traditional media outlets (Shaw 2008). This practice can, of course, have lamentable consequences on occasions. For example, in 2009, Shane Fitzgerald, a twenty-two-year-old student from Ireland, inserted a fake quote in the Wikipedia article attributed to Maurice Jarre – a quote that was subsequently published by a number of newspapers in their obituaries for the composer. Fitzgerald was quoted in *The Guardian*, arguing that the purpose of his hoax was 'to show that journalists use Wikipedia as a primary source and to demonstrate the power the internet has over newspaper reporting' (Butterworth 2009).

It is, of course, tempting to frame this obituary hoax as yet another Wackypedia story with which to denigrate the online encyclopaedia. However, there are also a number of lessons to be learned for professional reporters working to tight deadlines.

Wikipedia News: Encyclopaedia and/or Newspaper?

So far this chapter has established that Wikipedia has developed a role for itself in news dissemination. However, it is important to acknowledge that this does not necessarily mean that it is a news organization in any traditional sense of the term. Indeed, a Wikipedia article dedicated to this question states baldly that it is not an online newspaper. It also states that it does not welcome the kind of original research or first-hand accounts of events that are often presented by conventional war correspondents (Wikipedia F). It explains:

> You may see yourself as a daring investigative reporter, contacting everyone from anonymous sources to people in positions in power, hoping to learn the truth about a subject. Through your myriad of connections, you uncover the scoop of the century. Wikipedia is simply dying for this scoop, right? Wrong.

Like many things to do with Wikipedia, this issue is not necessarily as clear, however, as this statement would seem to imply. For despite these protestations, Wikipedia also provides incentives to its editors to create timely articles by providing coveted slots in the 'In the News' section on its front page. The main talk page of the '2008 South Ossetia war' article proudly notes that it was featured in the 'In the News' section on 12 August 2008 and 1 October 2009. The encyclopaedia also makes great claims for the value of the flexibility of its software platform. For example, in the Wikipedia article dedicated to the wiki itself (Wikipedia G), it argues that 'a defining characteristic of wiki technology is the ease with which pages can be created and updated.'

Furthermore, material produced to promote Wikipedia also makes reference to its role in news reporting. For example, the information provided to the Facebook group about the encyclopaedia trumpets the fact that 'Wikipedia has received major media attention as an online source of breaking news as it is constantly updated.' The '2008 South Ossetia war' article provided a very good example of how this constant updating process can used to respond to a breaking news story.

Waking Up to a War

The first entry to new article was made at 21:30 UTC on 7 August 2008 by a user called 'Chrystal Blue Moon'. At that time, it comprised of the title and a single sentence: 'A conflict started in 2008' (Wikipedia 11). This short stub was written within hours of the major events described in the timeline of events presented later in this article. However, since this humble beginning the article grew through hundreds of edits so that by October 2008 it was nearly 10,000 words long, with six specially prepared maps, six photographs and over 300 references to external websites. Furthermore, this main article was also associated with an extensive 'history' that records the various versions of this page. It is further associated with an archive of the discussion of the editors of this page, which provide a number of insights into the processes that have shaped (and continue to shape) this article. By October 2008 this 'talk' ran to just over 380,000 words. This article and its attendant discussion represent, therefore, a considerable collective effort on the part of its editors to provide information in a timely manner on a topical subject. It also provided a significant record of the cultural practices of the editors of this article.

At first sight, it might seem somewhat misguided to attempt to identify the definitive social practice for a site whose strap line was once the 'free encyclopaedia that anyone can edit' – mainly because the inclusion of 'everyone' appears to preclude any meaningful analysis of phenomena such as gate-keeping, hierarchy and social norms that have been used to understand more traditional news production institutions. Likewise, it might seem unwise to place too much importance on policies and procedures in structuring Wikipedia, when one of the policy pages states clearly that 'if a rule prevents you from improving or maintaining Wikipedia, ignore it' (Wikipedia I). However, despite these eye-catching phrases it is clear that Wikipedia has developed a number of procedures that are worthy of further investigation. Indeed, as Jeff Howe (2008: 115) pointed out, 'it's Wikipedia's dirty little secret that a manner of bureaucracy has evolved to maintain the site's editorial standards of truth and neutrality.'

It is also clear that in developing these procedures that Wikipedia is not as libertarian as its early rhetoric would suggest. Joseph Reagle, for example, argues that the site has 'instituted gradually more control'. Indeed, he is quoted in the *New York Times* as saying that 'the idea of a pure openness, a pure democracy, is a naïve one' (cited in Perez-Penia, 2009).

The development of the '2008 South Ossetia war' article and its associated discussion pages provide a number of examples of the role played by gatekeepers, the power of the administrators to control access to the database (as well as the power of individual users to circumvent some of these controls) and the role played by Wikipedia policy and guidelines in the framing the resulting article.

Gatekeeping New Articles

Returning again to the early stages of the '2008 South Ossetia war' article, the history files record that the next editor on the scene was a user called 'Christian Nurtsch'. Judging by their user profile page, this user was an experienced Wikipedian, as it described them as a 'rollbacker' for the English language version of Wikipedia (Wikipedia J). A rollbacker is a privileged user with permission to use the rollback functionality 'as a fast method of undoing edits that are blatantly non-productive' (Wikipedia K). According to SQL's Tools (provided as a link at the bottom of Nurtsch's user page), this user had performed nearly 1,000 roll-backs by the end of September 2008 (Wikipedia L). It is significant to note that this experienced user did not contribute to the text and instead served a warning on the face of the article that it might meet the criteria for speedy deletion (CSD).

This less-than-warm welcome for the new article demonstrated one of the obvious ways that Wikipedia functions as a bureaucracy. It has developed a number of procedures that monitor and control the creation of new articles on the site that are framed by the 'Speedy Deletion' process. The Criteria for Speedy Deletion include articles that involve: patent nonsense and gibberish; pure vandalism; recreation of deleted material; and pages created by banned users in violation of their ban, with no substantial edits by others (Wikipedia M).

In the case of this fledgling article, the experienced user merely issued a warning. The original users responded to this warning edit by promptly returning the article to its former glory, commenting: 'Wait!!!! Right now a war started. Please help to start the article' (Wikipedia N).

Some three minutes after the article was first edited, another experienced user 'Excirial' altered the article and re-established the CSD notice. Excirial's user page provides a useful insight into procedures and programs that enable 'gatekeeping' within the open architecture of a wiki. For example, the range of brightly coloured boxes displayed on this page in October 2008 told us that this user was a 'new page patroller', that they participate in the 'adopt-a-user program' and they are a member of the 'counter-vandalism unit' (Wikipedia O). Many of these processes are automated to support the effectiveness of the participating editors.

Sixteen minutes after being set up the article now read: 'A conflict started in 2008 between Georgia and South Ossetia. Fire between both sides lead Georgia to declare war. [1][2]' (Wikipedia P). It is significant that the fledgling article finally features the external links (denoted by the reference numbers) that are an important part of the verification process for a Wikipedia article. The article then grew rapidly so that by 22:18 on 7 August 2008 the article comprised 374 words, with a map, a list of belligerents and sixteen external links (Wikipedia Q). However, it nearly ceased to exist as an independent article at this stage, as an editor called

'Kober' attempted to merge it with a pre-existing Wikipedia page called 'Georgian-Ossetian conflict'. 'Chrystal Blue Moon', however, reversed this merge by using the revert function built into the wiki software. Turning to the associated discussion, it is possible to see 'Chrystal Blue Moon' pleading for the continuing independence of this article.

Bureaucratic Power

Another obvious way that bureaucratic control is exercised in Wikipedia is through selective access to the tools that control the site. These tools support processes such as page deletion, page protection, blocking and unblocking individual users, and access to modify protected pages (Wikipedia R). The Wikipedians who are granted these additional privileges are known as administrators or admins. Admins have a range of powers (Wikipedia R); however, the technological power of administrators to block users from editing an article is also used as a threat to discipline their actions. For example, on 17 August 2008 'Future Perfect at Sunrise' responds to a perceived problem with images by posting: 'Any account found uploading Ossetia-related war images with missing or wrong source or licensing information, here or on commons, will be blocked immediately, indef, and without prior warning' (Wikipedia S).

Wikipedia also has a number of levels of authority above the level of administrator, such as steward and founder, which further regulate the activities of the site. Arguably the most famous founder, Jimbo Wales, seeks to make little of these roles by stating publicly that being an admin is 'not a big deal'. However, it is clear that it is a role that is respected by many of the editors developing the page under discussion. For example, turning to Excirial again, we can learn from this user's page that they failed recently in their attempt to be made an administrator of Wikipedia (despite having made some 27,000 edits in the last year). In a moment of self-reflection they observed that: 'I have to admit that the errors and questionable edits I made are far above the level that can be tolerated as mistakes' (Wikipedia O).

Turning back to the further development of the '2008 South Ossetia war' article, the privileges granted to the administrators clearly played a part in deciding which users were able to participate in its further development. 'Chrystal Blue Moon', for example, disappears early on in the story; probably because they were exposed as a 'sock puppet'. According to Wikipedia, a sock puppet is 'an alternative account used deceptively. Some examples that clearly violate this policy would be using two usernames to vote more than once in a poll, or to circumvent other Wikipedia policies' (Wikipedia T). In the case of 'Chrystal Blue Moon', a Wikipedia administrator thought that this user was the sock puppet for another user called 'M.V.E.i'. On yet another Wikipedia page, dedicated to the supposed infractions of this user, it is possible to read that other sock puppets of M.V.E.i are 'Forward Belarus', 'Afro-Russian' and 'Moscovite Knight' (Wikipedia U). However, it is also clear when considering this example, that despite the administrators having the power to banish, a user with sufficient motivation and technical knowledge can sometimes circumvent the blocks imposed by the administrators.

The Power of the Policy: Online Governance

In re-reading the talk pages produced in August and September 2008, it is noticeable that editors cite Wikipedia policy and guidelines in key interchanges, much in the manner of lawyers quoting case law. This is particularly true when the editors are working on a contentious issue. For example, on archive page 15, the user, Grey Fox, seeks to establish a consensus with his fellow users, by noting: 'We have one image of a destruction in Georgia, and per the WP:UNDUE policy [...] not more than 1 for Tskhinvali should be presented in this article, even if there are a 1000 on commons' (Wikipedia V).

This quote flags up the fact the validity of the policies of Wikipedia were broadly accepted by most of the users involved. This is particularly true of its key policies, such as those requiring 'Neutral Point of View',

'Verifiability' and 'No Original Research' (which are often referred to in Wikipedia talk pages by the abbreviations 'WP: NPOV', 'WP: VER' 'WP:OR'). Indeed, the pointed references to these guidelines became more overt when there was an apparent conflict between differing interpretations of these policies, for example, in the interminable discussions about the name of this article.

Furthermore, it is clear when reviewing the user pages of these editors that they are, to varying degrees, disciplined as they become more familiar with Wikipedia. This process begins with a highly informal induction, but is then supported by technical sanction and promotion to administrator (discussed above), by continuing indoctrination and by ritual humiliation. For example, Wikipedia has articles on writing a first article and how to deal with 'newbies'. The Wikipedia article called 'Please do not bite the newcomers' (Wikipedia W) even notes: 'New contributors are prospective "members" and are therefore our most valuable resource. We must treat newcomers with kindness and patience – nothing scares potentially valuable contributors away faster than hostility.' However, Wikipedia also maintains a page called the 'village stock', which relies on humiliation to enforce norms of behaviour (Wikipedia X).

If it Looks and Sounds Like an Encyclopaedia, Then ...

In seeking to discuss the capability of Wikipedia to deliver the news, it is essential to bear in mind that the policies and procedures discussed above were primarily framed to facilitate the production of an ever-changing, up-to-date online *encyclopaedia*. As such, they represent a significant achievement. It is very striking that during the development of the article under discussion, there were endless claims of propaganda, bias, and manipulation. There were also many examples of rudeness, bordering on hate speech. However, it is equally striking that these confrontations were flagged up and dealt with using the policies of Wikipedia, even as the participants engaged in the very difficult process of providing an account of the war.

Of course, it should also come as no surprise that the faithful application of these policies had a significant impact on the way in which the editors dealt with an ongoing news event. This was particular true of the application of the policy that excluded original research as well as the policies, templates and technologies that designated the format of the article shown on the screen.

The impact of the 'no original research' policy (WP:OR), for example, can clearly be seen in an interchange on 10 August 2008 (Wikipedia Y). One user has located a relevant UN report that looks like a valuable resource for the developing article. However, rather than greeting this discovery as a possible opportunity to develop an interesting angle on the war, a fellow editor disciplines him, noting: 'We should not pick our own quotes out of the UN transcripts. That's WP:OR. Let the news organizations decide what's newsworthy.'

The obvious consequence of this policy is the large number of links displayed on the article page. This characteristic arises out the endless drive to create consensus by providing acceptable verification for the statements made. However, in holding verifiability as a core policy, the editors of this article have adopted, by default, a non-standard mode of news management in which readily accessible public domain sources are held out as the gold standard. Indeed, in marked contrast to traditional newsroom practice, the participants are actively discouraged from cultivating non-public sources (or even to provide an account of what is going on through personal experience or by interrogating the participants involved). In the Wikipedia model, verification is reduced to finding an acceptable link.

Likewise, the format of the encyclopaedia itself also had a direct impact on the ability of this article to tell a conventional 'news story'. Indeed, to state the blindingly obvious, the structure of this article is modelled on the conventions of an encyclopaedia article rather than a news article. For example, the '2008 South Ossetia war' page was based on a standard model provided by Wikipedia that was modified during its development by applying a series of layout templates. Some of the layout had been influenced by the military history style guides – WP:MILMOS and WP:MHMOS. Furthermore, it is striking that in their discussions the users often looked to structural precedents, models and *ad hoc* templates to solve contentious

issues, such as what to include in the timeline of the war. This understandable embrace of the encyclopaedic structure, however, had a significant
impact on the way in which subsequent events were framed. For example,
the highly contested 'pull-back' of Russian troops in October 2008 was
covered about one third way the page down of the article, in the section
dedicated to the six-point peace plan. It seems unlikely that many news
editors would place the top news story of the day in that location.

The Ends of Journalism

This chapter began by observing that a number of commentators had argued
that Wikipedia had a role to play in covering an ongoing news story. In
concluding, we might raise the stakes a little, by arguing that everyone
involved in making the news should take Wikipedia seriously.

This chapter is not arguing that every statement made in Wikipedia
should be taken seriously (mainly for the reasons discussed earlier). Instead,
one might suggest that the analysis provided in this chapter indicates that
the current popularity of the site, coupled with the obvious desire of some
editors to produce current events articles, will result in Wikipedia having
a significant impact on the public sphere if left unchecked. Furthermore,
the case study provided suggests that this impact is likely to asymmetric;
for whilst it is clear Wikipedia might indeed provide some opportunity for
real-time deliberation on important issues (coupled with the opportunity
for widespread dissemination) it does not make a significant contribution
towards the sourcing of the news beyond what is available in the public
domain. This suggests, therefore, that we might want to take this site seriously mainly because it is possible that it will have a destabilizing effect on
the more traditional parts of the fourth estate that are already struggling
to absorb the shock waves engendered by other new media forms. Some
of these additional challenges might be beneficial, as they will highlight
the inadequacies in current practice. However, the example presented here
also suggests that we should take this site seriously, mainly because it is very

easy for those outside the newsroom to be seduced into thinking that it provides a cheap alternative to investigative journalism. Only time will tell, but current wisdom suggests that secondary analysis and dissemination are not the only ends of journalism.

References

Aftergood, S. (2007). 'The Wikipedia Factor in U.S. Intelligence' in *Secrecy News: Secrecy News from the FAS Project on Government Secrecy*. Available at www.fas. org/blog/secrecy/2007/03/the_wikipedia_factor_in_us_int.html.

Benkler, Y. (2006). *The Wealth of Networks: How Social Production Transforms Markets and Freedom*. New Haven: Yale University Press.

Blue Hat SEO-Advanced SEO Tactics (2008). 'How To Overthrow A Wikipedia Result'. Available at www.bluehatseo.com/how-to-overthrow-a-wikipedia-result/.

Bowman, J. (2007). 'What To Do When Your Company Wikipedia Page Goes Bad' in *Search Engine Land Website*. Available at searchengineland.com/070627–094651.php.

Butterworth, S. (2009). 'Open door: The readers' editor on ... web hoaxes and the pitfalls of quick journalism' in *The Guardian*, 4 May 2009.

Chancellor, A. (2009). 'Wikipedia says I'm dead – well, that's news to me' in *The Guardian*, 17 December 2009.

Encyclopædia Britannica (2006). 'Fatally Flawed: Refuting the recent study on encyclopedic accuracy by the journal Nature'. Available at corporate.britannica.com/ britannica_nature_response.pdf.

Giles, J. (2005). 'Special Report Internet encyclopaedias go head to head' in *Nature* 438, 900–1.

Howe, J. (2008). *Crowdsourcing: Why the Power of the Crowd is Driving the Future of Business*. New York: Crown House.

Keen, A. (2007). *The Cult of the Amateur: How Today's Internet is Killing Our Culture and Assaulting Our Economy*. London: Nicholas Brealey.

Keen, A. (2006). 'Worse than Bad' in *Andrew Keen: On Media, Culture and Technology: The Future with a Twist*. Available at andrewkeen.typepad.com/the_great_ seduction/2006/02/w_g_winfred_geo.html.

Leadbeater, C. (2008). *We-think: Mass Innovation not Mass Production*. London: Profile Books.

Lih, A. (2009). *The Wikipedia Revolution: How a Bunch of Nobodies Created the World's Greatest Encyclopedia*. London: Aurum Press.

Liphshiz, C. (2009). 'Wikipedia editors: Coverage of Israel "problematic"'. Available at www.haaretz.com/print-edition/news/wikipedia-editors-coverage-of-israel-problematic-1.275285.

McCullagh, D. (2009). 'Michael Jackson's death roils Wikipedia' in *CNET News*, 25 June 2009.

Nature (2006). 'Britannica attacks ... and we respond' in *Nature* 440, 582.

Page, S. (2005). 'Author apologizes for fake Wikipedia biography' in *USA Today*, 11 December 2005.

Parr, B. (2010). 'Google Gives $2 Million to Wikipedia's Foundation'. Available at mashable.com/2010/02/16/google-wikipedia-donation/.

Perez-Pena, R. (2009). 'Keeping News of Kidnapping Off Wikipedia' in *New York Times*, 28 June 2009.

Rafiq, A. (2008). 'How to Move Over Wikipedia: How to Rank Higher than a Wiki SERP (Search Page Result)'. Available at www.blueverse.com/2008/12/21/how-to-move-over-wikipedia-how-to-rank-higher-than-a-wiki-serp-search-page-result/.

Rajan, A. (2009) 'Premature obituaries may force new Wikipedia rules' in *The Independent*, 27 January 2009.

Seigenthaler, J. (2005). 'A false Wikipedia biography' in *USA Today*, 29 November 2005.

Shaw, D. (2008). 'Wikipedia in the Newsroom' in *American Journalism Review*, February/March 2008.

Shirky, C. (2008). *Here Comes Everybody: The Power of Organizing Without Organizations*. London: Penguin.

Stewart, G. (2008). 'Selling Community: Corporate Media, Marketing and Blogging' in Gordon, J. (ed.), *Notions of Community*. Oxford: Peter Lang.

Sunstein, C. (2006). *Infotopia: How Many Minds Produce Knowledge*. Oxford: Oxford University Press.

Wikipedia References

A. History Page of '2008 South Ossetia war' article 21:47, 7 August 2008: en.wikipedia.org/w/index.php?title=2008_South_Ossetia_war&oldid=230489651.

B. Article Page for 'Criticism of Wikipedia': en.wikipedia.org/wiki/ Criticism_of_Wikipedia.

C. Talk Page (Archive 4) for the '2008 South Ossetia war' article: en.wikipedia. org/wiki/Talk:2008_South_Ossetia_war/Archive_4.

D. Talk Page (Archive 2) for the '2008 South Ossetia war' article: en.wikipedia. org/wiki/Talk:2008_South_Ossetia_war/Archive_2.

E. Article Page for 'Internet Censorship': en.wikipedia.org/wiki/Internet _censorship.

F. Article Page for 'Wikipedia: Wikipedia is not a newspaper': en.wikipedia.org/ wiki/Wikipedia:Wikipedia_is_not_a_newspaper.

G. Article Page for 'Wiki': en.wikipedia.org/wiki/Wiki.

H. History Page of '2008 South Ossetia war' article 21:30, 7 August 2008: en.wikipedia. org/w/index.php?title=2008_South_Ossetia_war&oldid=230486469.

I. Project Page Wikipedia: List of policies: en.wikipedia.org/wiki/Wiki pedia:List_of_policies.

J. User Page for User: Christian Nurtsch: en.wikipedia.org/wiki/User: Christian_Nurtsch.

K. Project Page Wikipedia: Rollback feature: en.wikipedia.org/wiki/ Wikipedia:Rollback_feature.

L. Wikimedia Toolserver – SQL's Tools Service for Christian Nurtsch: http:// toolserver.org/%7Esql/sqlbot.php?user=Christian+Nurtsch.

M. Project Page Wikipedia: Criteria for speedy deletion: en.wikipedia.org/wiki/ Wikipedia:CSD.

N. 'The Revision History of the 2008 South Ossteia war' page: en.wikipedia.org/w/ index.php?title=2008_South_Ossetia_war&dir=prev&action=history

O. User Page for User: Excirial: en.wikipedia.org/wiki/User:Excirial.

P. History Page of '2008 South Ossetia war' article 21:46, 7 August 2008: en.wikipedia. org/w/index.php?title=2008_South_Ossetia_war&oldid=230489598.

Q. History Page of '2008 South Ossetia war' article 22:18, 7 August 2008: en.wikipedia. org/w/index.php?title=2008_South_Ossetia_war&oldid=230495262.

R. Project Page Wikipedia: User Access Levels: en.wikipedia.org/wiki/ Wikipedia:User_access_levels#Administrators.

S. Talk Page (Archive 9) for the '2008 South Ossetia war' article: en.wikipedia. org/wiki/Talk:2008_South_Ossetia_war/Archive_9.

T. Project Page Wikipedia: Sock Puppetry: http://en.wikipedia.org/wiki/ Wikipedia:Sock_puppetry.

U. Category: Wikipedia sockpuppets of M.V.E.i.: http://en.wikipedia.org/wiki/Category:Wikipedia_sockpuppets_of_M.V.E.i.

V. Talk Page (Archive 15) for '2008 South Ossetia war' article: en.wikipedia.org/ wiki/Talk:2008_South_Ossetia_war/Archive_15.

W. Project Page Wikipedia: Please do not bite the newcomers: en.wikipedia.org/ wiki/Wikipedia:Please_do_not_bite_the_newcomers.

X. Project Page Wikipedia: Village Stocks: en.wikipedia.org/wiki/Wikipedia:Village_stocks.

Y. Talk Page (Archive 6) for the '2008 South Ossetia war' article: en.wikipedia. org/wiki/Talk:2008_South_Ossetia.

ALEC CHARLES

Attack of the Killer Squirrels: A Study of the Fantastical Symbolism of *BBC News Online*

There are a host of factors which distinguish online journalism from its print and broadcast counterparts. These include: its virtuality and its textual capacity (a news website's content is limited by its capacity for production rather than for reproduction; its potential editorial volume – in terms of both number and length of stories – is much greater than that of its broadcast or print equivalents); its news cycle (unlike its print counterparts, online news runs 24/7: its news cycle is continuous and fluid, even more so than those of rolling news channels whose hour-long cycles impose formulaic structures upon news provision); its mode of consumption (while television is traditionally viewed in familial groups and newspapers are often read in public spaces – trains, buses, pubs, cafés – online news is generally received privately at home or surreptitiously at work); its personalization (each online consumer generates a customized selection of stories); its permanence (the past appears perpetually retrievable); and its erasability (the past may in fact be deleted at a stroke). This therefore is a form of news unlimited by space and time, one which belongs to the World Wide Web's potentially subversive realm of virtually infinite memory: it is a secretive indulgence, a place of dreams. If the Internet offers postmodernity its collective dreamscape – an unbounded space of hidden fantasies (narcissistic, paranoid and pornographic) – then an online news service may similarly be seen as accommodating the unconscious mind of its parent organization: a private and personal realm liberated from the conscious, focused attention of regulatory forces, the home of taboo journalism and of what, for example, the section of the *Daily Telegraph*'s website which deals with such things calls 'weird news'.

Through the exponential developments in its spread and speed of operation, online news provision has at times disseminated and authenticated the wildest of fantasies, opening up the conventional, evidence-based realism of serious journalism to the outpourings of an unregulated, sensationalist dreamscape. Stories of entirely imaginary provenance have appeared in the output of nationally recognized news organizations. For example, as *BBC News Interactive* reported on 4 September 2009, 'two Bangladeshi newspapers have apologized after publishing an article taken from a satirical US website which claimed the Moon landings were faked. The *Daily Manab Zamin* said US astronaut Neil Armstrong had shocked a news conference by saying he now knew it had been an "elaborate hoax".' Another similarly surreal fiction – one which originated as a viral email and, somehow legitimized by its online ubiquity, appeared on the websites of various news organizations in January 2005 – concerned the antics of a Slovakian man who reportedly urinated his way to freedom after his beer-laden car was caught in an avalanche.

This chapter focuses upon the online news output of a self-consciously public organization, one which suffers the uncompromising prohibitions of a massive super ego (or mechanism of self-regulation) – the BBC. (The BBC's general editorial guidelines stretch to about 250 sections. The UK's Press Complaints Commission, by contrast, features only sixteen – rather shorter – sections in its Code of Conduct.) The more that one's desire is censored and repressed the greater that desire becomes: one might therefore expect that the BBC's extraordinary degree of self-control would propagate in its least regulated regions (in those private-public spaces of its online provision) a proliferation of its most fantastical and subversive outpourings.

The BBC's levels of repression may be evidenced in its journalists' enthusiastic adoption of the weblog as an arena in which to exercise their long-suppressed tendencies to editorialize. But to propose that blogging on its own heralds an end to the objectivity of journalism may constitute, as Tumber and Webster (2006: 171) suggest, an unrealistically extravagant claim. Indeed such forms of expression may be viewed as acts of catharsis, evidence of a self-correcting paradigm blip. Yet we might discover, in the

BBC News website's liminal spaces, modes of symbolic enunciation which more closely parallel the radical processes of the dreamwork itself.

This chapter deploys quantitative and qualitative methods of content analysis to survey a specific sequence of 143 stories which appeared on the *BBC News* website between 1 April 1998 and 1 April 2008: stories which relate the ethnic struggle between Britain's populations of red and grey squirrels through a stereotypical process of binary opposition, and the latter's demonization and threatened eradication. In doing so – and with extensive reference to materials gleaned from a series of interviews with journalists, programme-makers and politicians conducted for the purposes of this research – this chapter seeks to explore the symbolic resurgence of ideological taboos repressed by BBC's corporate super ego to reveal a latent fixation upon such subjects of populist media hysteria as immigration and terrorism. On 22 October 2009 the BBC courted controversy when it decided to allow British National Party leader Nick Griffin to appear as a guest on its flagship political debate series *Question Time*. This chapter suggests that the xenophobic perspectives embodied by the BNP may already have been visible, at a symbolic level, within the eccentric marginalia of the Corporation's news output.

Tall Tales

BBC News Interactive's daily chart of its most read and most e-mailed stories reveals the apparent unorthodoxy of its readers' prevalent tastes. Very often these stories expose adolescent or tabloid fascinations with such topics as female undergarments: 'Mystery over roadside underwear' (19 January 2007), 'Giant knickers put out house fire' (2 January 2008), 'Teenager finds bat asleep in bra' (9 July 2008), and 'Flying underwear causes power cut' (30 July 2009). Lavatorial and scatological subjects are also popular: 'Tasmanian paper made from roo poo' (15 February 2005), 'Row over Italian toilet artwork' (6 November 2006), 'Thief steals urinal from city pub'

(5 January 2007), 'How do you "go" in space?' (10 May 2007), 'Anger at Kenya donkey nappy plan' (17 July 2007), 'Dog mess CCTV squad nets human' (26 July 2007), 'Indian suspect in banana ordeal' (5 August 2007), 'City hit by legal to pee prank' (23 December 2008), 'Cow urine drink set to launch' (5 March 2009), 'Toilet row lowers space morale' (31 March 2009), 'Astronauts drink recycled urine' (22 May 2009), 'Zambia's peeing monkeys evicted' (1 September 2009), and 'Could poo power help heat the country?' (14 January 2010). These puerile tales, so at odds with the BBC newsroom's earnest public image, shift from the unsavoury to the taboo, invoking such subjects as abnormal amputations and unconventional methods for the disposal of the dead: 'North Carolina pair feud over leg' (2 October 2007), 'Thieves cut off man's holy leg' (13 December 2007), 'Diamond memories of the dead' (12 January 2004), 'Crematoria struggle with obese' (18 April 2007), 'Buyer finds mummy in Spanish flat' (16 May 2007), and 'Belgian guest finds frozen bodies' (5 July 2007). Botched penis enlargements also provide a curiously recurrent theme: 'Trying desperately to measure up' (24 May 2002), 'Penis operation left man in pain' (28 January 2003), 'Doctor struck off over penis surgery' (31 January 2003), 'Botched ops doctor wins appeal' (1 July 2004), and 'Most men unhappy with penis ops' (13 February 2006). Related (but less clinically sound) procedures also feature with surprising frequency: 'Woman jailed for testicle attack' (10 February 2005), 'Man cuts off penis in restaurant' (24 April 2007), 'Inmate cuts penis off with razor' (28 November 2007), 'Fire crew aid in penis operation' (6 December 2007), and 'Penis fire suspect is charged' (6 January 2009). In addition to these absurd accounts of genital mutilation, reports of inappropriate sexual conduct also appear regularly: 'Therapist shows woman penis photo' (13 February 2007), 'Pet camel kills Australian woman' (20 August 2007), 'Bike sex man placed on probation' (14 September 2007), 'Carrot joke sex attacker guilty' (7 November 2007), 'U.S. penis photo doctor loses job' (21 December 2007), 'Farm ban for sheep sex arrest man' (18 June 2008), 'Men guilty over fake penis scam' (25 November 2008), '60-foot penis painted on roof' (24 March 2009), and 'Man used penis to assault female police officer' (16 March 2010).

One of the most popular of these bizarre stories appeared on 24 February 2006 under the headline 'Sudan man forced to marry goat'. The goat's owner had discovered one Mr Tombe having sex with his goat; the owner had taken Tombe to a council of elders who had ordered him to pay the owner a dowry for the goat on the grounds that he had 'used it as his wife.' The website's World Editor Adam Curtis reported on his blog entry of 18 September 2006: 'That goat report was consistently showing up in our "live stats" box as the most widely e-mailed story on the site [...] during a single morning, the goat story was e-mailed by readers in Australia, France, Sweden, the US, Luxembourg, India, Malaysia, Tanzania, Estonia and many other countries.' The story was followed on 3 May 2007 by 'Sudan's famous goat wife dies'. The next day an obituary item recalled that the goat 'found supporters around the world who, thanks to the internet and particularly this website's "Most E-mailed" function, kept her plight in the public mind for much of her short marriage.' Adam Curtis (18 August 2008) has added in an interview conducted for this chapter:

> The goat story attracted attention because people were e-mailing it to friends around the world, thereby bringing it back into our daily 'most popular stories' slot from time to time. The weird and wonderful stories are part of the tapestry of coverage we provide. We take our job of reporting international news extremely seriously, but we do not believe our readers want an undiluted diet of geo-political news, so we try to vary the tone and subject matter of what we do. We include news of the entertainment world, science and technology, business and health. We also have a daily feature labelled 'Also in the News', which is normally a quirky, improbable or just plain funny story. The feature is very popular; so much so that we recently introduced a separate index to showcase such stories. Why are they so popular? Because most people enjoy something offbeat – a story to make them laugh or to pass on to friends.

The BBC newsroom's online presence provides a site for stories which would not normally feature as part of the its mainstream broadcast provision. These are tabloid tales; yet, like all that is repressed or consigned to the realm of the taboo, they express profound fears, desires and fixations. The carnivalesque revels of the red-tops would redden the public face of the Corporation; but in the privacy and anonymity of its online portal these dreams and nightmares can be explored. These are the subliminal fantasies of the unconscious mind, archetypes which Anslow (2008) has identified as prevalent in populist journalism, and which here seem to reveal the workings of a corporate unconscious. These online stories not only represent a fixation upon a range of general taboos and archetypes; they also express ideological perspectives which have been repressed by the self-imposed neutrality and sobriety of the Corporation's super ego. In these half-secret spaces, in stories whose writers tend to remain unnamed, and in the safety of symbolic rhetoric, neurotic fantasies may be performed – fantasies which the Corporation's less censorious, sensationalist competitors in the populist press are free to enact in more open and direct ways.

Native Beasts

The uncanny, for Freud, estranged the homely and familiar by bringing to the light of day that which was never meant to have been made public. *BBC News Interactive* also alienates safe domestic space, and it does so perhaps most strikingly in its portrayal of the native fauna of the British Isles. These creatures, at once domestic and undomesticated, represent an incongruous atavism within the artificial security of the news-consumers' homeland. They populate a symbolic idiom through which even the tamest newsroom might adopt the characteristics of what Tony Blair (on 12 June 2007) dubbed the 'feral beast' of journalistic sensationalism. They represent a primordial chaos within the quotidian order of things, and thereby manifest an expression of populist hysteria in response to perceived threats to the integrity of Middle England (such as paedophilia, immigration and terrorism), an angst elegantly epitomized by a headline from *The Times* of 19 April 2008: 'Giant owl casts shadow over village'. Two notable examples of this phenomenon from the *BBC News* site involve a rabbit and a fox.

The site has featured a pair of tales of British communities living in terror of rabbits: 'Wallace and Gromit spook island' (7 October 2005), 'Hunt for real life were-rabbit' (7 April 2006). These stories were inspired by the animated film *The Curse of the Were-Rabbit* (2005); but, while the former related a Dorset island's superstitious fear of our floppy-eared friends, the latter portrayed a real-life horror – a 'ravenous giant rabbit':

Four gardeners described the rabbit as having one ear larger than the other.

The main clues are oversized paw prints and sightings of what growers claim to be a cross between a hare and a rabbit [...] Grower Jeff Smith, 63, said: 'This is no ordinary rabbit. We are dealing with a monster.

'It is absolutely massive. I have seen its prints and they are huge, bigger than a deer. It is a brute of a thing.'

With its photofit description and its paw-print clues, the story deploys the language, and the ideological perspective, of crime reporting. As John Fiske (1989: 293, 296) reminds us, the 'textual devices that control the sense of news are all embedded in a narrative form'– 'stories are prewritten, they "write" the journalists [...] their meanings are already in circulation.' The journalist's art is to recognize and repackage traditional narratives. There are no new stories; it is all old news. This defining paradox of journalism can clearly be witnessed in the BBC's online account of a 'Girl bitten by fox' on 5 September 2003:

A four-year-old girl is recovering after she was bitten by a fox – as she slept in her inner London home.

Jessica Magnier-Brown was left with bruise marks on her arm after the incident.

It is thought the fox entered the house in Tufnell Park through an open patio door at about 2200 BST on Sunday.

Jessica's parents, Richard Brown and Corinne Magnier, heard her screams and went to her first floor bedroom to see the fox run out.

Ms Magnier, 37, said: 'I heard her screaming and thought she was having a nightmare so I went upstairs to her room on the first floor.

'Her door was ajar and I saw something coming out of the bedroom.

'It came rushing out. I thought it was a large cat. I couldn't imagine a fox would be in the house.

'Jessica held out her arm. We could see the teeth marks.'

Like the tale of the were-rabbit, this account invokes a number of popular cultural precedents (including, in its third paragraph, a continuing predilection for the clichés of the crime report). The invasion of the young girl's familial space by a ravening canine signals a modernization of the story of Little Red Riding Hood; but this is also a version of Bram Stoker's *Dracula*. Stoker's vampire Count not only poses as the companion of the wolf (Stoker 1979: 29) but can also transform himself into a giant dog (Stoker 1979: 99): he visits young ladies' rooms in the dead of night and leaves only bitemarks behind. As Franco Moretti (1997) has suggested, Bram Stoker's late Victorian novel can be viewed as warning against the invasion of immigrants from the East – and perhaps this fox can be seen as serving a similar symbolic function, two years after 9/11 and eight months before 2004's enlargement of the European Union. The fox is an invader from the countryside, an emblem of immigration, of the alien which penetrates not only our cities and towns but also our homes themselves.

The fox also embodies another area of media concern – the opposition of the urban and the rural – as witnessed in the controversy surrounding the ban on fox-hunting which came into force in England and Wales in February 2005. A third issue is visible here, a further focus of tabloid hysteria – the subject of paedophilia. The fiend in the child's bedroom invokes an icon of populist journalism, an image whose impact and ubiquity Jon Silverman (2003) acknowledges when he writes that 'every age has its monsters and one of ours is the paedophile. Not even the experts really know if there are more around than ever before [...] What we do know is that "paedophilia" has become a modern obsession.' These are of course issues upon which the BBC refuses to fixate; and yet, in the dreamscape of its online presence, echoes of this repressed tabloid hysteria may emerge – occurring, as in dreams, in these eccentric familiars, the nation's native animal guides.

The *BBC News* website has published a number of similar tales of children being attacked by foxes while sleeping in their urban homes. On 1 July 2002 the victim's mother gave another account reminiscent of a horror movie – 'I've seen all this blood coming down his face and the fox is just sitting there staring at us' – while on 7 June 2010 the language of the piece again echoed that of crime reporting: 'A police source said the fox apparently entered the house through an open ground-floor door before attacking the twins in an upstairs room.' A follow-up online story on 30 June 2010 went so far as to describe the fox's behaviour as 'brazen' – while *BBC News*'s television coverage of the same story the following morning observed that the family 'felt violated' by the attack. On 21 June 2010 the *BBC News* website had paralleled that story with an account of a boy who was bitten by a fox after he tried to stroke its tail, a report which is only newsworthy insofar as it refers back to the previous story. When a dog bites a man that is not news; but when it is perceived that the story of a dog biting a child is news, then journalists will continue to identify such stories as news.

The media hysteria around the 2010 fox attacks resulted in the production – and posting on the Internet – of a hoax video which appeared to show a vicious vigilante attack upon a fox in a London park. On 8 August 2010 the creator of the hoax film (and also the BAFTA-nominated director of the 2007 film *Taking Liberties*) Chris Atkins told the BBC that he 'made the film as a satirical swipe at the "ludicrous media coverage" of the dangers of urban foxes.' He added that 'the reporting, including by the BBC, was both irresponsible and misrepresentative. It never stressed that urban fox attacks were very rare and [foxes] are not dangerous'.

The reputations of other native British species have not fared much better at the hands of the BBC. In spring 2010, for example, the *BBC News* website featured a sequence of stories about the arguments surrounding the culling of badgers across the UK, stories which revealed ongoing tensions between farmers and animal rights campaigners similar to those seen in the fox-hunting debate. Even the fate of the humble hedgehog is not immune from controversy. On 5 September 2002 the *BBC News* website reported that 'animal welfare groups have [...] welcomed the move by McDonald's to issue "hedgehog-friendly" ice cream cups, after a spate of deaths. The animals were getting their heads stuck inside the McDonald's McFlurry containers while sniffing for food, ending up starving to death.' On 13 September 2006 the site returned to this story when 'a charity [...] won a six-year campaign to get McDonald's to change the design of an ice cream container because hedgehogs could become stuck in it.' This is a story in which a typically British creature (stunted, prickly and myopic) gets caught in an American imperialist contrivance. The fact that it started in September 2002 – a year after 9/11 and the month in which the British government published its dossier on *Iraq's Weapons of Mass Destruction* – is perhaps merely a coincidence.

Squirrels

Immigration, paedophilia, the rural-urban divide and even the War on Terror: these issues are also manifest in the representation of the humble squirrel in the news. The United Kingdom boasts two main species of squirrel: the red and the grey – *Sciurus vulgaris* and *Sciurus carolinensis*. According to the BBC's *Science & Nature* website, 'grey squirrels are an alien species and were introduced to the UK from the USA in the late nineteenth/early twentieth century. Their success has been to the detriment of our native red squirrels.' We may note that this politically neutral media organization (which has famously strived to avoid the use of a *them* and *us* formula in its reportage of international conflict) does not disdain from laying patriotic claim to the red squirrel in its deployment of the possessive pronoun: *our* squirrels. The BBC's patriotic identification with Britain's red squirrel population reflects the mainstream media position: the notion that, as a *Daily Telegraph* headline trumpeted on 10 July 2002, 'Grey invaders threaten island's reds'. In contrast to the nationalist fervour prompted by the squirrel debate in much of the mainstream press, however, the liberal-leftist credentials of *The Guardian* newspaper have (as one might have expected) fostered a rather more relativistic and pluralistic stance on the subject. As it announced on 21 February 2003 'the red squirrel may be an immigrant from America.' Like the grey, this native symbol of Britishness was once itself 'an economic migrant.' However, it seems that, despite the overt polarization of the squirrel debate around attitudes towards immigration, the jobbing journalist may for the most part remain blissfully unaware of the political symbolism of the red and the grey squirrel – as David Lister, the co-author of 'Squirrel wars: reds, greys and blacks battle for supremacy' (*The Times*, 26 April 2008), has confirmed (15 May 2008). Yet the fact that these analogies remain at an unconscious level may reinforce their ideological significance.

Though reporters may not always recognize these meanings, their readers may nevertheless acknowledge them. On 7 November 2005 the *BBC News* website published a sequence of photographs of squirrels taken by its readers, along with those readers' comments. Reader Rachel Harding asserted that 'the grey squirrels have as much right to life as any other immigrant' – while Peter Jones added that 'they didn't ask to be introduced to this country and we cannot subsequently cull them just because they're not native.' Indeed, it is not only this liberal cohort of citizen photojournalists who are cognizant of these symbolic relations. Natural history writer and broadcaster Chris Packham (2009) has written that 'there are some "conservationists" who have clearly lost the plot when it comes to purity and perfection [...] when it comes to the emotive issue of immigration plenty of people [...] are hell bent on cleaning up all the "non-native" scum and making Britain's countryside pure again, just like it was in the good old days.' Packham (in correspondence of 5 May 2009) has gone on to suggest that while we may draw apparently absurd parallels between the attitudes of militant conservationists ('the unimaginative and lazy legions who show no real depth of intelligence when it comes to conservation') and those of racist extremists, the 'gruesome reality' of such parallels is profoundly disturbing.

Indeed, the tensions between red and grey squirrels have provided an unlikely rallying cry for Britain's Far Right. On 18 August 2002 Michael Prestage of *The Independent* reported on a British National Party rally: 'One stall has bulk supplies of cards comparing immigrants to the grey squirrel that has ousted the native red squirrel.' The following month *The Observer*'s Andrew Anthony cited a BNP member on the subject of British Moslems: 'They will do to us what the grey squirrel did to the red squirrel in this country.' In April 2003 *The Independent* quoted another BNP activist: 'This town is turning completely into a foreign land [...] it's like the grey squirrels taking over. I'm a red squirrel, that's what I am.' On 3 December 2007 an article by Simon Bennett on the BNP's website explained: 'The red squirrel is the indigenous one, the grey one the colonizer. The grey squirrel will never be termed indigenous, no matter how long it has been here. The term indigenous has a precise scientific meaning. A species either is, or is not, indigenous; it cannot *become* indigenous.' There is even an ultra-right-wing website which promotes the *Red Squirrel's Nut-Cracking Nationalism*: 'Our Country is being invaded by fast breeding colonizers. Like the Red Squirrel was over run by the Grays [*sic*], we could become isolated in small pockets and face extinction.' There is, of course, an extraordinary irony (or moronity) in the use of an American spelling – *gray* – in response to a perceived threat of cultural invasion (the invasion of the greys) from the United States. The BNP's rhetoric also reveals several issues which suggest a deep-rooted racism beneath the nationalist guise: the belief that nationality is defined by dominant ethnicity and determined by colour; the argument that indigenous ethnicity is based on a unique and incontrovertible historical originality (the fallacious premise that the reds have been here forever) or primacy (the reds may have not been here forever, but they did get here first); the notion that black and white people are as different as red and grey squirrels and therefore that racial difference is as absolute and unbridgeable as the species gap (from which perspective miscegenation becomes equivalent to an abomination); and the intention not only to limit the influx and spread of minority ethnicities, but also to expel or eradicate those ethnicities from the body politic. It would appear, therefore, that the squirrel issue has come to symbolize the cuddly, naturalized, 'acceptable' face of racism. When BNP leader Nick Griffin controversially appeared on the BBC's political discussion programme *Question Time* (22 October 2009) he proposed, rather unusually, that his definition of indigenous Britishness included only those people whose ancestors had been in the country at the time of the last Ice Age. In 2010 the Zoological Society of London played upon this conceit when it advertised an attraction featuring animals which once lived wild in the UK with an image of a lynx, wolf, bear, moose and bison strolling down a British high street and the slogan 'We lived here before you.'

The extreme Right's symbolic deployment of the squirrel in its discourses of racial hatred are painfully reminiscent of the anti-Semitic propaganda promulgated by the Third Reich, and specifically of the juxtaposition of rat and Jew in Fritz Hippler's *The Eternal Jew* (1940). A comparison between the Final Solution and the fate of the grey squirrel, though grossly inappropriate, seems outrageously inevitable: on 3 October 2007 the *BBC News* website referred to grey squirrels as 'tree rats' in a story headlined 'Can the squirrel problem be solved?'. The BBC had already advanced the notion of the grey squirrel as 'tree rat' on 29 May 2003 in a story which addressed the issue of 'the parapox virus – a disease to which [grey squirrels] are immune but one that is fatal to reds.' Like the Reich's Jewry, the grey squirrel is portrayed as a breed of disease-ridden vermin – one perhaps ripe for the cull.

Glad to be Grey?

The year 2009 witnessed a stark framing of the discourse of ethnic opposition within the *BBC News* website's ongoing narrative of the British squirrel population. On 20 January 2009 the site noted the rise in the UK of a new cousin of the grey squirrel: 'It seems possible now that the grey squirrel has had its day and that black squirrels could become the dominant species across the UK.' By contrast, on 6 November 2009, the BBC's online readership were informed that 'residents of a Surrey town have set up a shrine and an online tribute page after a "celebrity" albino squirrel was run over.' On 23 November the *BBC News* site added that 'residents in a Surrey town have expressed their amazement at the global response to the death of an albino squirrel in a road accident [...] "It is amazing. We have had e-mails from all over the world," said Rick Parish, chamber of commerce president. [...] In the United States, Fox News covered Albi's death, with anchorman Shepard Smith describing the "recent tragedy in the small town of Dorking, England".' It appears that, in terms of media attitudes to these arboreal rodents, colour increasingly counts.

Between 1 April 1998 and 1 April 2008 the *BBC News* website ran 143 stories directly related to the activities of squirrels. As Figure 1 demonstrates, there is a sharp rise in the incidence of such stories in the years after 2001. As Figure 2 demonstrates, this increase is not related to total numbers of stories appearing on the website: there are relatively insignificant increases in total volume over the same period. It seems that squirrels may have become improbably prominent emblems in the discourses of ethnic tension and intolerance, but whether the rise in these squirrel-based stories is related to an atmosphere of heightened paranoia or xenophobia that has developed in the media since 9/11 is perhaps impossible to demonstrate; although the nature of some of these stories does suggest a connection.

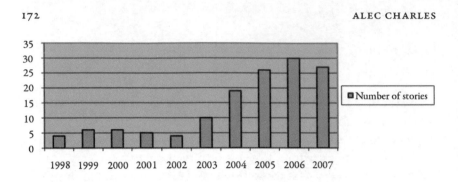

Figure 1 Squirrel stories appearing on the *BBC News* website: 1998–2007.

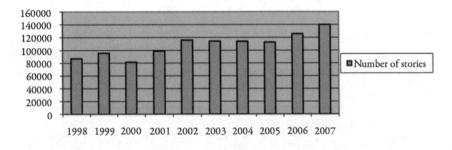

Figure 2 Total number of stories appearing on the *BBC News* website: 1998–2007
(data courtesy of the BBC).

As Figure 3 demonstrates, there is a marked bias in the BBC's online coverage of red and grey squirrel stories. Between 1 April 1998 and 1 April 2008 red squirrels were portrayed positively in 82 stories and negatively in none. By contrast, over the same period, 98 negative stories about grey squirrels were countered by only five positive ones. As Figure 4 shows, positive stories about squirrels were overwhelmingly skewed in favour of the reds.

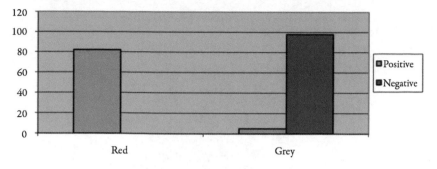

Figure 3 Numbers of positive and negative stories about red and grey squirrels on the *BBC News* website: 1 April 1998–1 April 2008.

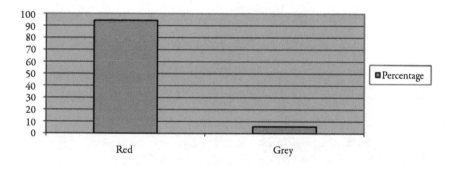

Figure 4 Proportional share for red and grey squirrels of total number of positive stories: 1 April 1998–1 April 2008. Margin of error (calculated at 95% confidence level): 4.89%.

Figure 5 displays the main themes which characterize stories about red squirrels. Most address the issue of the species' rarity and the fact that it is indigenous to Britain. Some refer to the various schemes to protect the species, and many allude to the threats posed to the red squirrel (either through territorial competition or disease) by their grey cousins. It is notable that in every story which refers to the parapox virus the greys are explicitly blamed for the spread of that disease.

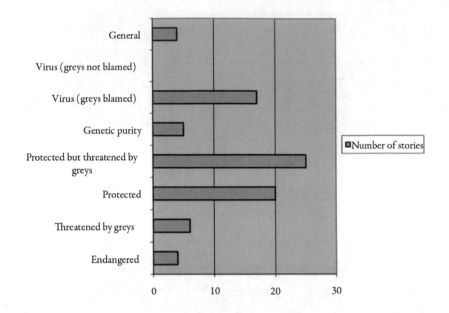

Figure 5 Themes of stories about red squirrels on the *BBC News* website: 1 April 1998–1 April 2008.

In a number of the BBC's stories these creatures become overt symbols of collaborations and divisions within British politics. On 1 April 1999, twelve months on from the Good Friday Agreement, Alex Kirby's 'Stormont squirrels bridge the divide' offered events in the grounds of Stormont Castle as a metaphor for the Northern Ireland peace process: 'a rare example of co-existence – grey and red squirrels living together in harmony.' By 2 October 2006, eleven days before the signing of the St Andrews Agreement, while the relationship between red and grey squirrels still symbolized Irish cooperation, it had evolved somewhat more sinister overtones: 'the governments on both sides of the border are planning to enter the squirrel war with a controversial culling plan.' Inter-governmental anti-terrorist initiatives are paralleled by a draconian cross-border rodent hunt.

Squirrels have also come to reflect issues of Anglo-Scots relations: 'An imaginary "Hadrian's Wall" is to be set up to stop infected grey squirrels crossing the border into Scotland and wiping out their red cousins' (*BBC News Interactive*, 20 September 2006). One year on, on 24 September 2007 (a few months after the Scottish Nationalists had swept to victory at Scotland's parliamentary elections) the BBC quoted Scots parliamentarian Murdo Fraser on the subject of his nation's purebred arboreal rodents: 'Scotland is the principal stronghold of the red squirrel on mainland UK and we must do everything possible to protect it.'

Mr Fraser has commented (12 August 2009): 'To me, the red squirrel is a native British species which symbolizes British natural heritage. The red squirrel is an endangered species under particular threat due to the encroachment of the non-native American grey squirrel.' Although Deputy Leader of the Scottish Conservative Party, Fraser denies that his support for the red squirrel is related to 'the conservation of a traditional way of life' but continues to stress that 'the survival of the red squirrel is about the conservation of a native British species which is under threat due to a non-native invader.' Politicians, conservationists and journalists may disavow nationalist agendas, yet their discourse on this subject is infused with an increasingly prevalent xenophobic rhetoric; vocabularies laden with threats of encroachment and invasion reveal the resurgence of a wartime insularity.

Like the Scots, the Welsh have honed in on the figure of the red squirrel as a model for the delineation and naturalization of national identity: 'Conservationists believe Wales may have its own "pure" race of red squirrels' (*BBC News Interactive*, 10 October 2004). Once more the racial purity of one's squirrel population seems to be a matter of (or a metaphor for) national pride. On 20 January 2001 *BBC News Interactive* quoted the BBC Wales wildlife presenter Iolo Williams in surprisingly intemperate terms: 'I would like nothing more [than] to see the greys eliminated; I always see it as a tree rat. I am old enough to remember reds all over mid Wales and I think they are magnificent creatures.' Mr Williams (25 August 2009) has spoken of the red squirrel's 'symbolism in terms of Welshness' with a nostalgia which resonates throughout this discourse:

> For me, the red squirrel is a reminder of my childhood. I grew up in the heart of mid-Wales during the late 1960s and 1970s and I remember red squirrels as common mammals in the coniferous woodlands surrounding the village. From the mid-1970s onwards, however, grey squirrels flourished and the reds quickly disappeared. I saw my last one in the area in 1985. The red squirrel therefore has become a symbol of lost youth, along with quiet country lanes, hay meadows and vibrant rural communities. I am a staunch supporter of red squirrel conservation because it is a beautiful, native mammal that is endangered because of the introduction of an alien species. Personally, I would love to see grey squirrels completely eradicated from these islands and reds, once more, found throughout Britain.

There is something hauntingly familiar in the way in which this discourse shifts so smoothly from a nostalgic romanticization of natural and national history into plans for the extermination of a race. On 21 November 2004 Charles Dutton, spokesperson for Anglesey's red squirrel conservation project, added his voice to the *BBC News* website's increasingly immoderate clamour: 'If we can rid our forests of the alien grey squirrel, it is possible for the native reds to re-establish themselves. The grey squirrel has now colonized 90 per cent of England and Wales and is widespread in Scotland. It is a carrier of a disease that is deadly to red squirrels. History [...] has proved that it is impossible for the two species to live together.' Regardless of one's views as to the rights of rodents, the portentous rabidity of this rhetoric – and its avowed and unabashed historical awareness – may suggest some cause for concern.

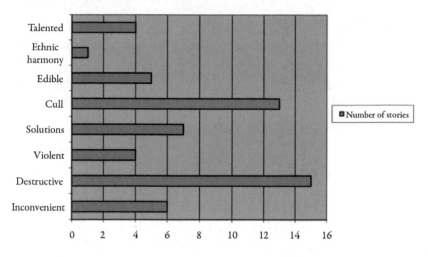

Figure 6 Themes of stories about grey squirrels on the *BBC News* website: 1 April 1998–1 April 2008.

In contrast to the celebration of the racial purity and indigenous Britishness of their red counterparts, the overwhelming majority of stories about grey squirrels portray them in negative, derisory and contemptuous lights. Online stories on 8 November 2003, 14 August 2006 and 27 June 2007 blame squirrels for chewing through electricity cables and causing major power cuts. Indeed on 7 June 2005 (exactly a month before the Al-Qaeda strikes on London) similar activities were said to have caused a 'massive explosion'. It appears these illegal aliens are not only undermining traditionally British ways of life but are even targeting the nation's industrial infrastructure.

The greys are portrayed as hooligans and criminals. Such headlines as 'Fat squirrel trapped behind bars' (25 October 2007) and 'Burglar squirrel ransacks house' (16 August 2006) speak for themselves. On (what Figure 6 shows to be) those very rare occasions on which a grey squirrel's talents or virtues are celebrated, there are usually provisos to this praise. When a 'Water-skiing squirrel steals the show' (31 December 2002) it is notably an indigenous American grey – rather than an illegal alien in the UK. Even when a 'Squirrel helps police crack case' (30 May 2002) the BBC's account emphasizes how uncommon it is for these greys to support the criminal justice system: 'Police investigating a burglary in Bath had an unusual ally – in the form of a law-abiding grey squirrel.' The unfortunate implication is that these immigrants tend rarely to abide by the laws of this land.

The War on Terror

The squirrel has endured a poor reputation for a number of years. The urban myth of the squirrel addicted to crack cocaine, a legend which appears to have originated in New York and Washington DC, reached the UK in 2005 with online tales of junkie squirrels 'terrorizing' London. As *The Guardian* reported on 8 October 2005, 'squirrels in south London could have become addicted to crack cocaine, say residents of Brixton, who suggest the rodents have dug up drugs buried by dealers or nibbled residues of crack on pipes and vials discarded by addicts.' Like the tale of the Slovakian man who urinated his way out of a snowdrift, this apocryphal tale comes to prominence through the Chinese-whisper system of the Internet, a process of ideational evolution by which the fittest memes (those notions which best suit our paradigms and prejudices) survive and proliferate. The Internet not only disseminates these stories – through its processes of cultural selection – it hones and fashions them. Since 11 September 2001 those reports of the activities of this immigrant underclass which have become most widespread through the online media are those which have best fitted the public mood in relation to the prevailing themes and imagery of the War on Terror. On 26 November 2001 *BBC News Interactive* published the following tale:

> A part-time inventor from West Yorkshire suffered whiplash injuries when a squirrel landed on his head as he was testing out a feeding tray mounted on a hat.
>
> Mike Madden, 48, was walking through woodland when the grey squirrel spied the nuts on the headwear.

The squirrel landed with such force that Mr Madden was knocked to the ground and injured his neck.

He said: 'It felt solid when it hit me but I was lucky really because it could have taken my head off.'

The 48-year-old welder has been taking pain-killers and wearing a neck brace since the accident near his home in Crackpot Cottage, Honley, in Huddersfield.

He said: 'I was out walking through the woods with my friend Craig Bailey.

'We had only just started the walk when 'kaboom' – I was on the floor.

'I didn't see much of what happened but Craig told me he saw the squirrel flying through the air and land right on my head.

'The next morning I was in so much agony.'

Mr Madden designed the hat so that birds could feed from it while he was out walking, because he was concerned about their winter food supplies.

But he did not think other inhabitants of the woodlands would take an interest in it.

Mr Madden said: 'Someone told me afterwards that with it coming up to winter and food being so short, squirrels can be quite aggressive and opportunistic.

'I wish I had known that before.

'I've always liked squirrels – but once you've had one land on your head travelling about 30 mph you can easily go off them.

'I couldn't tell you exactly how much it weighed but I think it was about the size of a small puppy or kitten.'

Mr Madden does not plan to continue with his plans for a bird-feeding hat.

The date is not insignificant: this is just a couple of months after the Al-Qaeda attacks on New York. One is reminded in this context of one of Slavoj Žižek's reflections on 9/11 (Žižek 2002: 14–15; revisited in Žižek 2008: 153–4):

> Is not the endlessly repeated shot of the plan approaching and hitting the second WTC tower the real-life version of the famous scene from Hitchcock's *Birds* [...] in which Melanie approaches the Bodega Bay pier after crossing the bay in her little boat. When, as she approaches the wharf, she waves to her (future) lover, a single bird (first perceived as an indistinguishable dark blot) unexpectedly enters the frame from above right and hits her on the head. Was not the plane which hit the WTC tower literally the ultimate Hitchcockian blot [...]?

For the bird (or plane) read squirrel. The story is the same, an instant of unforeseeable, unbelievable shock, an attack from a constituency the Western world had believed it could tolerate – a sudden high-speed crash with unimaginably traumatic consequences. As Mr Madden says: *kaboom.*

If the grey squirrel had already come to symbolize an illegal alien, then in the xenophobic, scaremongering climate of the British mass media in the wake of 9/11 its transition to terrorist was perhaps inevitable. On 7 November 2002 *The Guardian*'s Rebecca Allison announced that 'householders in Knutsford, Cheshire, are being plagued by the unlikeliest of foes – a vicious grey squirrel with a penchant for human flesh.' The following day *The Times*'s Russell Jenkins declared that 'the rogue squirrel who attacked residents in Knutsford is dead – shot by the grandfather of a child bitten by the rodent.' *BBC News Interactive* also covered the story (on 7 November 2002) beneath the uncompromising headline – 'Granddad guns down terror squirrel' – and supported by the sub-header 'Community terrorised':

> A vicious squirrel which terrorised a Cheshire town has been shot dead by a grandfather seeking vengeance. The animal had already attacked a man mowing his lawn and woman walking down the street, in Knutsford.
>
> But when it sank its teeth into Kelsi Morley's face, her grandfather Geoff Horth decided to act.
>
> He went out and killed it.
>
> Two-year-old Kelsi was attacked as she took a morning stroll with her mother.
>
> She stopped to admire the squirrel before it pounced on her face and sank its teeth into her forehead.

Kelsi's mother Karen had to pin the girl to the floor and pull the animal off her face.

The youngster was left bleeding heavily from a deep gash.

Mr Horth said he was unrepentant about his vigilante action.

On Thursday his wife said: 'When Geoff saw what had happened, he just wanted to put a stop to it.

'He said if it had bitten a child's face this time, what would it do next? He didn't want any more children getting hurt.' [...] Mrs Horth added: 'This squirrel had been terrorising people around here for weeks.'

It seems curiously significant that in the attacks upon both Mike Madden and Kelsi Morley the ground (the outdoors space) is referred to as 'the floor': *I was on the floor*; *Kelsi's mother Karen had to pin the girl to the floor*. The external has uncannily transformed into domestic space; the threat has been transplanted into our homes. The squirrel is portrayed as an insidious alien invader and a child-molester; its nemesis a vigilante. But more significantly it is, as this story repeatedly emphasizes (with its four instances of variants on the word), a terrorist. *It had bitten a child's face this time, what would it do next?* Hijack a plane, perhaps. It may even have been accumulating WMDs. For *Grandfather Geoff Horth* read *President George W. Bush*.

The story had been broken on 6 November 2002 by the *Knutsford Guardian*'s account of 'the squirrel from hell'. According to its publishers (on 28 November 2002) the story went on to make 'headlines throughout the world'. Local historian Joan Leach (who advised one interested news agency on the background of the town) recalls on her website that the story even reached the United States via CNN. Ms Leach (15 August 2009) has added that 'it caused a stir at the time as it happened in a popular open space. The Beatrix Potter image of a cuddly, cute animal was shattered.' The story was covered in the *Knutsford Guardian* by reporter Andrew McCreaddie. McCreaddie comments (12 August 2009):

I had been working as a reporter for less than a month when I discovered the 'terror squirrel' story. It came in very late on deadline day and we decided to splash on it simply because of the sheer strangeness of it. It was treated seriously, but I think most people also saw the bizarre side (residents scared to go outside to their cars or leave windows open). Within two days of the story being published I had received calls from regional, national and even international media organizations. I remember having to answer questions from journalists in Australia from my desk in Cheshire.

McCreaddie believes there were three main reasons for the international interest in this story:

The first – especially for the red-top tabloid nationals – was the amusing link between K-*nuts*-ford, the food a squirrel is supposed to eat and the fact the squirrel went 'nuts'. That helped them with many headlines, straplines and intro puns. Secondly, the girl who was attacked was adorable. Never underestimate the public's love of stories that involve cute kids and animals (even though the animal was not so cute this time). The pictures we got (with scratches across the girl's face) were particularly attention-grabbing and helped with the serious side of the story. The third reason was the sheer strangeness of it all. Residents were scared to leave their homes without an implement such as a broom. I remember one woman telling me how her husband was sent out first to check the path to the car was clear. The fact that all these residents' lives were being affected by one nutty squirrel was really bizarre.

McCreaddie's explanation of the story's success is persuasively pragmatic; and yet his depiction of the town's absurd reign of terror seems to mirror the surreal state of heightened paranoia which followed the attacks upon the World Trade Center. The international reach of this story may to some extent be explained by the way in which it so closely captured the zeitgeist of the first year of the War on Terror; but it should also be emphasized that its symbolism – and its global dissemination online – contributed to the exacerbation of that paranoia.

The first squirrel assault – the attack upon inventor Mike Madden – took place two months after 9/11; the events in Knutsford took place almost exactly a year later, the month after the US Congress had passed a resolution to authorize military intervention in Iraq. The next major outrage would take place the following year. On 13 August 2003, with American and British forces now entrenched in Iraq, *BBC News Interactive* reported the terrorists' retaliatory strike – 'Marauding squirrels invade estate':

Fearless grey squirrels are terrorising the residents of a West Midlands housing estate [...] One woman says she was cornered by the creatures in a local park [...] Resident Ivor Pershall, who is disabled, says he has been unable to open the windows of his West Bromwich flat during the heat wave because the animals keep getting inside to look for food.

'I'm frightened of them. They jump on the balcony and then try to get in a hole in the brickwork in my flat which leads into the living room.

'They run along the fence and everywhere round here and they play up and down the street. I just can't stand them [...] I don't want any harm to come to them, but I am frightened of them.'

Bob Evans, a borough councillor in Sandwell, said a number of other people living in Hawkstone Crescent had asked for help. '[...] This is the first time I've had to deal with squirrels, but since the problem came to light recently lots of people have spoken to me.

'When I was a lad you didn't see squirrels coming into town – now we're inundated with them.

'One woman told me she got surrounded by six squirrels in a park in Wednesbury.

'One's OK, but five or six is a bit of problem.'

Fearless grey squirrels are terrorising the residents of a West Midlands housing estate – this story revisits the discourse of terror, but what is most striking about this account is its normalization of the rhetoric of racism: *now we're inundated with them.* The story takes place within a journalistic culture in which, two years into the War on Terror (and less than a year before the EU enlargement of May 2004, which was already causing panic in the tabloid press – see Cook 2005: 79–90), such language had already been naturalized. The message directly echoes the sentiments not only of the BNP but also (by this time) of Britain's mainstream political parties: individual immigrants may be acceptable; immigration en masse is no longer to be accommodated.

The atmosphere of terror and the ideologies prevalent in this era of terror are relentlessly perpetuated. On 25 March 2009 *BBC News Interactive* reported the case of a woman called Oonagh Nutt (inevitably) whose home was overrun by squirrels: 'They chewed their way through my roof in several places, they tunnel through the cavity walls, they live under the floor boards, they go to the toilet in the attic. Up close they are quite frightening – they look like puppy dogs with big hands, they growl and bark at you, they're vicious things. They'll go for you.' Again, then, one's home territory is threatened by alien invasion. On 3 August 2006, the summer after the Al-Quaeda attacks on London, the same website had announced that 'a mother and son were attacked by a grey squirrel as they walked near to their home in Swindon.' Suburban Britain continues to languish beneath the terror threat. The irony is that we fail to recognize that the actual provenance of this threat (the grey squirrel or the War on Terror) is our closest ally, the United States itself.

Genocide

This is all, of course, very silly. It would be easy to forget that it has all happened before, and that, at the start of the twenty-first century, the insidious discourses of ethnic cleansing and of civil tyranny continue to underlie democratic postmodernity. On 6 February 2009 Britain's Channel 4 screened Luke Sewell's documentary *Squirrel Wars: Red vs. Grey*. The film follows the crusade of patriotic pest control officer Paul Parker to eradicate the entire grey squirrel population of Northumberland. Sewell depicts Parker as halfway between Churchill and Rambo:

> I had heard about a man who roamed the Northumberland countryside twelve hours a day, seven days a week, fighting for a cause that many thought futile. Some said he was mad, a maverick, a lone guardian of the countryside. Some even suggested that he was a Gulf War vet unable to leave the conflict behind. I found this man at a time in his life when he had sacrificed everything to pick up arms and fight for something he truly believed in. This was a fight bigger than the man himself, it was a fight against two million American grey squirrels, a battle that embodied what it meant to be British and proud, a war to save the native red squirrel.

Resplendent in his khaki combat gear, Parker has managed to exterminate over 20,000 (or about one per cent) of the country's grey squirrel population – or as he puts it himself, in his quasi-Churchillian way, 'never before has so much been done by so few.' Filmmaker Luke Sewell (21 August 2009) comments:

> Undeniably the image of the grey and red squirrels has been hijacked by the extreme Right as highlighting some kind of race war. I was aware of this from the start of production. I never felt that Paul [Parker] was particularly ideological. Although he was patriotic and suspicious of outsiders, it wasn't as if he was a member of the BNP. Primarily he was interested in saving a species that he cared deeply about. However he did often talk about the red and grey battle within the framework of right-wing rhetoric. I believe that he was confused about the nature of immigration and patriotism and was a sucker for *Daily Mail* sensational nonsense about immigrants coming to Britain and getting loads of handouts. However he was a simple man and it felt unkind to single him out as a total bigot – his racism was born out of a lack of education, poverty, a small town mentality, laziness, and just being spoon-fed total nonsense in the media. I thought it would be interesting to send up the right-wing hijacking of the red squirrel and people's fear of immigration. In a strange way in this context Paul is to some extent a victim of this kind of crass sensationalism and ends up becoming more sympathetic as a result. The tongue-in-cheek story of his war with 'immigrant grey' was perfect for highlighting the absurdity of right-wing rhetoric.

It is significant not only that Sewell recognizes the political symbolism within the representation and perception of the squirrel debate, but also that he sees the dissemination of the related rhetoric, and therefore also of the ideologies which underpin it, as the responsibility of the mass media. Paul Parker's xenophobia seems symptomatic of a shift in populist discourse, and the news media's toughening perspective upon the future of the grey squirrel appears to reflect an increasingly intolerant attitude towards all aspects of immigration. Parker's genocidal tendencies may have been provoked in part by a normalization of the language of racial, religious and cultural intolerance which has pervaded the popular media since 9/11, one which is paralleled in even the BBC's (let alone the *Daily Mail*'s) growing acceptance of draconian solutions to the grey squirrel problem. On 20 January 2004 *BBC News Interactive* had announced that 'calls for a cull of grey squirrels in Cumbria are being considered.' On 3 June 2005 it added that a pub near

Worcester, the Hadley Bowling Green Inn, had introduced a grey squirrel terrine to its menu. (One might note in passing that research for this chapter has uncovered one minor consolation for the greys: the pub is now under new management and stresses that 'we have not anything of that kind on our menus.') On 21 January 2006 the *BBC News* site added that 'a massive cull of grey squirrels is to take place across England to try to halt declining numbers of the endangered native red population.' On 23 March 2006 it revealed Conservative peer Lord Inglewood's proposal that celebrity chefs 'should encourage schoolchildren to eat grey squirrels in an effort to save the endangered red species.' Baron Inglewood of Hutton announced that 'unless something radical and imaginative is done Squirrel Nutkin and his friends are going to be toast.' Lord Inglewood (21 August 2009) has added that 'the idea of culling greys is much more widely accepted because the evidence of the last few years shows unequivocally that a failure to cull will lead to the eventual elimination of the reds.' Like Iolo Williams, Richard Inglewood suggests a relationship between the plight of the red squirrel and the values and traditions of the British countryside: 'For me the red squirrel encapsulates something to do with my home area and its distinct qualities and character. Equally the grey represents a series of forces which are threatening it. The distinction is analogous to [...] the urban-rural divide.'

On 11 June 2006 the *BBC News* website publicized Scots parliamentarian Murdo Fraser's suggestion that 'bounties should be paid for the shooting or trapping of grey squirrels.' On 5 July 2006 it described an MP's plan to eradicate grey squirrels by eating them. On 15 August 2007 it reported that 'people on Anglesey have been urged to call a phone line to report sightings of grey squirrels as part of a cull.' On 24 January 2008 it stated that 'almost 12,000 grey squirrels have been killed in Northumberland in an effort to save the red squirrel.' On 15 February 2008 it added that 'woodland areas of County Durham are being targeted by teams aiming to cull grey squirrels [...] Volunteers predict about 100 greys a day will be trapped in the operation.' On 15 April 2008 the BBC's Raymond Buchanan profiled Paul Parker of the Red Squirrel Protection Partnership (the pest-control protagonist of Luke Sewell's documentary): 'His ambition is to take his skills south and eventually clear the last grey squirrel out of London's Hyde Park.'

The Observer Magazine's cover story of 19 October 2008 saw reporter Tim Adams joining Paul Parker and his patron Lord Redesdale on the hunt for grey squirrels in Northumberland. In the course of his story Adams (2008: 32) begins to draw parallels between the squirrel issue and wider ethnic tensions: 'The longer you spend in Northumberland the more you realize what a very long way from anywhere it is. *The Observer*'s photographer [...] and I are staying in a curious country house hotel [...] that was recently converted into a hostel for asylum seekers. When there was a local protest at the prospect of the incomers, however, it reverted to being a hotel [...] Overnight, I begin to develop a theory that the suspicion about incomers has also fuelled some of the zeal of the squirrel operation.' Adams quotes RSPP Chairman Lord Redesdale: 'We only call ourselves the Red Squirrel Protection Partnership because if we called it the Grey Squirrel Annihilation League people might be a little less sympathetic [...] we do nothing with red squirrels apart from save them by killing grey squirrels!'

This euphemization of genocide is hardly new. George Orwell (1962: 37) wrote that 'the Hitlers and Stalins find murder necessary [...] but they don't speak of it as murder: it is "liquidation", "elimination", or some other soothing phrase.' Primo Levi (1989: 18) pointed out that 'the well-known euphemisms' of the Final Solution were meant to prevent [the] public 'from finding out what was happening.' Lucy Dawidowicz (1990: 172) has added that 'the names given to these institutions for killing [...] were originally intended as a camouflage to conceal from the general public these systematic programmes of murder. This neutral terminology [...] no doubt later reinforced [...] delusional traits among the killers.' However Lord Redesdale (in correspondence of 2 September 2009) has stressed that, despite its name, the Red Squirrel Protection Partnership is very open about its methods: 'Other groups [...] did not like the use of the word *kill*. We have used it in every interview as that is what we do. [Otherwise] we would be vulnerable to the charge that we are killing large numbers of animals but hiding the fact.'

A Liberal Democrat peer and a member of the illustrious and once controversial Mitford family (perhaps best remembered for Diana and Unity Mitford's brief flirtation in the 1930s with Adolf Hitler), Lord Redesdale is understandably sensitive to the publicity his campaign has garnered.

While he emphasizes that 'Paul [Parker] has a real talent for getting the press on his side' he remains conscious of the ambiguities within media representations of their crusade. Redesdale notes that their final meeting to secure their £148,000 grant from the Department for Environment, Food and Rural Affairs lasted an hour and a quarter – 'an hour of which was over the potential bad publicity.' While he recognizes that the media attention has resulted in increased support and funding for his cause, he remains uncomfortable with depictions of their endeavour as a nationalist enterprise:

> The *Observer* article by Tim Adams garnered a lot of Press interest though no donations and led to the Channel 4 documentary. The documentary raised £15,000. The response from people who saw the programme was really positive with a very large number of small donations, mostly from older people who remembered having reds. The response on the ground also helped as we were invited into areas that had been hesitant before. TV really helps with improving people's trust that you are doing what you say. However, although Paul was happy with it, the link to killing grey squirrels and questions of them coming over here from abroad I found unfortunate. Paul was given a slant such as a shot of an England flag on his window that was unfair, especially as the flag was not even on his house.

In February 2006 Donald Rumsfeld proposed that 'some of the most critical battles' of the War on Terror would be fought in the newsrooms. Rupert Redesdale demonstrates a similar understanding of his own campaign's need to capture hearts and minds through sympathetic headlines:

> Two years ago as a way of dealing with the bodies we launched our 'eat a grey save a red' campaign. This was linked to our supply of greys to the local butchers Ridley's of Corbridge. This was covered on BBC One's *Breakfast*. This really caused a press stir, with stories then also on CNN and CBS as well as all the national papers. The eating of greys was intended to change perception of the grey from furry animal to organic free range food. Those who question our cause seem quite happy if we say we are selling the bodies for £2 each to eat.

Redesdale's alternative to euphemism is a functionality which makes his solution to the squirrel problem seem inevitable: extermination (once more) as productive industry. On 29 May 2009 *The Guardian* reported that Lord Redesdale's protégé Paul Parker was planning to expand his operations in response to a growing demand for squirrel meat. Talk of the mass slaughter of grey squirrels has shifted from the controversial to the casual and incontrovertible. On 10 February 2009 the *BBC News* website quoted a representative of the Scottish Wildlife Trust: 'I can understand and empathise with those people who do not like the prospect of killing wild animals, but it is disingenuous to say that there are viable alternative solutions to saving the red squirrel in Scotland.' No dissenting voices were cited.

The eradication of the grey squirrel enjoys even royal assent. A cause long supported by the Duke of Edinburgh (*BBC News Interactive*, 6 June 2000) has now been adopted by his eldest son (*BBC News Interactive*, 5 June 2009). The culling of the grey squirrel has become ideologically naturalized – to the extent that the *Daily Mail*'s Harry Mount could propose (on 12 June 2009) that 'if you want to preserve British woodland, and the real Squirrel Nutkin, too, stick a grey in your pot today, on a low heat, for eight hours.' Mr Mount's *Daily Mail* article includes a photograph of the reporter standing alongside squirrel exterminator extraordinaire Paul Parker, and brandishing a brace of slaughtered greys. Harry Mount is, coincidentally, the cousin of British Conservative Prime Minister David Cameron. In his *Daily Mail* story, Mount laments the fact that, as he sees it, 'the law [...] is in the greys' favour. Although you can be fined £5,000 for freeing a trapped squirrel and you can shoot them any time of year, they still aren't classed as vermin like mice and rats; so there is no statutory duty to get rid of them.'

Harry Mount (13 August 2009) has, however, expressed his personal opinion on the subject rather more moderately than the rhetoric of his *Daily Mail* piece would suggest: 'I think it's perfectly OK for foreign species to make their way over here. Didn't the apple tree make its way over here several thousands of years ago? It's only when they start picking on the things that are living perfectly happy, quiet lives that my anger starts to rise.' This might simply be interpreted as a difference in tone (the caring face of Cameronite Conservatism which, some fear, might harbour deeply Thatcherite tendencies within); but it may be that Mount's *Daily Mail* rhetoric reflects its context – not only the *Daily Mail* but a culture in which a militant reaction to perceived external threats has become a standard of journalistic, political and public discourse.

Conclusion

Symbolic discourse, of course, impacts upon what becomes consciously acceptable. This odd little brand of genocide has crept up on the nation almost unremarked. The British do, after all, have larger problems to contemplate. Yet could it be the case that these events, in serving as metaphors for those vaster political and ideological concerns, might also allow us to see the possible outcomes of the historical trends they shadow and foreshadow?

The language of politics and of the media has changed since 9/11: the boundaries of the acceptable, of the thinkable, of the speakable and of the possible, have been extended. Restrictions upon civil rights and immigration have accompanied this period of unrelenting war. *Deportation* has become a politically unobjectionable term. *Extraordinary rendition* no longer seems quite so extraordinary. Extremist ideologies have long tended to insinuate themselves into popular consciousness by means of euphemism and metaphor. This is not necessarily a conscious process. These nightmares of terror and these fantasies of genocide may therefore (as dreams do) reveal much that cannot otherwise be expressed about the present and about the future. Without the regulations and prohibitions of an ideological super ego (a United Nations of thought), the Internet – with its speed of communicational transfer and therefore of ideational mutation and evolution – develops and disseminates the unconscious imperatives of *homo sapiens* on a global scale. Its predilection for conspiracy and pornography not only reflects, but also exaggerates to the point of caricature, the fears and desires of the species. It not only reveals our absurdities: in that it shapes who we are, it may also make those absurdities real.

What then might this situation suggest about the nature and the future of 'quality' journalism and of its self-proclaimed status as an objective, literalist and unambiguous mode of public and professional communication? Could online provision offer the possibility of a *new* new journalism: a journalism which is no longer constrained by the outmoded imperatives of its own bloated super ego, one whose falsely formal notions of objectivity may be superseded by a self-conscious subjectivity (or an approach to objectivity which invokes and nominates plural subjectivities) – journalism as a fluid, vibrant, reflective and analytical narrative, as a discourse which courts reinterpretation – journalism as an ongoing organic history? John Fiske (1989: 307–8) writes that

> arguments that news should be more accurate or objective are actually arguments in favour of news's authority, and are ones that seek to increase its control under the disguise of improving its quality [...]. In a progressive democracy, news should stress its discursive constructedness [...] it is politically healthy for news to encourage its readers to negotiate (often stubbornly) with it, to use its discursive resources to provoke and stimulate viewers to make their sense of [...] the social experiences it describes.

Could a mode of reportage which renounces its own ideological repression – which celebrates its carnivalesque dreamspace, which relishes its symbolic freedom and challenges the notions of established power enshrined in the conventionality of official and formal discourse, which returns to the light of day all that has been squirreled away – offer precisely such interactively post-authorial, post-authoritative and post-authoritarian possibilities as Fiske suggests? Or would it just give us somewhere new to hide our nuts?

References

Adams, T. (2008). 'They shoot squirrels, don't they?' in *The Observer Magazine*, 19 October 2008.

Allison, R. (2002). 'Flesh-eating squirrel stalks streets of Knutsford' in *The Guardian*, 7 November 2002.

Anslow, J. (2008). 'Myth, Jung and the McC women' in *British Journalism Review* 19:2, 58–65.

Anthony, A. (2002). 'Flying the Flag' in *The Observer*, 1 September 2002.

Buchanan, R. (2008). 'Grey squirrel hunting' in *BBC News Interactive*, 15 April 2008.

Charles, A. (2004). 'Racist, or just animal crackers?' in *British Journalism Review* 15:1, 68–72.

Cook, C. (2005). 'How the British Press Reported Enlargement' in *EU Enlargement – One Year On* (ed. Charles, A.), Tallinn: Audentes, 79–90.

Dawidowicz, L. (1990). *The War against the Jews*. Harmondsworth: Penguin.

Fiske, J. (1989). *Television Culture*. London: Routledge.

Freud, S. (1985). *Art and Literature*. London: Penguin.

Jenkins, R. (2002). '"Yosemite Sam" puts down rogue squirrel' in *The Times*, 8 November 2002.

Kirby, A. (1999). 'Stormont squirrels bridge the divide' in *BBC News Interactive*, 1 April 1999.

Levi, P. (1989). *The Drowned and the Saved* (trans. Rosenthal, R.). London: Abacus.

Lister, D., and Smith, L. (2008). 'Squirrel wars: reds, greys and blacks battle for supremacy' in *The Times*, 26 April 2008.

McCreaddie, A. (2002). 'Squirrel attacks girl, 2' in *The Knutsford Guardian*, 6 November 2002.

Moretti, F. (1997). *Signs Taken for Wonders*. London: Verso.

Mount, H. (2009). 'Anyone for grey squirrel risotto?' in *The Daily Mail*, 12 June 2009.

Orwell, G. (1962). *Inside the Whale*. Harmondsworth: Penguin.

Packham, C. (2009). 'Ecological Cleansing'. Available at wildlifeextra.com

Prestage, M. (2002). 'A nice day out of face-painting and bigotry' in *The Independent*, 18 August 2002.

Silverman, J. (2003). 'Paedophiles: Who are they?' in *The Independent on Sunday*, 19 January 2003.

Stoker, B. (1979). *Dracula*. London: Penguin.

Tumber, H., and Webster, F. (2006). *Journalists Under Fire*. London: Sage.

Žižek, S. (2002). *Welcome to the Desert of the Real!* London: Verso.

Žižek, S. (2008). *Violence*. London: Profile Books.

JAMES MORRISON

Spin, Smoke-Filled Rooms and the Decline of Council Reporting by British Local Newspapers: The Slow Demise of Town Hall Transparency

If there is one realm of public life in which the provincial press has long justified the mantle 'fourth estate' it is in fulfilling its time-honoured role as principal scrutinizer (and critic) of local government. For generations, regional newspapers in the UK, mainland Europe and the United States have been our primary sources of information on the deliberations and decisions of local authorities – and our channels for dissent over wayward procedures, policies, and politicking.

Yet, as we enter the second decade of a new century – a brave new digital world in which it should be easier than ever for journalists to keep us abreast of the activities of councillors and officials – in England and Wales at least, local papers appear increasingly neutered. Surveys point to a dramatic decline in the amount of space and time they are devoting to council coverage and the steady demise of dedicated local government correspondents.

This chapter argues that these developments can be blamed, in part, on recent reforms to the way councils in the two countries conduct their business. Tony Blair's Local Government Act (HM Stationery Office 2000a) ushered in cabinet-style council executives based on the model used by the UK's national administration, at the same time exempting them from meeting in public unless discussing major decisions they intended to take collectively. Two new leadership options were introduced for authorities covering populations of 85,000 or more: executive leaders or US-style directly elected mayors. Meanwhile, whispering in their ears, came a new generation of media managers and political assistants modelled on the ministerial special advisors for which Blair himself became so notorious.

More recently, as the interface between provincial press and local government comes to resemble that between Britain's national papers and the Prime Minister's Cabinet – with reporters, barred from the meetings at which policy decisions are actually taken, forced to rely on carefully managed statements and briefings – council PR machines have moved a step closer to silencing the critical voice of local journalism. Not content with managing the messages they send out to the external media, all but a handful of UK local authorities now produce their own publications – many closely resembling commercial newspapers or magazines (Newspaper Society 2009; Local Government Association, April 2009). Staffed by pro-fessionally trained, well-paid journalists whose salaries the private sector cannot hope to match, this new breed of title reaches far more households than the conventional press, and is increasingly out-competing it in the pursuit of a dwindling pool of paid advertising.

This chapter uses a mix of primary and secondary research to examine the effects of three key developments that are undermining local author-ity accountability in England and Wales: increasing secrecy in executive decision-making; the decline of council reporting by independent news-papers; and the growth of proactive council PR strategies, including the use of self-funded journalism to promote campaigns and policies.

Cabinet Government and the Demise of Open Debate

The most notable recent change to the hierarchical structure of councils in England and Wales was the introduction of 'executive arrangements' for those covering populations of more than 85,000 (HM Stationery Office 2000b). In a move portrayed by Ministers as a means of speeding up local decision-making, authorities were given a choice of two new leadership options: a directly elected mayor or executive leader. Councils taking the mayoral route, subject to prior approval in a local referendum, were initially allowed to choose between a cabinet and an alternative model under which mayors would take day-to-day policy decisions on the advice of council managers (senior civil servants likely to be their authorities' incumbent chief executives). This approach would have reduced elected councillors to a second-tier role under a 'presidential' mayor and his/her unelected aide (Heinelt and Hlepas 2006). Only one council, Stoke-on-Trent, adopted it, and, when it subsequently abandoned this in favour of a leader and cabinet, the Government amended the law to remove the option altogether (HM Stationery Office 2007). Meanwhile, executive leaders – normally drawn from the party with most seats after a local election – were permitted to form cabinets, prime minister-style, appointing executive members to specific portfolios and (since 2007) vesting all executive power in themselves (HM Stationery Office 2007). Post-2007 leaders therefore have broadly the same executive powers as mayors.

The advent of cabinet government was contentious enough for some councillors, who argued it broke the longstanding tradition that each member should have an equal say in policy-making, irrespective of whether they were in the ruling party. Though key decisions (those affecting two or more electoral wards) still had to be taken at full council meetings, and published in monthly forward plans, with strong cabinet backing they would encounter little challenge.

Of even greater concern was the freedom authorities were given to limit the meetings their cabinets held in public. Ministers had originally proposed that cabinets should not be obliged to meet publicly at all – a break with years of practice in full council, committee and sub-committee meetings following the Local Authorities (Access to Information) Act 1985 (HM Stationery Office 1985). A House of Lords amendment moderated this freedom, stipulating that cabinets should meet in public whenever discussing key decisions they intended to take collectively. However, a loophole, yet to be addressed, enabled them to convene in private even on key decisions – if they had been delegated to individual cabinet members (Campaign for Freedom of Information 2001). So executive decisions delegated to individual councillors – or, in some cases, unelected officers – were rendered subject to less scrutiny than collective ones.

The climate of secrecy surrounding cabinet meetings has greatly irritated 'backbench' councillors – many of whom, despite long years of service, find themselves locked outside the inner-circle of the leader/mayor and his/her frontbench confidants. But why, beyond this, does it matter? One outcome is that many issues of public interest are slipping by unnoticed. In February 2010, Woking Borough Council stretched the definition of commercially sensitive matters qualifying as 'exempt' that have therefore traditionally been heard in private (HM Stationery Office 1985) by holding a series of closed meetings at which it finalized the purchase of a shopping-centre for £68 million (Rider 2010). The first local residents knew of any negotiations – secured with a loan from the Public Works Loan Board which will take fifty years to repay – was a press release on the council's website issued *after* it signed on the dotted line. It is established practice for councils to exclude press and public from meetings (or parts thereof) concerned with negotiating commercially sensitive contracts, but to hold a final vote and conclude a deal in private is somewhat unusual.

Much more seriously, the recent scandal about inadequate child protection procedures in Doncaster was exposed only after a local newspaper, the *Doncaster Free Press*, doggedly followed a trail starting with a reference to 'deep-rooted' issues around its services for children and young people in an otherwise routine Audit Commission report on the council's overall performance. A series of follow-up stories led to the paper's revelation nine months later that a serious case review into a ten-month-old baby had exposed a 'chaotic and dangerous situation' in the council's children's services department. When this story was finally published, and it emerged that six further serious case reviews were under way, councillors outside the cabinet accused the town's elected mayor, Martin Winter, of presiding over a 'culture of secrecy' (Ahmed 2009). Mr Winter eventually resigned, and a new management team for children's services was parachuted into the authority by Schools Secretary Ed Balls in March 2009. While the story did finally get out, then – through the tenacity of a local paper – how much sooner might it have been exposed if the case reviews had been discussed more openly in council meetings?

The Decline of Council Reporting

Evidence suggests that the spread of cabinet government is acting as a disincentive to an increasingly financially straitened local media to continue staffing any but the most important meetings of their local authorities. A 2009 survey of local newspaper executives by the Press Association, Britain's national newswire service, found that nearly two-thirds were devoting less time and fewer staff hours to council coverage than in 1999, and more than one in five employed fewer dedicated local government reporters than a decade earlier (Fowler 2009). Half of all editors surveyed admitted the 'level of scrutiny' to which they subjected their principal local authorities had been reduced by these factors.

One of the most common reasons given for newspapers' failures to attend meetings routinely was the fact that, with the advent of cabinet government, many newsworthy decisions are no longer made in public. After all, why send a reporter who could otherwise be providing vital copy for the web and overnight editions out of the office to report from a meeting at which little is debated or voted on – and any matters that are will merely be rubber-stamped, having been all-but decided in the privacy of the cabinet room beforehand? Comments from respondents surveyed included claims that 'cabinet structure has diminished debate, independence, political rows and committee activity' and that 'decisions in local government are made less and less in full council and our coverage reflects this.' A significant admission made by some weekly editors was that the councils they covered least were ones with the biggest majorities – i.e. those most needing to be held accountable for their decisions, due to the weakness of opposition parties. Their rationale was that the unassailability of ruling parties in these authorities rendered the quality of debate at meetings negligible.

The decline in the reporting of council meetings was not solely attributed to the advent of cabinet government. Budget pressures and staff reductions were repeatedly cited, particularly by the editors of smaller daily newspapers – with some identifying the closure of district offices as a logistical issue that made it difficult to staff district council meetings (let

alone those of parish councils – the lowest tier of UK local government).
Others pointed to reductions in the number of daily editions their papers
produced, and the resultant loss of space for council stories.

In many cases, councils receiving the least coverage were upper-tier
counties (those with the biggest budgets and responsibilities). Papers continuing to provide the most comprehensive coverage of their local authorities were those fortunate enough to only have one to worry about: i.e. those
whose previous two-tier structure had been replaced by a unitary one as a
result of the rolling reorganization which began in 1992. One respondent
lamented: 'Staff shortages mean readers not in the heart of our circulation
area get a worse service and many local authorities are not held to account
as they once were.'

Evidence for declining council coverage also came from local authority media managers, who generally revelled in their newfound ability to
take controversial decisions without fear of press exposure. Metropolitan
boroughs, in particular, said they had to deal with fewer 'embarrassing' stories than previously, simply because journalists no longer attended enough
meetings or dug sufficiently deeply for stories. More than one respondent
described specialist council reporters as a 'dying breed' which they did not
expect to see replaced once those in post had retired. Some said their press
releases routinely appeared in print almost verbatim – reviving charges of
'churnalism' (Davies 2008).

Growth of Proactive PR and Council-Run 'Newspapers'

As if financial cutbacks and declining openness in council policy-making
were not obstacle enough to effective scrutiny, the adoption by many councils of aggressive media strategies, including increasingly professionalized
news publications, is having an even more deleterious effect on independent news reporting of local government business. According to two 2009
surveys local authorities – one by the Newspaper Society of 436 across

the UK (Newspaper Society 2009), the other by the Local Government Association of all 353 in England (LGA 2009) – between 95 and 98 per cent of councils publish regular newspapers, magazines or newsletters. While many of these are bimonthly or less frequent, dozens are monthly, and seven are fortnightly (six of these in London alone). At least three, *Greenwich Time*, published by the London borough of Greenwich, Tower Hamlets' *East End Life*, and *Inform*, an email newsletter from Bath and North East Somerset Council, are weekly.

Critics of council papers are concerned that well-produced local authority publications – particularly those covering traditional newspaper stories, as well as those related to their own councils – are poaching readers from commercial papers. Furthermore, an increasing number of local authority publications accept paid advertising – including the councils' own statutory notices – thereby depriving commercial titles of appeal and valuable revenue. Meanwhile, council-run publications are increasingly being professionalized, with trained and experienced local journalists recruited for generous salaries to staff them – in so doing draining expertise from the independent sector. The combined effect of these factors, the critics argue, is to slash profits for traditional titles, endanger jobs, and threaten the survival of an independent, plural media.

Poaching Readers

Council-run publications in some areas are making serious inroads into the circulations and readerships of their commercial rivals. *East End Life* is posted free through the letterboxes of 81,000 homes in Tower Hamlets, while its independent competitor, the *East London Advertiser*, also published weekly, struggles to sell more than 6,800 copies with a fifty pence cover price (Greenslade 2009a). Between 1993 and 2010, its circulation fell from 20,000 to 7,500, while in the year to April 2009 alone it dropped by nearly a quarter. Hackney Council's *Hackney Today*, which boasts 'the

largest reach in the borough of any local paper' in media-packs it sends
potential advertisers, was distributing 108,000 copies a fortnight to local
homes in April 2009. Its commercial rival, the *Hackney Gazette*, was selling barely 8,000 copies a week (Greenslade 2009b). Malcolm Starbrook,
editor of the *East London Advertiser*, blames 'a large proportion' of his
144-year-old paper's sales decline on *East End Life*, citing its non-council
coverage as a major cause for concern: 'It carries court reports, seven-day
TV listings, sports, has local advertising – all the things you would expect
to find in a local newspaper. The difference being that it's all heavily sub-
sidised' (Tryhorn 2010).

Accepting Paid Advertising

Recent surveys of the growing local authority newspaper and magazine
market have highlighted the proliferation of paid-for advertising in some
titles – and the threat this poses to commercial ones long dependent on
advertising revenue for their profits (Newspaper Society 2009; LGA 2009).
With many of these titles increasingly outstripping traditional ones in
terms of distribution, recession-hit companies can hardly be blamed for
choosing to advertise in them.

    While the LGA states that six out of ten council titles in England
devote 10 per cent at most of their space to advertising, and a quarter
contain no adverts (LGA 2009), the Newspaper Society interprets things
differently. Its survey found that 90 per cent of London authorities either
already contained or would accept third-party advertising and a third of
those outside the capital ran adverts (Newspaper Society 2009). *H&F News*,
for example, distributed fortnightly to 87,000 homes in Hammersmith
and Fulham, boasts in its media pack 'more readers, more news and more
influence than any other paper'. It suggests that 'if you are looking for a way
to reach homes in Fulham, Hammersmith and Shepherds Bush which is
cost effective and reliable, then look no further' (Belam 2009).

But it is the migration of councils' own statutory notices to local authority-run publications that most concerns many editors. Under existing law, councils must advertise all major planning applications, announcements, and other notices in their local press. While newspapers were initially cheered by a recent ruling by Ministers that this condition should remain (Day 2009), certain councils are now placing these notices in their own titles, in preference to commercial ones. This gives them the advantage of appearing prudent: by negotiating free or cheaper advertising space than traditional papers would offer, and in so doing easing the burden on council taxpayers. In one sense, they are also meeting their publicity obligations more fully, by placing notices in the most widely distributed local titles, rather than ailing paid-for papers. *Hackney Today*, *H&F News*, *Brent Magazine* and *Living*, published by the borough of Havering, are among those running both internal and external ads.

The rates council-run publications charge their advertisers are also eye-opening. As of May 2009, *Haringey People*, printed ten times a year by Haringey Borough Council, was selling full-page adverts for £2,500, while its neighbouring local paper, the *Ham and High*, charged £2,000 (Belam 2009). While this made the latter's rates more competitive, it could only boast a 12,000-strong circulation – compared to the 224,500 claimed by *Haringey Life* (which, unlike commercial titles, is not required by law to certify its sales figures).

Rates charged by council publications, then, are sufficiently lucrative to offset (at least in part) their cost to council taxpayers. Hardly surprising, then, that they are courting advertisers so assiduously – to the alarm of commercial papers. Replying to a Freedom of Information Act request on 5 January 2010, Tower Hamlets Borough Council revealed that *East End Life* had earned £1.45 million in advertising in 2008–9 – £825,000 of which was raised from external advertisers who would otherwise have had to buy space in the press. In addition to running numerous council job advertisements (another traditional preserve of paid-for papers), the borough confirmed *East End Life* also took ads from NHS primary care trusts and voluntary organizations. Its advertising sales team numbers 6.6 people – collectively earning £249,000 – and it came in £231,000 under budget, only narrowly avoiding a profit.

The closure of some sixty local newspapers in 2008 alone (Toynbee 2009) can arguably be largely attributed to loss of advertising revenue. In 2009 a collapse in media advertising – exacerbated by the recession – saw Trinity Mirror make 1,700 redundancies and sell or close thirty titles; another regional group, Johnston Press, put the *Yorkshire Post* and *The Scotsman* up for sale; and the Guardian Media Group axed 153 local jobs. In March 2009 Northcliffe Media cut 1,000 local jobs after suffering a 37 per cent year-on-year drop in advertising revenue (Toynbee 2009). Even the LGA conceded in 2009 that 60 per cent of London boroughs had reported local commercial titles closing or struggling in the previous year, with three-quarters attributing this to falling advertising revenue (LGA 2009).

Professionalization of Council Publications

The final major concern raised by the newspaper sector in relation to council-run publications relates to their increasing professionalization. Unlike the poorly photocopied A4 newsletters of old, today's local authority newspapers and magazines are glossy affairs, produced using industry-standard desktop publishing software. Many boast mastheads, headline styles, and fonts closely resembling those of commercial titles, meaning that 'they are not easily distinguishable from independent press' (Newspaper Society 2009). The resemblance between council-run publications and 'real' papers is growing all the time: by 2009, 54 per cent of those distributed outside London ran non-council news, such as court reports and charity appeals (Newspaper Society 2009). This can add to the impression for less media-savvy consumers that they are reading genuine newspapers, rather than council PR bulletins.

Another factor contributing to the professionalization of council-run publications is that many staff now working on the former once worked – or *would* be working now, if market conditions were different – on the latter. Recruitment websites such as www.journalism.co.uk and www.gorkana.com

regularly carry job ads posted by councils offering £30,000-plus per annum. We know from the previously cited Freedom of Information request to Tower Hamlets that *East End Life* was employing 7.6 editorial and production staff, including four reporters, collectively earning £379,000 in January 2010. By contrast, as of September 2009, a typical starting salary for a local newspaper reporter was around £12,000 (according to www.prospects. ac.uk). With many papers no longer recruiting anyway, and some shedding jobs, it is easy to understand why applying to work on a less pressurized council publication can be so attractive to low-paid senior reporters on independent titles – particularly those saddled with substantial personal debt after self-financing a degree and the National Council for the Training of Journalists certificate widely regarded as the minimum requirement for entry-level jobs in the British provincial press.

For some, the professionalization of council publications is merely the latest stage in a gradual shift in communications strategy for local authorities, which has seen them move away from the largely reactive press officer approach of old to more proactive, Westminster-style 'media management' (Harrison 2006: 180). Kate Bond, corporate communications manager for Telford and Wrekin Council, has justified the use of aggressive PR tactics to counteract negative press stories – and publicize bread-and-butter information residents arguably need to know (cited in Harrison 2006: 180). This view finds sympathy with frustrated councillors like Darlington's Nick Wallis (2009): 'It's precisely the one-eyed nature of a lot of the local press that generated the growth of council magazines, because councils wanted to talk directly to their residents, and avoid the hostile spin continually imposed by the media.'

Cabinet Government and the Decline of Council Reporting

Primary research conducted for this chapter focused on a qualitative questionnaire sent to editors of twenty-four of the UK's 1,270 local newspapers – around two per cent of the total. Titles were targeted to give a representative geographical spread. Short commentaries were also solicited from the group political editor of the Kent Messenger Group and the Newspaper Society. Of the twenty-four questionnaire recipients, twenty replied. Although their geographical spread was representative on the whole, with two Scottish titles and 18 from England, no responses were received from Welsh papers.

The most valuable findings were the anecdotes received from survey respondents – in some cases editors, in others news editors or political reporters. The following comment from a reporter on a Devon evening paper reflects many of those received in response to a question asking about the impact of the Local Government Act (2000) on newspapers' ability to keep tabs on council decisions: 'The Cabinet makes its decisions at a public meeting, but meets in private before that. The public meetings are usually very quick, with little useful comment and no opposition from Cabinet members. Decisions are clearly agreed in advance.'

Like many other respondents, this reporter insisted that most commercial newspapers were savvy enough to overcome barriers to scrutinizing the workings of their council – in his case, by attending scrutiny meetings at which bigger issues were examined by backbench councillors. However, while a Hampshire-based weekly also robustly defended its reporters' ability to distinguish between real news and council propaganda, it added of the Local Government Act (2000) reforms: 'The changes have been bad for coverage of councils, which councils have tried to overcome by trebling their number of PR staff who pump out rubbish "puff stories" about their council.' A similarly exasperated response came from a Yorkshire-based morning paper: 'cabinet responsibility has made it harder to question decisions and we have to rely on FOI [Freedom of Information Act (2000)] more than I would like.' Even where cabinets are meeting in public, at least nominally, there is a sense that items have often been agreed in advance. The editor of a Surrey weekly, who admitted its council coverage had fallen by 10 per cent since 2000, commented that 'there is definitely a sense that all the key discussions and decisions are agreed in advance in private.'

On a more positive note, however, the less 'ready-made' nature of council stories in an era of behind-closed-doors deal-making is encouraging some to adopt a more imaginative approach to sourcing ideas. A respondent from a Kent daily said that 'increasingly we are using the meetings as a reference point to get an idea for a story, rather than doing a straightforward report of what was said.' A journalist from an evening paper in the North East concurred: 'We have enough contacts gained over many years to ensure we hear about even those discussions held in private.'

Both commentators broadly echoed the concerns identified by questionnaire respondents regarding a loss of accountability. Lynne Anderson, Communications Director of the Newspaper Society, said of the impact of the Local Government Act (2000): 'It can be harder these days for the local paper to get the information they need from the council, either because the important decisions are made behind closed doors or because everything is routed through the press office.'

While arguing that the use of council procedural devices to limit scrutiny of council business is nothing new, Paul Francis, political editor of the Kent Messenger Group, argued that he believed opposition parties in particular were finding it increasingly difficult to 'get their voice heard' under the new regime: 'In one sense, councils are doing what they always did but the concept of council chambers being arenas for meaningful democratic debate has all but vanished.'

Growth of Proactive PR and Council-Run 'Newspapers'

Paul Francis was bullish about the prospect of his newspaper group falling foul of aggressively marketed council media, describing their impact as 'negligible'. He dismissed Kent County Council's broadband television station, Kent TV!, and pointed out that *Yes!*, its twice-yearly magazine, has been closed.

Questionnaire respondents seemed generally unfazed by the threat of council-run publications – with many arguing the public is intelligent enough to distinguish between spin and genuine stories covered by commercial papers. A typical response, from a Lancashire-based paper, read: 'There is a quarterly council magazine. I would say its impact is minimal because council-related stories have a positive spin or are mainly information-based.'

As a deliberate decision was taken to elicit UK-wide responses, rather than focusing on London (where council papers have had the biggest financial impact), this response was perhaps to be expected. Moreover, the nature of respondents – journalists, rather than advertising executives or owners – meant their comments were inevitably going to focus on editorial, rather than financial, concerns. However, one East Midlands newspaper respondent, though dismissive of its current council-run competitor, added that 'our county council and police are presently looking at joining together to produce a monthly newsletter. That may have an impact on sales.' The Newspaper Society's Lynne Anderson sounded a similar note of concern:

> The industry has no complaint with the traditional council newsletter, published two or three times a year and offering helpful information to residents about services such as refuse collection. But this new breed of council-run 'newspaper' or magazine, often monthly or more frequent, is nothing more than propaganda in the guise of independent news reporting. Many of these titles compete head to head with independent local papers for readers and advertising.

Surrey County Council's Media Manager, Paul Marinko, who consented to a telephone interview for the purposes of this chapter, confirmed that *Surrey Matters* – distributed free four times a year to local addresses – will only hire NCTJ-trained journalists. Though it is staffed by just two people (an editor and writer, both of whom perform other communications duties between issues), the salary scale for the former is £32,169–£36,912, while the latter's is £36,615–£41,592.

Marinko (himself NCTJ-trained) does not want *Surrey Matters* to compete editorially with other media, let alone cover non-council stories. But he argues councils have a responsibility to give local taxpayers value for money – and commercial activities, such as courting advertisers, can be part of that: 'It's not for us to just tell people how great Surrey County Council is, but at the same time we need to make sure we get certain information out to them, and in doing so give them value for money. So we are taking advertising revenue.'

Research for this chapter also included two sets of Freedom of Information requests relating to local authority transparency. One was a two-part request sent to twenty-four councils in England and Wales (approximately

5 per cent of the total), asking about council procedures, staffing and publication production costs, and the salaries earned by any political assistants they employed. The other was a more targeted request focusing on the use of political assistants, sent specifically to all eleven local authorities currently with directly elected mayors (excluding the Mayor of London).

Replies received presented a mixed picture on publication costs. Tower Hamlets Borough Council revealed newly employed reporters were earning £31,152 as of March 2010, and average starting salaries on the *H&F News* were even higher (£33,994). Hammersmith and Fulham revealed its paper's advertising income had risen fivefold between 2006–7 and 2008–9 – from £86,681 to £431,711.

Most mayoral authorities confirmed they employed political assistants. Salaries appeared to differ widely, though. Middlesbrough Council has adopted the egalitarian approach of allowing each of its main political groupings – Labour, Conservative and the Middlesbrough Independent Members Association – to employ one assistant, at a cost of between £27,052 and £28,636. In contrast, Watford Borough Council has a single assistant to represent the authority itself (earning £51,793).

Conclusion

This chapter has argued that local authority accountability in England and Wales is being jeopardized by changes to the ways in which councils conduct their business. It has cited both primary and secondary evidence to support the contention that council decision-making in many areas – notably those operating under post-2000/2007 executive arrangements – has become more secretive, and to demonstrate the genuine threat some commercial newspapers face as a result of the competitive recruitment, advertising, and editorial policies adopted by a new generation of professionally produced council publications.

However, it would be wrong to suggest there is no cause for optimism for provincial papers as they emerge, battered, from the deepest post-war recession. Various initiatives are under way to ensure thorough, objective reporting of council-related matters continues. These include everything from hyper-local news sites – some staffed by enthusiastic amateurs, others by professional freelancers – to the Press Association's launch with Trinity Mirror of a new council reporting scheme (Oliver 2009). Meanwhile, the National Union of Journalists passed a motion in November 2009 calling on its national executive committee to lobby for an amendment to the Local Government Act (2000) enabling councils to co-fund independent news organizations. And some newspapers – including one surveyed here – are trying other strategies, including distributing their local authority's free-sheets inside their own paid-for titles.

In the meantime, faced with ever tighter editorial budgets, some papers are harnessing new technology to cover council meetings without the need to send reporters in person. As the Newspaper Society's Lynne Anderson explains, 'live webcams of council meetings, Twitter and blogging are also changing the way council news is reported. Local papers continue to cover council news and scrutinize council decisions but not necessarily in the same way as before.'

References

Ahmed, M. (2009). 'Secrecy and Turmoil at the Top Behind Doncaster Crisis' in *Community Care*, 20 January 2009.

Belam, M. (2009). 'Local Newspaper Week – Council Newspapers'. Available at www.currybet.net/cbet_blog/2009/05/local_newspaper_week_4.php.

Campaign for Freedom of Information (2001). *Access to Information in Local Government*. London: Campaign for Freedom of Information.

Davies, N. (2008). *Flat Earth News*. London: Random House.

Day, E. (2009). 'Council Ads Move Does Not Tackle Propaganda Sheets' in *Press Gazette*, 22 December 2009.

Fowler, N. (2009). *Enhancement of Service Study: Local Government, the Courts, and Regional Newspapers*. London: Press Association.

Greenslade, R. (2009a). 'Council Papers are Bad for Local Journalism and Bad for Democracy' in *London Evening Standard*, 22 April 2009.

Greenslade, R. (2009b). 'Are Councils Publishing Newspapers Beginning to See the Financial Light?' in *The Guardian*, 6 August 2009.

Harrison, S. (2006). 'Local Government Public Relations and the Local Press' in Franklin, B. (ed.), *Local Journalism and Local Media: Making the News*. Abingdon: Routledge, 175–89.

Heinelt, H., and Hlepas, N.-K. (2006). 'Typologies of Local Government Systems' in Back, H., Heinelt, H., and Magnier, A. (eds), *The European Mayor*. Wiesbaden: VS Verlag für Sozialwissenschaften.

HM Stationery Office (1985). *Local Government (Access to Information) Act 1985*. London: HM Stationery Office.

HM Stationery Office (2000a), *Local Government Act 2000*, London: HM Stationery Office.

HM Stationery Office (2000b), *Local Authorities (Executive Arrangements) (Access to Information) Regulations 2000*, London: HM Stationery Office.

HM Stationery Office (2007). *Local Government and Public Involvement in Health Act 2007*. London: HM Stationery Office.

Local Government Association (2009). *Local Authority Newsletters and Magazines Survey*. London: LGA.

Newspaper Society (2009) 'Council Newspapers: Anti Democratic in Spirit and Practice'. Available at www.newspapersoc.org.uk/Default.aspx?page=4372.

Oliver, L. (2009). 'PA to Trial Public Service Reporting Project with Trinity Mirror'. Available at www.journalism.co.uk.

Rider, N. (2010). 'Woking Council Buys Wolsey Place Shopping Centre', in *Woking News and Mail*, 22 February 2010.

Toynbee, P. (2009). 'This is an Emergency. Act Now, or Local News Will Die' in *The Guardian*, 24 March 2009.

Tryhorn, C. (2010). 'War Rages over Council-run Newspapers' in *The Guardian*, 25 January 2010.

Wallis, N. (2009). 'Having it Both Ways'. Available at darlingtoncouncillor.blogspot.com/2009/8/having-it-both-ways.html.

SONYA YAN SONG

The End – or the Genesis – of Journalism?
The Online Extension of Chinese Print Media

In discussions about the Chinese media, journalism is often associated with propaganda, censorship and the imprisonment of journalists. But if the Chinese media, especially print media, appear to be a long way from maturing because of these obstacles and are seen as 'the last bastion of China's planned economy' – then the emergence of the Internet is dramatically changing this picture. Its rapid penetration into a mass audience is fast changing the rules of the game, both for media and the government.

The Chinese media environment is still marked by boundaries set by the government, some in the form of explicit taboos on what can be reported, others in unspoken taboos that must be probed and tested. Moreover, the practice of journalism is circumscribed by two fundamental realities: 1) even in China's so-called commercial media, investment does not guarantee control over content; 2) at some level, all media organizations are state-owned. Nevertheless, the development of online media in China is proving to be a major testing ground for print media seeking to enlarge these boundaries, both politically and commercially.

Chinese print media view the Internet as the inevitable next step in the advancement of journalism in the country. But the approaches they are taking differ significantly. This chapter will explore the political, legal and commercial boundaries within which Chinese media operate, and how they are moving to the Internet to create opportunities they do not have in print – often employing subtle means to cross these boundaries. An overview of the Chinese media market will be followed by brief case studies based on extensive interviews with representatives of Chinese media companies. The three cases examined are: *Sanlian Life Week*, which is the most cautious among traditional media about investing online; *Beijing*

Lifestyle, the website has positioned itself to implement a uniquely localized strategy on the Internet; and *Beijing Youth Daily*, whose affiliated website is among the pioneers of the use of the Internet and one of the most successful news sites in China.

Restrictions or Opportunities?

Traditional Western offline media are fully matured and the space for further development in their original pre-Internet sphere is limited, so they have been expanding their presence to the online battlefield. For them, the decision to go online is tantamount to one between evolution and extinction.

Since the economic reforms that started in 1978, Chinese media have experienced considerable advances both in terms of what they have been allowed to do and what they have sought to do. More recently, the media sector has received a boost from the emergence of the Internet, which possesses the ability for the first time genuinely to reach a mass audience. As such, the situation for the Chinese media could not be more different. Longtime government restrictions on traditional media have retarded their development in the offline sphere. Viewed from another perspective, that means these restrictions, which are slowly lifting, have left a lot of potential for the Chinese media to grow. What Chinese media now face is quite different from traditional Western media – it is not a story of a sad ending but rather a happy beginning, both in the offline and online media sectors.

Unlike developed Western countries, China has been in a process of economic transition over the past three decades, and as a result the country's media industry has evolved in an economic environment very different from its Western counterparts. Since 1978, China has witnessed significant changes, most notably a gradual move from a centrally planned economy to a market economy. However, in spite of liberalization in the economic sector, China's media remain heavily controlled by the state, which imposes on the media a state-ownership regime, and a growing number of rules and administrative regulations. Qian Gang (8 April 2008), co-director of the China Media Project at the University of Hong Kong, argues that the transition of the Chinese media market is being carried out in a fashion that is 'even worse than the most awkwardly "transformed" state-owned enterprises' and calls the media industry 'the last bastion of China's planned economy.'

The unique situation of the Chinese media industry in a rapidly growing and reforming economy can be attributed to two major, and sometimes contradictory, roles – one is as a mouthpiece of the state and the Party (thus, serving a political cause, rather than functioning as a business), and the other is as a watchdog for society, reporting news (and in doing so, seeking to make a profit). However, the first role of the Chinese media has been so dominant that it has prevented the development of that second role.

State-Owned and Party-Controlled

Chinese news media are owned by the party-state and are distributed by approval of the government. A 1999 ruling governing publications stipulates that all Chinese media companies are ultimately state-owned, no matter who has invested in them or at what level that investment was made.

The notion that the ownership or control of an enterprise is determined by the level of an investor's investment in the enterprise is a well understood concept of corporate ownership in the West. But, in a landmark dispute in 1999 over the ownership of *Beijing Lifestyle*, three departments of the central government jointly declared that this principle is not applicable to the Chinese media field, which they defined as comprising news publications, radio, television and film. Wang Yan, then the investor in, and the owner of, *Beijing Lifestyle*, was thereby stripped of his job and deprived of his ownership of the media company. The case of *Beijing Lifestyle* illustrates that any capital other than state capital cannot be certain of control over any Chinese media enterprise under current circumstances. Since the *Beijing Lifestyle* case, the party-state has reaffirmed the party's leadership, and therefore ownership, of the news media – in spite of China's accession to the World Trade Organization (WTO) in 2001.

In 2002, the General Administration of Press and Publication (GAPP) published the *Implementing Rules of the Several Opinions on Strengthening the Reform of News Publications, Radio, TV and Film*. According to the Rules, endorsed by the Propaganda Department, selected pilot media enterprises were allowed to receive state capital from government institutions inside the media field and outside it – such as from large state-owned enterprises and government-affiliated institutions – as well as from non-state Chinese organizations and foreign investors. The proportion of state capital is stipulated to be no less than 51 per cent. Moreover, neither state capital from outside the media field nor foreign capital is allowed to finance any editorial activities. In 2005, China's State Council published an administrative order affirming that non-state capital is barred from investing in and managing all forms of news media, including news agencies, newspapers, publishing houses, television stations and news websites. While the party-state has always maintained ownership of the news media, this is the first time that restrictions have been formally enacted in the form of an administrative code with enforcement power (cf. Wei 2008).

The position of the Chinese government with regard to the Internet has shifted over time, with authorities initially asserting that websites were not considered a part of the media, then acknowledging that they were, and finally embracing the Internet as a medium that could have a positive impact on society, provided it was properly regulated. Indeed, the 17th National Congress sought to define a role for the government in the development of the Internet, proclaiming that its responsibility was 'to well maintain, utilize, regulate and develop Chinese websites.'

Free Trade

Unlike many other services such as telecommunications, which have been opening up according to a fixed schedule after China's accession to the WTO, no provision has been made concerning the media sector (cf. World Trade Organization 2001). Without violating any rules, the Chinese media field remains unchanged after the internal structural adjustment and several rounds of trade negotiations with the external world.

However, some scholars expect changes to take place in the Chinese media industry as a result of the irresistible opening set in motion by accession to the WTO. For instance, Xie Xinzhou (2003) points out that 'with China's increasing participation in the WTO community, the Chinese media are being more frequently requested to join contests on a worldwide scale and thus the armor [of the hefty governance] will definitely be whittled away.' Xie Xinzhou noted in 2003 that seven licenses were required to launch a Chinese news website. Indeed, as time passes, even more permits have been required to launch Internet businesses in China.

Many different government entities are involved in issuing such permits, including the State Council (encompassing the Information Office), the General Administration of Press and Publication (GAPP), the Ministry of Industry and Information (encompassing the dissolved Ministry of Information Industry), and the State Administration of Radio, Film and TV (SARFT). The basic permits (listed on the front page of Sina.com) required to launch a news website in China are: the permit for providing Internet content (ICP); the permit for online cultural businesses; the permit for Internet publication; the permit for audio-video content services; the permit for Internet news publication; the permit for Internet information service on drugs; the permit for Internet information services on education; the permit for electronic bulletin services; the permit for wireless value-added service (VAS); the permit for telecommunication services; and the permit for Internet information services on health.

Commercial Factors

According to official statistics, as of July 2009, there were 9,549 magazines and 1,943 newspapers published in China. There is, however, some evidence to suggest that the government's statistics may understate the number of print publications. For example, 14,118 magazine and newspaper titles, 2,626 more than the combined official figures of periodicals, have been counted on Gotoread.com, the most popular website providing print subscription services. Many Chinese media practitioners say they believe that there are, in fact, around 30,000 magazine titles circulating in China, many of them published without a legal license.

Whatever the number of publications, what is clear is that readership is climbing in China. According to a report by the World Association of Newspapers (WAN), global paid newspaper circulation rose by 2.6 per cent in 2007, with China and India registering the strongest growth. China was shown to be the biggest newspaper market by circulation, with a daily distribution average of 107 million. Chinese newspapers witnessed advertising revenues rocketing in 2002, although this growth has since somewhat plateaued. Nonetheless the momentum in this area remains strong, with the overall revenue hitting RMB 90 billion in 2009.

One of the threats that Chinese newspapers face – which magazines do not – is that much of what they offer readers can be replaced by the Internet. Online media can promise the same comprehensive content as a daily newspaper, but can deliver it faster and often at no cost to the reader. Magazines, on the other hand, occupy a somewhat different space in the news ecology. They generally target a more specialized audience, sometimes with more in-depth content, and this makes them more attractive to advertisers seeking to reach a specific demographic.

Samir Husni (1998: 25) wrote that magazines 'must be sold not once, but twice: first to the readers and then to the advertisers'. Steve Greenberger, a senior vice president at Zenith Media, wrote (in the company's 2005–6 report) that magazines are an especially attractive medium for advertisers to promote their products, adding that 'when consumers buy a magazine, they consciously buy it with the understanding that there are ads inside. A large percentage probably buy the magazine predominantly for the ads.'

China's rapid economic development in recent decades has substantially improved the living standards of many Chinese people and has sustained a number of magazines focused on fashion, lifestyle and personal finance. Between July 2007 and June 2008 the fashion magazine *Trends Cosmo*, one of twenty titles published by the Trend Media Group, generated advertising revenue of RMB 613.2 million. In 2009 China's magazine advertising market reached RMB 10 billion.

Analysis International estimates that the total size of the Chinese advertising market was RMB 174 billion in 2007, of which online ads accounted for RMB 10 billion, or less than 10 per cent. Television continues to dominate the advertising market: in 2007, for example, the combined annual revenue of Sina.com and Sohu.com (which together comprise nearly 50 per cent of the online advertising market) represented only about 20 per cent of CCTV's advertising revenue for that year. However, between 2003 and 2007, the revenue of the Chinese online advertising sector increased far more rapidly than the overall Chinese advertising market. Revenue from the Chinese online advertising market exceeded RMB 20 billion in 2009. This growth is likely to continue insofar as the Chinese online advertising market remains relatively underdeveloped., In 2007, for example, spending on online advertising amounted to USD 6.90 per capita in China compared to USD 98.10 in the United States.

News Online

Ten years ago, the conservative approaches to the Internet of Chinese offline media provided Chinese web portals with big opportunities. Today it is much easier for Chinese commercial sites to recruit top talent and develop and promote complex applications financed by venture capital and stock markets than it is for news sites affiliated with the Chinese print media. As Internet pioneers Chinese web portals have far more experience in, and have developed far more sophisticated approaches to, the publication of online news than their print counterparts, and as a result they are far more popular among Chinese online audiences. Figures published by Alexa, the most widely used online traffic monitor, demonstrate that the daily distribution reach of the five largest Chinese web portals is roughly eight times that of the most popular Chinese news sites affiliated with traditional print media. The huge gap between Chinese web portals and news sites affiliated with print media means there are a lot of obstacles for Chinese print media to overcome in order to find their footing in the online media arena.

The number of Chinese Internet users has been growing rapidly for over a decade. By the end of 2009, the total figure had reached 384 million, according to the Statistical Report on Internet Development in China released by the China Internet Network Information Center (CNNIC). This figure could well make China the world's largest national Internet market. In 2009 North America had only 259.5 million Internet users.

Despite the large number of Chinese Internet users, China's Internet penetration rate in June 2009 was just 28.9 per cent (see Internet World Stats 2010), only slightly higher than the world average of 25.6 per cent, and much lower than the 74.1 per cent of the United States. In other words, the Internet in China still has huge scope for expansion. Among the 25 per cent of the Chinese population who access the Internet relatively frequently, a large portion are under 25 years old and/or have at least a high school education. CNNIC figures also show that the online appetite for news in China is substantial, with news sites ranking second to those that provide music, instant messaging services and videos. In the CNNIC survey, 81.5 per cent of the respondents claimed to read online news. To meet the demand, Chinese news sites, especially one-stop news providers, offer both breaking news and less time-sensitive items such as infotainment, which may appeal to a younger audience.

A key question for offline media companies in developed countries is how to make full use of their websites and how to implement synergies between offline and online aspects of their production and publication practices. However, in China many traditional news outlets continue to question whether it is really worthwhile to go online. The publications that have adopted a conservative approach toward investing in online operations have well-considered reasons for this perspective, while those that have embraced the Internet also appear to have strong rationales for their strategies – as the following case studies demonstrate.

Sanlian Life Week: Reluctant to Invest Online

Sanlian Life Week is China's most popular news magazine. Indeed, its circulation exceeds the combined reach of its two closest rivals. Despite the relatively low cost of maintaining the magazine's website, which was only RMB 30,000 (USD 4,400) in 2007, its editor-in-chief Zhu Wei says he remains sceptical about the commercial value of the site. Indeed, Zhu remains dubious about the need for the publication to maintain an online presence at all. Since the site's launch, network traffic has never been significant, nor has the site generated much in the way of advertising revenues. Zhu argues that news websites are still struggling to discover viable revenue models and that web portals and their news integration services are already being out-competed by fast-growing Internet services like Google and Wikipedia. In explaining his reluctance to embrace the Internet, Zhu cites three reasons:

> The return on investment in online media is inadequate. This problem is not confined to *Sanlian Life Week* but is common to all Chinese media seeking to generate revenues through Internet channels. The existing print business model is what works for them, as it does for *Sanlian Life Week*.

The online market for niche publications has limited growth potential. Since 2007 *Sanlian Life Week* has been cooperating with Sina.com to allow the republication of their content through this portal. By appearing on Sina, the magazine's articles can increase their rate of page views tenfold (compared to publication on the magazine's own website), but Zhu is not convinced the articles are reaching the right readers: 'The majority of Chinese online readers still lack interest in our content and the magnification effect created by Sina.com is thus quite limited, because the audience is low-end, whereas the magazine's target audience and content is high-end. My observation tells me that most viewed blogs are either written by celebrities, or related to sex or sensational topics. It's so hard for decent Chinese media to grow well off the cultural soil here.'

Zhu argues that the appetite for news among Chinese online readers has actually declined in proportion to the number of users coming online each year, although he has not provided hard data to support this point. In the pre-Internet era, when Chinese people had few alternative channels of information other than governmental mouthpieces, Chinese people longed for an abundance of news and information. After the Internet was introduced, their thirst for information was overwhelmed by Chinese web portals whose news aggregation provided their audiences with much more news at a much higher speed than any other news outlets or television stations could. However, as time passed, Chinese online users gradually lost their passion for massive news consumption. In particular, they are tired of what Zhu calls 'news derivations' or the web portals' habit of providing hundreds of versions of news reports around one core story. As a result, Sina.com and other Chinese web portals have inevitably begun to experience a fall in their page views.

Beijing Lifestyle: Prudently Following the Lifestyle of Beijingers

Beijing Lifestyle is a weekly newspaper which serves as a consumer guide in Beijing. Its circulation started dropping in 2003, the main cause of which was not the Internet but the changes in Beijingers' lifestyles. Since then, private car ownership has boomed in Beijing and the paper's middle-class readers have been commuting to work by car rather than by public transport. Because people mostly read the paper on the bus or on the subway, this shift in commuting habits had a considerable impact on the publication's circulation. Furthermore, the municipal government has been trying to make the city look neater by removing newsstands from streets. This measure further worsened the paper's circulation figures. However, the good news is that increasing numbers of readers are accessing the paper's content over the Internet. As reading offscreen is rather more discreet than reading a newspaper in the office, the paper's website has seen a boom in network traffic during working hours.

The paper is valued by many advertisers because it reaches precise demographics within their potential consumer base. For this reason, *Beijing Lifestyle*'s online provision targets only a Beijing audience and the website invests only in Internet connectivity to the Beijing area. Access from South China is quite slow but this does not matter to the newspaper or its advertisers at all.

Beijing Youth Daily: Forerunner to an Affiliated News Site

Beijing Youth Daily, the official newspaper of the Beijing Communist Youth League (subordinate to the Beijing Municipal Committee of the Chinese Communist Party), was launched in March 1949. In December 2004, Beijing Media, the publication's parent media group, was listed on the Hong Kong stock market as the first ever Chinese media group to go public overseas. Ynet.com was the first website to be derived from this core print business of the media group. Ynet was launched by three members of *Beijing Youth Daily*'s technology department who wanted as much as possible to disassociate the website from its parent publication, because they felt that the name tainted the site with its state-owned and conservative heritage.

However, in 2007 Ynet.com was obliged to merge with Qianlong, a regional news website supported by – and a mouthpiece for – the Beijing municipal government. This merger was an overtly political act, according to Xu Jian, CEO of the Ynet site. Xu was struck by Qianlong's lack of drive and self-development, a cultural hangover from an era of state-ownership. Furthermore, Qianlong had a very different vision of newsworthiness from that pursued by Ynet: Qianlong would judge news according to how the municipal government (which grants funding to Qianlong) might react to it, while Ynet would seek to follow the demands of its audience when generating and publishing content. However, alongside his company's ongoing collaborations with 375 Chinese offline media companies, Xu now aspires to build partnerships with a host of international Internet organizations. Ynet.com has already started to cooperate with MSN, MySpace and eBay, in the hope of promoting its content by exploiting their high levels of popularity among Internet users. Ynet now provides a daily diet of 1,000 news updates manually input by online editors, and a further 40,000 automatic news updates, which service a daily traffic of 40–50 million page views.

The Expansion of Print

China's print editors are often reluctant to invest in online provision because they believe that their print product still holds significant scope for expansion and that the Chinese print media market is far from fully developed or saturated. Yang Daming, Managing Editor of *Caijing Magazine*, for example, argues that 'China's fast economic growth is able to nourish more news outlets of this kind.' Yang's optimism is matched by his magazine's booming advertising revenues.

Income levels are a key indicator of reader quality (Summer and Rhoades 2006: 58) – and specifically of the value of readerships to advertisers. Almost all of the magazines whose representatives were interviewed for this chapter believe their readers have above-average incomes. They assume so because subscriptions to magazines cost more than those to newspapers: for example, the annual subscription to *Caijing Magazine* is RMB390, whereas the annual subscription to the daily newspaper *Beijing Evening* is RMB216.

Yet – despite the sector's significant increases in access to advertising capital – one of the key factors underpinning the current prosperity of this magazine market is the fact that the Chinese media market is not completely free. The total number of published titles is strictly controlled under the country's publication licensing policy. The existing players, irrespective of their publications' quality, are able to prosper because of the absence of competitive pressures.

As a result of this, China's traditional print media sector – unlike China's online commercial news sector – lacks both the motivation and the designation of resources for marketing activities. When, for example,

Sina.com spent over RMB 300 million on a marketing campaign in 1998, traditional Chinese media companies viewed this as an astonishing act of 'cash burn'. Xu Jian, CEO of Ynet, however, argues that the establishment of Sina's leading position in the Chinese online world may owe something to its costly marketing initiatives, and therefore may well have been justified.

Starkly different positions and viewpoints regarding the nature of online journalism are held by major Chinese web portals and the news websites maintained by offline media companies. While some of these differences can be attributed to the early-mover advantages enjoyed by the major web portals, the political and commercial factors described in this chapter also appear to play a determining role in why Chinese offline media view the Internet with greater scepticism than do the stand-alone online media outlets. These differences prevail even in those cases where print media companies have been eager to embrace the Internet through such ventures as People.cn (the website launched and maintained by *People's Daily*) and have thus sought to emulate the success of their web-only counterparts.

Meanwhile, some Chinese newspapers, such as *Beijing Lifestyle* and *Economic Observer*, have deliberately chosen a development path that orients them closer to magazines in what they offer their readers. According to interviews with executives at these newspapers, such an approach has protected them from being undermined seriously by the Internet. *Beijing Lifestyle* has, for instance, developed a strong reputation for reaching a targeted audience in Beijing, encouraging that audience to translate what they read into their patterns of consumer spending. This strategy is clearly highly valued by advertisers. While circulation is a key factor in determining a magazine's advertising rates, demographic factors are also attractive to advertisers. For example, advertisers will generally pay a premium for readers of the same sex (mostly men or mostly women). The audience of *Beijing Lifestyle* is predominantly female, holding a college degree or above, with a white-collar job, aged between 20 and 38 (with the bulk of those aged between 27 and 32), according to Sheng Xiaojing, general manager of the affiliate website of *Beijing Lifestyle*. This is crucial for the publication's major advertisers (cosmetics and fashion companies), who mainly target female consumers.

Zhang Jinghua, Deputy Editor-in-Chief of *Economic Observer* argues that if traditional print media are ever going to be able to break through to China's online market and take on the web-based news sites that have dominated the Internet in China for a decade, they will have to analyze the situation rationally, position their websites properly, efficiently exploit the advantages they already possess, and budget their investments to address the fact that 'making a website profitable isn't easy.' However, these challenges appear to hold Chinese print media companies back from launching ambitious initiatives to expand their online presences. The interviews conducted for the purposes of this chapter suggest that China's high-quality and high-end print publications will endeavour to maintain their positions in the lucrative niche markets they currently occupy rather than take on the well-established commercial news sites in the online sector.

References

Husni, S. (1998). *Launch Your Own Magazine: A Guide for Succeeding in Today's Marketplace*. Nashville: Hamblett House.

Internet World Stats (2010). 'Internet Usage in Asia'. Available at www.internetworldstats.com/stats3.htm.

Summer, D., and Rhoades, S. (2006). *Magazines: A Complete Guide to the Industry*. New York: Peter Lang.

Wei, Yongzheng (2008). 'The Citizen Enjoys Freedom; the Media Belongs to the State'. Available at yzwei.blogbus.com/logs/24178629.html.

World Trade Organization (2001). *Report of the Working Party on the Accession of China*. Geneva: WTO.

Xie, Xinzhou (2003). 'Analysis of the Competition in the Online Media Sector' in *Journal of International Communication* 2:3.

GAVIN STEWART

Afterword: An End of Journalism Studies

Towards the end of his poetic career, T.S. Eliot penned an often-quoted section of 'Little Gidding' that seems tailor made for the framings of ends. Eliot (2001: 40) suggests that we shall not 'cease from exploration' insofar as 'the end of all our exploring / Will be to arrive where we started / And know the place for the first time.'

So should we explore some more? Have we wandered in circles? Do we finally know our own intent? In seeking to provide an endnote to the chapters in this collection, it seems necessary to speculate a little on our original purposes.

Looking back to the earliest drafts of our call for contributions to this project, it is interesting to note that at that stage we intended the project to be 'an opportunity to re-assess' the 'status and purpose' of journalism. From the moment we received the first suggestions from contributors it became clear that this re-assessment was going to be polyphonic affair, with many themes sounding at the same time. Likewise, it was also clear from an early stage that these re-assessments were going to be wide-ranging, as many of our participants were keen to address specific geographical and technological issues within and beyond the confines of contemporary professional practice. Furthermore, as the conference which inspired this collection came closer it was obvious that their contributions would come from many differing perspectives as we had made a deliberate point of inviting both academics and practitioners to contribute to our discussions.

In our original call we sought to harmonize our proposed themes using the concept of the 'journalistic function'. We deployed this construction as a piece of pragmatic shorthand to bundle together those activities, institutions, technologies and outcomes traditionally associated with journalists (and others with access to, and/or control of, the media). In re-sounding this call, it has to be said that the concept of the 'journalistic function' is a rather neat one. For example, one can imagine this key function valorized through certain modes of theory, with its obvious associations with lofty notions such as the fourth estate and the public sphere. Likewise, one can imagine this key function being monitored for malfunctions – in accusations of bias, blindness, bigotry, churnalism, and trivialization.

It was probably remiss of us that we did not provide a fuller explanation of our purpose in deploying this term. However, its understated vagueness suited our aims as it helped us to escape from such unproductive binaries as the 'bloggers versus journalists' debates that have sometimes clouded thinking in this area. It was also useful in that it helped us to get beyond the endless jeremiads that often fail to interrogate their own assumptions about the ends of journalism.

Technology was an obvious starting point for discussion. Fortunately, however, the contributions made to this book require us to reach beyond a reductionist technological determinism by insisting that we should not isolate the discussion of technology from the other conditions of journalism. Marcus Leaning and Jon Silverman, among others, challenge us to get beyond the obvious assumptions about new media technologies; to engage with the complexities of emerging practices and social usage. Likewise, the examples provided by Richard Junger, Clive McGoun, Roy Krøvel and Sonya Yan Song demonstrate that it is important to look beyond the assumptions of a particular culture, class or generation.

Taking a slightly wider frame, many of our contributors also remind us that we should not seek to abstract the 'journalistic function' from the intimate details of its context. James Morrison, for example, invites us to be more vigilant as we consider the complicated relationship between journalism and other related functions, such as politics, advertising and public relations. Likewise, it is also important we stay ever-vigilant when dealing with our unexplored assumptions of our subject; for example, when dismissing those joke or taboo subjects that are deemed too ridiculous for serious interrogation. Indeed, it is evident from our own contributions, that we believe that the investigation of the rhetoric of the squirrel story or the rise of the online encyclopaedia (that none of us would ever admit to using) tell us something of interest about the functioning of journalism.

In stepping back a little further again, it is also possible to see the contributions to *The End of Journalism* as part of an on-going process to establish the ends of journalism studies. Indeed, when you look in detail at the methodologies and the chosen subjects presented in this collection, it becomes evident that these contributions are also examples of possible practice. Indeed, in the varied approaches adopted by the contributors to this collection, it is plain that they believe in argument, quotation and the well-chosen case study; that many of them believe that we can be enriched by an awareness of history, and that we can benefit from understanding social practices beyond the confines of professional journalism. Likewise, many of them – including Ivor Gaber and Andrew Calcutt and Philip Hammond's chapters on the debate between objectivity and subjectivity – also believe in the value of theory. Furthermore, their carefully chosen vocabulary suggests that they believe that it is possible to philosophize about our chosen subject, even as we seek to be ever pragmatic. Taken together, the various approaches enacted in this collection frame journalism studies as a subject (not a discipline) based on an attempt to look beyond the obvious to make things obvious.

Attempt is, of course, a key word in this context. In his introduction to this book, Alec Charles turns to the *Myth of Sisyphus* and suggests that journalism might never be able to find all the answers. It is quite likely, given its relationship to this subject, that journalism studies will also share this Sisyphean condition. It is also likely that it will be have the same opportunities to demonstrate its own limitations, even when it strives to reach high ideals. Indeed, it is likely to be a subject characterized by its shortcomings as well as its successes.

But is this a problem? Maybe it will be beneficial if we are aware that our studies are limited; that nothing we write is ever truly definitive. Likewise, maybe it will help us if we embrace the fact that our arguments are contingent and always reflect particular points in time and space. Indeed, it might well be essential that we acknowledge the limits of our current positions, as this will allow us to stay alert to future changes. Our subject of study is rich and restless. It will no doubt provide endless challenges for those seeking to assess it.

Of course, we should also keep in mind the impact of all this endless-ness on one possible end of journalism studies: namely (as David Cameron reminds us) the education of the next generation of journalists. This is the point, of course, at which Power and Truth come very close to home. For, although it seems obvious that we should seek to encourage the next generation to develop the skills they will need to negotiate their own end of journalism, it is far less obvious as to what these skills might be. Like-wise, while it is often required by powerful institutional players that they engage with the requirements of mainstream media industries to validate their skill set, it is far from clear what the state of these industries will be in the near future. Maybe it is important therefore to question whether deep analysis, investigation, insight and adaptability are also important skills for future journalists. In looking to our own practice, it is clear that we believe that the academic traditions of journalism studies have a role to play in the development of our subject.

Turning once again to the obvious expectations raised by the Eliot quote above, it seems likely that we will never fully know the ends of jour-nalism. However, we must guard against the delights of despair, so that we do not fall prey to the ends of endlessness, or to take the gifts of the future as an unwarranted punishment. Moreover, it seems important to guard against overt disinterest and to strive, so that we can at least have some knowledge about our aims and beliefs. 'Little Gidding' is often described as a poem about religious ends. Judged from this perspective, it seems likely that the ends of journalism will be more like Valhalla than total enlighten-ment or redemption. Of course, it is hard to be sure of a subject that does not appear to recognize an end.

Reference

Eliot, T.S. (2001). *Four Quartets*. London: Faber and Faber.

Notes on Contributors

ANDREW CALCUTT is Principal Lecturer in Journalism at the University of East London, and coauthor, with Phil Hammond, of *Journalism Studies: A Critical Introduction* (2011). He was news editor, and later culture editor, of *Living Marxism*, and commissioning editor of one of the first online magazines produced in the UK, *Channel Cyberia*. He is currently editor of *Proof: Reading Journalism and Society*.

DAVID CAMERON teaches at the University of Newcastle in Australia. He has also worked as a freelance web designer and has consulted with commercial and government clients on social media training and integration. He co-edited *Drama Education with Digital Technology* (2009).

ALEC CHARLES has worked as a journalist in Eastern Europe and a documentary programme-maker for BBC Radio 3. He has taught at universities in the UK, Japan and Eastern Europe, and currently serves as Principal Lecturer in Media and Sub-Dean of the Faculty of Creative Arts, Technologies and Science at the University of Bedfordshire. He is the editor of *Transatlantic Cooperation: Europe, America and the Baltics* (2004), *EU enlargement – One Year On* (2005) and *Media in the Enlarged Europe* (2009). His recent publications include papers in *British Journalism Review* (2004), *Science Fiction Studies* (2008), *The Journal of Contemporary European Research* (2009), *Colloquy* (2009) and *Eludamos* (2009), and chapters in *The Films of Tod Browning* (2006), *Time and Relative Dissertations in Space* (2007) and *The Films of Edgar G. Ulmer* (2009).

IVOR GABER is Professor of Media and Politics at the University of Bedfordshire and Professor of Political Journalism at City University London. He is also a broadcaster, writer, and media consultant. As an independent radio producer he makes and presents programmes for Radio 4 and the World Service. His main field of academic expertise is political communications.

He has co-authored three books and numerous articles on this topic and is a frequent expert contributor to BBC 5Live, Radio 4, the World Service BBC TV, ITN, Sky News and a host of foreign broadcasters. He is an Independent Editorial Advisor to the BBC Trust, the UK representative on the UN's Inter-Governmental Council of the International Programme for Development Communication and an Academician of the Academy of Social Sciences. He has served as a media consultant to a variety of governments, international bodies and organizations including UK Government departments, the European Union, the Council of Europe and UNESCO. His journalistic career has included senior editorial positions at the BBC, ITN, Channel Four and Sky News. He was part of the launch team of Channel Four News, the televising of Parliament and Radio 5Live's political coverage.

PHILIP HAMMOND is Reader in Media and Communications at London South Bank University, and co-author, with Andrew Calcutt, of *Journalism Studies: A Critical Introduction* (2011). He is also the author of *Media, War and Postmodernity* (2007) and *Framing Post-Cold War Conflicts* (2007) and co-editor, with Edward Herman, of *Degraded Capability: The Media and the Kosovo Crisis* (2000).

RICHARD JUNGER is a former news reporter and is a Professor of Journalism at Western Michigan University. He specializes in American journalism history and law. He is the author of *Becoming the Second City: Chicago's Mass News Media, 1833–1898* (2010) and numerous other books and articles, and is currently writing a book on the American Civil War.

ROY KRØVEL is Associate Professor of Journalism in the Faculty of Journalism, Library and Information Science of Oslo University College, Norway.

MARCUS LEANING is Senior Lecturer and Programme Leader for Media Studies at the University of Winchester. He has published numerous articles and chapters on the contextual study of new media. He is also the author of *The Internet Power and Society: Rethinking the Power of the Internet to*

Change Lives (2009) and the editor of *Issues in Information and Media Literacy: Criticism, History and Policy* (2009) and *Issues in Information and Media Literacy: Education, Practice and Pedagogy* (2009).

CLIVE MCGOUN is a Senior Lecturer at Manchester Metropolitan University, where his research centres on alternative media, public spheres and the uses of communication for social change. He is currently affiliated with CREATE, a research, development and consultancy group at Manchester Metropolitan University which investigates digital cultures, emerging technologies and radical educational change.

JAMES MORRISON is Senior Lecturer in Journalism at Kingston University, and a freelance journalist and writer. As a staff journalist, he has worked for various local and national newspapers, including *The Daily Mail* and *The Independent on Sunday*, where he spent three years as arts and media correspondent. Since November 2003, he has lectured in journalism and public affairs at several colleges and universities, while continuing to freelance for a range of publications including *The Guardian, The Independent, The Times* and *The Daily Telegraph*. He has also worked as a freelance consultant for the Collections Trust and the Jordanian Media Institute, and as a trainer for the British Council and the Periodical Publishers' Association. He is currently a senior examiner for the National Council for the Training of Journalists, and is the author of *Essential Public Affairs for Journalists* (2009).

JON SILVERMAN is Professor of Media & Criminal Justice at the University of Bedfordshire. He is also a freelance journalist, broadcaster and author. He is a frequent contributor to BBC radio and television programmes and was criminal justice analyst for *BBC News Interactive*. From 1989 to 2002 he was the BBC Home & Legal Affairs Correspondent and before that (1987–9) was a correspondent in Paris and at Westminster. In 1996, he won the Sony Gold Award as Radio Journalist of the Year. He is the Author of two books – one on crack cocaine and the Yardies (1994) and one on sex offenders, media and society (2002). He is a trustee and media adviser to the charity, Fair Trials International and a member of the

Editorial Advisory Group of the *Howard Journal of Criminal Justice*. He spoke at a Council of Europe forum on free expression and the media in Reykjavik in 2009 and has given evidence to a House of Commons committee on the media and the police. He is an authority on international war crimes tribunals and has a consultancy with the BBC World Service Trust, mentoring journalists from Sierra Leone and Liberia covering the trial of Charles Taylor in the Hague. He has reported on trials at both the ICTY and ICTR and trained journalists in Rwanda, Sierra Leone, the Central African Republic and Macedonia.

SONYA YAN SONG is an experienced researcher in online news media, emerging technologies, the digital music industry, and electronic publishing, distribution and circulation in China. During her studies at the University of Hong Kong's Journalism and Media Studies Centre, she conducted research in comparative business models of online media companies in China. In particular, she explored the ways in which the development of China's online media sector mirrors, and diverges from, developments in the online sector in North America and Western Europe. She holds Bachelor's and Master's degrees in Computer Science from Tsinghua University in Beijing. She has also spent eight years working as a journalist and columnist focusing on the Internet, online media and technology sectors at *China Internet Weekly* (Beijing), BlogChina.com, *New Weekly* (Guangzhou), and *Sanlian Life Week* (Beijing). Her work as a journalist has touched on various aspects of China's new media sector, including coverage of companies as diverse as CCTV, Google China, Baidu.com, Sohu.com, QQ.com, Sina.com and Taihe Rye Music. Song is currently pursuing her doctoral degree in the College of Communication Arts and Sciences at Michigan State University.

GAVIN STEWART is Lecturer in Digital Media and course leader in BA Media Production at the University of Bedfordshire. He formerly worked as a project manager for the Narrative Laboratory for the Creative Industries at De Monfort University and as a project manager for the trAce Online Writing Centre project at Nottingham Trent University. His research interests are the aesthetics of digital texts and the impact of corporate digital media on our understanding of community.

Index